IN THE WEEDS

IN THE WEEDS

AROUND THE WORLD AND BEHIND
THE SCENES WITH **ANTHONY BOURDAIN**

TOM VITALE

hachette
BOOKS   NEW YORK

Hachette Books
Hachette Book Group
1290 Avenue of the Americas
New York, NY 10104
HachetteBooks.com
Twitter.com/HachetteBooks
Instagram.com/HachetteBooks

First Edition: September 2021

Published by Hachette Books, an imprint of Perseus Books, LLC, a subsidiary of Hachette Book Group, Inc. The Hachette Books name and logo is a trademark of the Hachette Book Group.

The Hachette Speakers Bureau provides a wide range of authors for speaking events.

To find out more, go to www.hachettespeakersbureau.com or call (866) 376-6591.

The publisher is not responsible for websites (or their content) that are not owned by the publisher.

Print book interior design by Jeff Williams.

Library of Congress Cataloging-in-Publication Data

Names: Vitale, Tom, author.
Title: In the weeds : around the world and behind the scenes with Anthony Bourdain / Tom Vitale.
Description: First edition. | New York : Hachette Books, 2021.
Identifiers: LCCN 2021022682 | ISBN 9780306924095 (hardcover) | ISBN 9780306924071 (ebook)
Subjects: LCSH: Bourdain, Anthony—Travel. | Vitale, Tom—Travel. | Television cooking shows—United States. | Travelogues (Television programs)—United States. | Food habits—Anecdotes. | Anthony Bourdain, parts unknown. | No reservations (Television program)
Classification: LCC TX649.B58 V58 2021 | DDC 641.5092—dc23.
LC record available at https://lccn.loc.gov/2021022682.

ISBNs: 978-0-306-92409-5 (hardcover); 978-0-306-92407-1 (ebook)

Printed in the United States of America

LSC-C

Printing 4, 2022

To my loving family, for their unwavering support and steadfast belief I was worth the effort, despite all evidence to the contrary

CONTENTS

PART THREE

AUTHOR'S NOTE

I DON'T KNOW IF MY LIFE ENDED OR IF IT BEGAN WHEN I STARTED WORK-
ing with Tony. Whatever the hell I did for a living was so vivid and
spectacular, it all but consumed me. Then, without warning, it was
over forever, reduced to nothing more than a memory.

In my case the old cliché that life has a funny way of turning
the tables when you least expect it rang uncomfortably true. Each
two-week shoot contained a lifetime's worth of adventures, and
there'd been so many trips, I'd lost count. Accustomed to the adrenaline rush of making split-second decisions with far-reaching consequences, I now found myself unemployed, with nowhere to go and
poorly suited to handling simple everyday tasks. I still wrote 2006
on checks. I still wrote checks, for Christ's sake. Even more disori-
enting, I went from the comfortable position of hiding behind the
camera to struggling to articulate my own story.

And by struggling to articulate, what I really mean is that I
found every excuse not to write this damn book. I grew a pandemic
mustache. I consolidated, then organized, my extensive matchbook
collection. I researched the nesting habits of a threatened species of

birds that I didn't have the heart to evict from my chimney. I learned how to make mulberry jam. The one thing I didn't do was write.

It's not like I had a lack of stories to tell. In fact I had too many and spent almost all of my waking hours silently reliving them. Truth told, I was afraid I wasn't up to the challenge, worried I'd get the story all wrong. When I eventually did the math and realized procrastinating would only lead to a self-fulfilling prophecy, I stayed awake for days straight in an attempt to make up for lost time. In the process I inadvertently discovered the only way I could get anything down on paper was by replicating the extreme intensity and overstimulation of my old job. Like an unhinged detective determined to crack a case, I surrounded myself with souvenirs from my travels, scoured the four corners of my house for transcriptions, travel itineraries, even old receipts. I cross-referenced everything against shoot notebooks, logs, schedules, and emails. But none of it compared to my vast archive of unedited raw film footage. Much of my entire journey with Tony, my whole life really, had been recorded. It was a TV show, after all. I sat, curtains drawn, oblivious to the passing of time, obsessively watching my life play back on an endless loop.

Some memories were so powerful that I was convinced they should have yielded documentary evidence; but of course not everything was filmed, or preserved via email or text. What follows is my best attempt to paint an honest picture of my experience traveling with Tony, the highs and lows, and the bizarre as shit situations in which we constantly found ourselves. It's a story told by someone who is still trying to make sense of it all.

P.S. INCIDENTS INCLUDED IN THIS book are not intended to glamorize or endorse acts of cannibalism, drug use, smuggling, torture, extortion, bribery, wire fraud, attempted vehicular manslaughter, or the poaching of endangered species.

IN THE WEEDS

PART ONE

PART ONE

Chapter One

AFTERMATH

JUNE 8, 2018, I WOKE UP AT FIVE A.M. TO MY CELL PHONE AND LANDLINE ringing at the same time. It was Chris, owner of the production company. In a quivering voice he said, "Tom, I'm so sorry . . . Tony killed himself last night . . . "

Hanging up the phone, I couldn't make sense of what he'd just said. Tony had just emailed me a routine note about the edit we were wrapping up; he'd confirmed a haircut appointment, leaving as we were in a few days for India. When I'd seen him last week for a voice-over session, he'd been jovial, asked me to join him for a smoke in the men's bathroom. "What are they gonna do, fire me?" he'd said.

I stumbled over to the TV, turned it on, and there was Tony's smiling face along with an incongruous banner headline reading, "CNN's Anthony Bourdain Dead at 61." My hand shaking, I lit a cigarette, called the producer Josh on location with Tony in France, and asked him what the fuck was going on.

"Tony's gone," Josh said through tears. "He hung himself; we're flying back to JFK."

The room started spinning. Tony was bigger than life. Super-human. This couldn't be happening, but somehow it was.

"I'm going to hang myself in the shower stall" had been one of Tony's longest running jokes, the sort of dark humor he might have interjected on any occasion he found even mildly uncomfortable or displeasing. As in, "My hotel room is so awful I'm going to hang myself in the shower stall if the cheap-ass curtain rod doesn't collapse under my weight." When he said that sort of thing, I'd always laughed.

THERE WAS NOBODY ELSE LIKE him. College dropout, sharp-tongued, anti-host, Tony was *the* accidental celebrity, an honest voice in a field of saccharine, an "I'll do whatever the fuck I want," wild kind of guy. God forbid the network conducted a focus group; he'd instinctively go the opposite direction. But whatever he was doing, it was working. Tony had transformed himself from chef to author, then again into a television personality, ultimately maturing into something resembling an elder statesman, all while maintaining a countercultural New York City punk rock hard edge.

Starting life as the Food Network's redheaded stepchild—low-budget and almost exclusively about food and travel—the show had shape-shifted into a bizarre cinematic geopolitical mashup that won Emmy Awards for CNN. Tony was constantly increasing the stakes. Each season he pushed further, slowly steering toward less traditional (and often riskier) destinations. For those of us on the show, Tony wasn't just the guy with his name in the title, he was a friend, mentor, and more.

I didn't know who Tony was when—back in 2002, fresh out of college—I got a job on his first TV show, *A Cook's Tour*. At the time Tony was new to TV as well. The surprise success of his book *Kitchen Confidential*, an insider exposé on the restaurant industry, had landed him a deal with the Food Network. Tony wasn't famous yet, at least in a recognizable TV personality sort of way. Bondain, Bonclair—back then everyone always messed up his name.

My official title was "Edit Room Assistant," a fancy name for logger, which meant I made notations on the raw footage for the editors. It was an entry-level position, but I was electrified at having landed a job in the industry so quickly. From pretty much the first tape, I was hooked. I remember watching Tony fight with the producer over a walk-in shot at a beach bar in St. Martin.

"Walk-in shots are totally conventional man, free your mind," he said in a mock hippie falsetto. But Tony lost his cool when the producer made the mistake of asking for the shot a third time. "Oh my god! Why can't you get this through your thick little dinosaur skull?!" he shouted. "Film the kids playing by the fishing boats, the surf, or even a fucking palm tree, for Christ's sake. Literally *everything* else here would make a better and more interesting introduction shot than my bony ass!"

Tony was naturally telegenic, possessing an unmistakable star quality; that much was clear. But even more alluring was his antagonistic, devil-may-care, combative relationship with the very machine that created his fame. The more Tony shirked the camera, the more I wanted to see. It wasn't that I enjoyed watching him squirm; he was just so brilliantly witty and sarcastic when backed into a corner.

In addition to logging tapes, my job responsibilities included doing anything else I was asked. Pick up dry cleaning for the producer, manufacture props for a fake infomercial, and on occasion assist with research for upcoming shoots. I didn't have to wait long for the most exciting assignment yet. When I heard that a rough cut of the St. Martin episode I'd been working on needed to go to Tony's apartment, I jumped at the chance. Naïve, impressionable, twenty-two years old, and desperate to make a good impression, I spent the whole taxi ride clutching that VHS tape for safekeeping while nervously rehearsing what I hoped was something intelligent to say.

Arriving at Tony's rent-controlled Morningside Heights walk-up, I took a deep breath, but before I even knocked the door opened. There he was, barefoot, wearing a black Ramones T-shirt with the sleeves cut off, looking just like he did on TV. Tony never looked up; instead he took the tape from my outstretched hand, and before I could say a word, slammed the door in my face. Despite that inauspicious first impression, I would work my way up the ladder, ultimately producing and directing nearly 100 episodes of TV with Tony. In the process I traveled to more than fifty countries and won five Emmy Awards. It was pretty much the definition of a dream job.

On paper I would've seemed like an unlikely candidate: a camera-shy introvert desperately afraid of flying, meeting new people, food with bones, and terrified of things with scales. Like snakes, and fish. Yes, fish. Yet somehow I ended up spending my entire adult life working on the four incarnations of Tony's ever-evolving travelogue, flying on countless puddle jumpers of questionable airworthiness to almost every snake-infested corner of the globe, constantly meeting strangers, often at some sort of barbeque involving ribs or a seafood extravaganza. Though the job required regular exposure to all of my known phobias (and added a few new ones to the list), the whole insane adventure beat the hell out of working for a living. I felt like I'd run away with the circus; I realized I'd been living my whole life in black-and-white.

Growing up, my sister Katie and I replayed *The Wizard of Oz* from a well-worn cassette tape. It was my favorite movie despite my problem with the ending. Thirty years later and I still didn't believe anyone would choose to go back to Kansas after having experienced Oz in Technicolor. That's what travel was like for me. Transported by mechanical tornado to adventures through colorful, amazing, and sometimes scary lands, I hadn't worried about a return to black-and-white because the trips to Oz didn't end, and Tony was the wizard. But better. He was a humbug with a supernatural power to control the forces of nature and alter reality. All the dazzling places we went seemed like a fitting backdrop for the most fascinating person I'd ever met.

This isn't to say the job was all tap dancing on sunshine, but I worked well under pressure and found the emergency-room intensity addictive. I guess in a way the whole thing gave my life purpose. Although I wouldn't have dared admit it, deep down I was Tony's number one fan. Which was sort of a precarious place to be, because he didn't really like adoration. But over the years I became adept at rationalizing a host of seemingly mutually exclusive contradictions.

"How do I get a job like yours?" is something you get asked a lot when you travel the world for a living. Roughly five times a year I experienced the sort of trips that someone might work their whole life to experience even once. From the outside it looked like an all-expenses-paid vacation—and in a lot of ways it was—but watching the show was nothing like living it. For all the outward simplicity of the show's concept—a camera crew and I followed Tony around the world while he basically did whatever he wanted—it was actually quite complicated behind the scenes. By the time I worked my way up to the role of senior director, "just another day at the office" had come to include a host of wildly varying responsibilities depending on the time of day, type of scene, country, Tony's mood, or even the prevailing headwind. It kept you on your toes and required a strong stomach, a tremendous amount of planning, negotiating, cajoling, and winging it off camera. Basically, each shoot often meant actual blood, sweat, tears, and doing absolutely anything that was necessary to get the best results. Between all the high-octane escapades in far-flung locales, navigating a constant minefield of "international incidents," not to mention countless other challenges involved with working in a new and unfamiliar environment each episode, the job demanded I be part diplomat, part labor leader, and part strike buster. Oh, and as the director, the ultimate creative success or failure of the show was riding on my shoulders.

We regularly worked in unstable or outright hostile countries. Each year we took Hazardous Environment Training that included checkpoint exercises and hostage-situation training. It was a given that the production team would be followed by government minders in communist countries and harassed by tourism boards in others. I found myself in morally dubious positions when our objectives were at odds with the locals who helped us make the show; in fact, sometimes just our presence could endanger their lives.

At the beginning, at least, I either didn't mind or didn't realize how isolating, all-consuming, overstimulating, and morally taxing it could be having "the best job in the world." Growing up, I'd been a quiet kid without a lot of friends, so being part of Tony's pirate crew was an alluring proposition, to say the least. But traveling for work is a lot lonelier than you would imagine, especially when you get home. Frankly, the whole thing was a mind-fuck. I'm fully aware how many people would kill to have these sorts of problems, but I'm not sure the human brain was designed to handle such a rapid succession of extreme experiences and emotions. For me—as well as for Tony and other longtime members of the crew—the show increasingly seemed like a one-way ticket to insanity. By the end, the work was taking a heavy personal, physical, and emotional toll, and it felt like there was no escape, even if I wanted one. But who could walk away from a job like this? Who on the outside would even understand?

AFTER NEWS OF TONY'S DEATH broke, it didn't take long for the condolences to start pouring in from everyone I knew as well as a significant number I didn't. When my message icon blinked above 100, I turned off my phone.

That afternoon I headed to our production office just off Herald Square. The new grand entrance framed an impressive Apple Store–like floating steel staircase, and light from two-story-high windows shined off highly polished concrete floors. The reception kiosk was empty, and I'd never heard the place so quiet. There was the distant hum of midtown traffic, and from somewhere down a hallway lined with framed posters of Tony I could hear the repetitive *whirrrshhhhhhhccchhh* of a document shredder. Zero Point Zero, or ZPZ, as everyone called it, had grown over the years as the company branched out to produce other food- and travel-centric shows and had recently completed an ambitious expansion and renovation project. There was a staff of about seventy-five now, including a full-on equipment department, accounting, and office management in addition to countless other changes. But Chris and Lydia, the husband and wife team who'd worked with Tony since *A Cook's Tour* and subsequently started ZPZ, were still in charge. From across the atrium I stood staring up at them in the fishbowl conference room one floor above. The plate glass walls did a good job of isolating sound, but seeing Chris pace and Lydia with her head in her hands, I could imagine what was being discussed.

"My father killed himself last year," said a voice from behind me. Startled, I turned around to find a guy named Austin who did something with computers and was the only person at the office who knew how to operate the espresso machine. "Dad was about Tony's age, he had a good job, well respected in the town where I grew up."

"I'm sorry, I didn't know," I said.

"It's gonna get harder. This is the easy part, when everyone is together, all grieving at the same time. But a couple months from now, once everybody goes their separate ways, and life settles back into a normal routine—but you don't feel normal—that's when it's really gonna suck."

The full weight of things hadn't sunk in yet, and some part of me must have wanted to keep it that way. I stiffened at his words, not liking the way Austin was talking to me as if we were now in the same sad club. At that moment there was only a very small group of people I wanted to be around, and I knew exactly where to find them.

Along with much of the road crew, I set up shop at a nearby bar we jokingly referred to as our New York office and embarked on a week-long bender of an Irish wake. A general state of intemperance and liquor-soaked disbelief prevailed.

"When Tony wakes up tomorrow, he's really gonna regret what he did last night," I recited between double shots of Johnnie Walker Black with a Coke chaser. There was confusion, sobbing, and anger too.

"We fucking risked our lives making that show," someone slurred. "And do you think Tony even knew your kids' names?"

"How could he do this to his daughter, she's only eleven," came another whinge.

"This is all Asia's fault, she fucking killed him," was a popular opinion.

The name Asia Argento came up a lot that evening. Tony had started dating the beautiful and mysterious Italian actress after meeting on our Rome shoot two years before. It was a passionate and volatile on-again, off-again relationship that had supposedly ended for good a few days before when paparazzi photos surfaced of Asia with another man. And then Tony had killed himself.

It didn't make sense. I played back a litany of "lasts." Last scene I filmed with Tony on my shoot in Indonesia a few weeks ago. We'd had our last "real conversation" that day. The last time we talked had been at a voice-over session the day he left for France. A few days before that he'd invited me to dinner for the last time. I'd declined, a decision I was very much regretting. Our last communication was an email about my Bhutan edit sent only hours before he died. "I don't like the cold open and would replace it," was all he wrote.

The shock and alcohol were bubbling a lot of emotions to the surface. "Tony hated me," I professed to anyone who would listen. I knew that he'd kept me around because I worked hard; I was confident of that. But as a human being, I was sure he hated me. Now, so consumed by grief and denial, I didn't have the capacity to think about what any of it really meant.

In the real world—the one that made sense, where the sky was up and the ground was down—I was supposed to be getting ready to leave to direct an episode in India. Instead I found myself in a totally fucked alternate reality standing in front of Tony's former restaurant, Les Halles. The shuttered brasserie on Park Avenue South had become a makeshift memorial, overwhelmed with pictures, chef paraphernalia, flowers, letters, and a mix of fans and restaurant industry professionals. Seeing it all, arrayed there against the windows and door of the storefront, I was confused. Who were all these people carrying on like it was Christmas Eve and Santa Claus had just been killed in a fucking suicide bombing?

I read a note left by a woman who drove all the way from Tennessee:

> Thank you for being real in a world where everyone seems so fake. I hate to idolize "famous" people that I don't know, but you are different. I love you and thank you for giving me hope. Thank you for showing me how I want to live my life, you set a great example for some of us "misfits."

Tony meant the world to those who knew him personally, and I was aware he possessed a militant faction of superfans, but they couldn't account for such a large number of complete and total strangers. Could it be possible that Tony really was *that* famous, beloved, and inspirational on such a mass scale? If true, had Tony even been aware of this development? Because if he was, he certainly never acted like it. As long as I knew him, Tony seemed to exhibit a real inferiority complex, under the impression that the attention was fleeting and could disappear at any second. Blindsided by the tremendous outpouring of grief, I might have been forgiven for thinking Tony had been mistaken for some kind of Kitchen God. And maybe he was. Nearby stood a group of line cooks who'd arrived after their shift, still in uniform. They were quietly sobbing.

The next day I took a taxi to JFK to meet the crew returning from France. I couldn't imagine what it had been like that awful morning, getting set up for Tony, expecting him to arrive any second, but instead getting the news that he wasn't coming. He would never be coming . . . I both wished I'd been there because maybe I could've done something, and was so thankful I wasn't.

In the roughly hundred shows and thousand scenes I'd filmed with Tony over the years, he'd only ever missed his call one time. We were shooting in Manila, and when he didn't show up at our location for the day's shoot, I'd called him up and gotten no answer. This was unusual, but not unheard of. I dialed him back five minutes later and five minutes after that. His phone just rang and rang. His hotel phone also went unanswered. I rushed back through Manila's painfully slow gridlock traffic and in a panic explained to the front desk I needed to get into Tony's room immediately. While riding up in the elevator I thought about how easy it had been to convince them. I hadn't been asked for ID or any corroborating evidence that I wasn't some "Squeaky" Fromme or Sirhan Sirhan type. I rang the buzzer and knocked loudly; no answer. I stepped back, and the bellman unlocked Tony's door. Inside, the room was pitch black, blinds drawn. A shaft of light from the hallway illuminated Tony lying motionless in his bed. As my eyes adjusted, I could see he was naked, partially covered by twisted sheets. Something smelled like sour milk, and I was convinced he was dead. Maybe it was the light or my involuntary exclamation, but Tony finally woke up. He looked right at me, blinked, then bellowed, "Get the fuck out!!!"

Practically running downstairs, I wiped the tears from my face and tried to steady my breathing. Not ten minutes later, Tony strolled into the lobby, ready to be on TV. He didn't mention anything about what had happened, and I never brought it up. From what I understood, that's pretty much how it happened in France. Except this time, Tony wasn't in the lobby ten minutes later.

After an emotional reunion at the airport, we all went back to the Brooklyn home of our longtime director of photography, Todd, where we started drinking or, more accurately, continued drinking. While we got plastered, Tony was waiting. Tony hated waiting, he'd be furious, I thought. But this time he was waiting on a refrigerated tray in a far-away morgue while his family figured out who was in charge. Word eventually came that he was to be cremated in France and sent home via messenger. There would be no body. There would be no funeral. He just . . . disappeared.

Tony had always been fascinated by Eastern legends of the hungry ghost—a spirit stranded in the netherworld due to a tragic death or lack of a proper burial—and in keeping with everything in his life playing out like a book, movie, or legend, now in some horrific twist of fate he had become a hungry ghost himself.

Eventually I went home to sleep off what was sure to be a Godzilla of a hangover. At the door was my suitcase, ready for the trip to India. That's when I all but came unglued. Even though by this point I was a travel professional, I habitually waited until the day before leaving, then in a frenzy I'd haphazardly grab whatever was at hand and stuff it into my luggage. Strange irony that I'd packed early for a trip that would never happen.

Over the years, few others had clocked more miles on the road with Tony or had as much opportunity to know, trust, fear, admire, and learn from him as I did. Tony was complex, so much had to be gleaned by paying attention, by filing away some offhand remark, or cataloguing some slip of the veneer, details to be analyzed and interpreted at a future point. In more than a decade and a half, what had I learned? Staring at that suitcase, I thought about how my privileged position, my years of access, also meant I had something else few others had: an opportunity to see the warning signs. So how had it ended up like this? What had all of it really meant? Tony used to say that the questions were more important than the answers. I had plenty of questions. Answers, however, were in short supply.

Chapter Two

READY FOR PRIME TIME

"YOU CAN'T *FUCKING* BREATHE A WORD OF WHAT I'M ABOUT TO TELL YOU!" Tony said when he spotted me waiting for him curbside at Santo Domingo Airport. In accordance with post-flight ritual, he lit up a Marlboro Red, taking a long—nearly half the cigarette long—drag before continuing, "If this gets out the WHOLE deal could BLOW UP. I just came from a meeting. It was so, so beyond secret they brought me up in the GOD DAMN freight elevator. It was total cloak and dagger ass shit!"

Tony's eyes darted back and forth as he talked, one slightly larger than the other, giving him the tweaked-out look of a squirrel on amphetamines. This was an unusual greeting—even for the predictably unpredictable Anthony Bourdain.

"We can kiss those fuck-tards at Travel Channel goodbye . . . *No Reservations* is . . . OVER!" Tony said, finishing the smoke and tossing it to the pavement.

Struggling to keep up, I lit a Red and noticed my hands were shaking.

"*Congratu-FUCKING-lations*, Tom, we're moving the FUCKING show to FUCKING CNN! Can you FUCKING believe it?!?!?"

Seven months later in November 2012 we touched down in Burma, or Myanmar, depending on who you were talking to, for the *Parts Unknown* pilot episode. Real life doesn't offer clear beginings, of course. At least, we rarely recognize them as such at the time. But looking back, our trip to Burma seems like as good a place to start this story as any other. I was thirty-two years old at the time, and for the last six years I'd been on the road with Tony getting paid to goof off and travel the globe while eating and drinking. Emphasis on the drinking. Which is maybe why I still couldn't believe CNN had given Tony—a countercultural, mostly uncontrollable ex-heroin addict in his mid-fifties—a blank check to go anywhere and do pretty much anything he wanted. It sounded insane to me, and I was the show's director. Marching orders from our new television masters were simple, at least: "Just keep doing what you're doing," citing the *No Reservations: Mozambique* episode's blend of history, culture, and personality as an example of what they hoped we'd deliver. But Tony being Tony, he wasn't going to settle for what worked last week, let alone last season, forget last network.

HAVING SPENT THE PAST FIFTY years under an oppressive military regime, Burma had been all but closed off to outsiders for decades. First impressions on the ground, though, were that Yangon, the country's largest city, was far from the time capsule I'd been told to expect. Moldering colonial Art Deco buildings from the days of the British Empire were everywhere, but the vibrant street life overflowing with a swirl of colors was anything but caught in time. Pedestrians, vehicles, and monks in scarlet robes fought for space with food vendors, sidewalk haircut stands, and tea stalls. Women wore thanaka on their faces, a natural sunblock made from tree bark, while men chewed betel nut and spat bloodred on the sidewalk. The ringing of bright green sugar cane juice carts was audible over the general din of shouting vegetable hawkers and the grunt of diesel buses bursting at the seams with passengers. Nested in an impossible tangle of sagging power lines, telephone pole megaphones broadcast what sounded like Burmese country-western music. The off-key vocals competed with overmodulated chanting emanating from loudspeakers at the many Buddhist temples and gold stupas. The chaos was almost symphonic.

For nearly half a century, not much had gotten in or out of Burma. Since 1962 a junta ruled the Southeast Asian nation with an iron fist, suppressing almost all dissent and wielding absolute power in what was the world's longest-running military dictatorship. The government possessed an appalling human rights record of child labor and ethnic cleansing, gagged the press, trafficked in heroin and blood rubies, and was waging an unending civil war in the north. Monks, artists, activists, and journalists were imprisoned for having an opinion. One in four Burmese was said to be a secret agent or informer. While the government was busy ensuring complete lack of personal freedoms through a vast bureaucracy powered by carbon copy, typewriter, and fear, the economy collapsed. Forget the lowest cell phone and internet penetration of any country— including North Korea—three-quarters of the Burmese population didn't even have electricity.

Then in 2011 something unheard-of happened. Long-ruling military general Than Shwe stepped down, and the junta, fearing an Arab Spring–style revolution, gave the country back to the people. Just like that, generations of totalitarian rule were over. Wildly popular Aung San Suu Kyi, Nobel Peace Prize winning leader of the opposition, was released from house arrest; Obama visited; trade sanctions were lifted; and for the first time in forty-nine years Coca-Cola was for sale on store shelves.

Now, thanks to a well-timed move to CNN, somehow we were going to be the first TV show of our type to come to the notorious hermit kingdom and work without restrictions. In order to do justice to what was an all too rare success story, we pursued an ambitious lineup of former political prisoners and democracy advocates to appear on camera. And much to our amazement, nearly everyone agreed enthusiastically.

Modern conveniences, and even necessities required to make a travel TV show, however, were proving difficult to put in place. Transportation was unreliable and complicated. With Burma having just opened up, there was a lot of demand and nearly zero tourist infrastructure. Hotels had a nasty habit of selling out six months in advance. Arranging domestic flights had to be done within the country, and Myanmar Airways didn't comply with international safety standards. Due to continued civil unrest, sudden government travel restrictions were a concern. Outside the hotel, there was no internet whatsoever, and our phones didn't work.

"Afghanistan has better cell service," Tony complained.

Most difficult of all, there was no banking system. Burma was a cash economy with no ATMs, and nobody took credit cards. We'd been warned that the only acceptable currency were perfect, unblemished US hundred-dollar bills, which money changers examined like diamond merchants. One fold, one imperfection, one stain, one tear would result in a rejection. We arrived with $30,000 worth of crisp new bills in our carry-on.

"ONE HOUR TO TONY, ONE HOUR TO TONY," came over the walkie. The countdown to Tony's arrival always had the effect on my nerves of hearing a ticking time bomb. Eleven a.m. and the pressure was rising right along with the temperature in downtown Yangon. This being the pilot episode of our new show, the stakes were high to get things right. One hand holding a Marlboro Red, the other fumbling to untangle Tony's microphone, I surveyed our location. It was the type of locals-only street-side restaurant Tony loved; low plastic stools, bustling and noisy. But it was also exactly the sort of place that made filming and recording audio nearly impossible. Even though we'd been through this drill literally thousands of times, the crew was especially frantic preparing for Tony's arrival. Mo was our most daring cinematographer. He was a human avalanche who'd come along on the pilot to operate an additional third camera and was currently vibrating like a massively overcaffeinated hummingbird to get shots of the customers. Veteran producer Josh—code name "Magical Giant" due to his good humor, heart of gold, and larger-than-life proportions—had just returned from making a donation to a nearby temple, hoping they'd turn down music blaring from their loud-speakers. Zach and Todd, our longtime directors of photography, were—as usual—butting heads over where to seat Tony. Along with their local assistant cameramen, they'd spent the last hour franti-cally lugging sandbags, hanging lights, rearranging tables, blocking shots, checking audio levels, calibrating back focus—in the process transforming an otherwise functioning restaurant into a cluttered and dangerous film set. These highly trained television professionals running around like chickens with their heads cut off were literally the best in the business and had become, over years spent traveling together, my closest friends.

"FORTY-FIVE MINUTES TO TONY, FORTY-FIVE MIN-UTES TO TONY," crackled over the walkie. Amid the increas-ing commotion, it wasn't hard to spot our fixer, Patrick, wearing a shell-shocked expression to complement the dark circles under his eyes. Predictably, he'd chosen the most inopportune time to ask a chagrined restaurant owner to sign our three-page release (a terrifying document indemnifying the network against litigation resulting from physical damage, personal injury, or defamation of character). As if on cue came a *KER-THWAP-SMASH*, the noise of someone tripping over an extension cord, knocking over one of our light stands.

Patrick already seemed to regret having taken the job, but I had faith he'd hold it together. I needed him to. Fixers were our lifeline, helping us navigate the often challenging complexities of each new location we filmed. They were almost always locals, but unlike pretty much anywhere else we'd worked, Burma lacked any recognizable film industry. So that left us with Patrick from North Carolina. But beneath the freckles, auburn hair, and button nose beat the heart of a hard-core investigative journalist. He was based in Bangkok, where he reported on Southeast Asia's illicit drug trade, and most recently he'd been undercover writing about government-sponsored heroin trafficking in the Golden Triangle. Over the two months of pre-production leading up to our trip, Patrick helped plan travel logistics, shared his contacts, assisted with our visa application, collaborated on the storyline, scouted locations, and recommended high-quality locals and experts for Tony to interact with on the show. The "side-kicks," as we called them, were Tony's window into whatever location we were visiting. Tony's experience, and therefore the show, was only as good as the people he spent time with on camera.

With Burma just emerging from fifty years of Big Brother, I'd worried that the local population would be paranoid and afraid to open up to the camera, yet midway into the shoot everyone we had filmed with thus far had been shockingly candid. Instead it was Tony who seemed off his game and generally dyspeptic. Several days ago, he'd greeted me with a stinging accusation. "This show is *grievously* lacking some quality food porn! All I've eaten is the color brown."

Unfortunately, he'd been right. So far we'd featured what had inadvertently turned out to be a string of monochromatic dishes. Attention had been paid to the "must-have" dishes in Burma, what restaurants were appropriate for which sidekicks, and what they wanted Tony to try. Research had been done on what foods told a story, and everything was carefully cross-referenced with what would fit into the schedule. But in the process an obvious detail had been overlooked: what the food actually looked like. Neglecting color and variety in the food was an amateur screwup.

The truth is, the food part of our food show never ceased to trip me up. It was a central element of each episode, but food was a fleeting and perishable resource that was logistically difficult to work with. Worse, I didn't actually like a lot of it. I found most of what Tony ate on camera, well . . . less than appetizing. In fact, I was probably the only person in the world who could go on an all-expenses-paid food tour with Anthony Bourdain and lose weight. Before you judge, please know I considered this a shameful handicap given my job. It wasn't that I was just some picky eater, although I sort of was. For some reason I've still yet to determine, I suffered from a myriad of food phobias since childhood. It was a constant struggle I was forced to deal with on a daily basis, especially when it came to fish. I did my best to keep it a secret from Tony as well as overcompensate for my deficiencies.

But sometimes I dropped the ball. Point was, the show needed at least *one* glorious food scene, and after Tony's recrimination, it was clear we needed it fast.

"Maybe Ma Thanegi would reconsider if Tony reached out to her directly?" Patrick had suggested. "He could promise to keep away from politics and focus on the food."

"Wait, do you think that might work?" I asked. "Why the hell didn't we try that before?"

Ma Thanegi was the one that got away. Preeminent expert on Burmese cuisine, she was the author of books on the subject as well as former aide to the leader of the opposition, Aung San Suu Kyi. She'd spent time in prison for her pro-democratic leanings and spoke perfect English. As far as I was concerned, Ma Thanegi was the *perfect* person to walk Tony through the nuances of Burmese politics and food. Unfortunately she'd also refused multiple requests to appear on the show, citing a desire to "keep a low profile."

Apparently, Ma Thanegi had served only three years of a ten-year prison sentence. Given the extremely unclear definition regarding what was and wasn't permissible to say, I could understand she didn't want to risk rocking the boat.

Sending an elderly woman to prison was not something I wanted on my already checkered résumé, so I'd reluctantly accepted that Ma Thanegi wasn't meant to be. But that was before I found myself halfway through the shoot teetering on the edge of yet another food-related cataclysm. So I'd explained the situation to Tony, who rolled his eyes and asked for a pen.

I would be most grateful for the opportunity to do real justice to the extraordinary cuisine of this country and would like to portray it in the best light—as explained by the most qualified person. That would, of course, be you. I am a fan of all your books which I found inspiring and hope we can arrange to meet for a meal of prawn curry or something similarly delicious. I would honor any restrictions you care to impose as regards to subject matter.

And that's all it took. After two months of saying no, Ma Thanegi agreed to be in the show. Somehow Tony possessed a devilry that made people do whatever it was he wanted.

Ma Thanegi had outlined two conditions, however.

"Don't say good things about me, just that I write on things, Myanmar and food," she said. "And don't say that I was once assistant to Ms. Suu Kyi . . . too many people 'use' her name for reflected glory and I am not from that group."

Back at the café, the walkie clacked, *"THIRTY MINUTES TO TONY, THIRTY MINUTES TO TONY."* Time was running out fast, and there was still a lot left to do. I took a deep breath and went over to check on Ma Thanegi. Pushing seventy years old, she was dressed in black and peered up at me skeptically through Coke-bottle glasses from under the shade of a black parasol. Despite her small frame, Ma Thanegi radiated authority, and her patrician commands had kept the restaurant staff nervously hurrying about all morning.

"Have you had time to think about paring down the menu?" I asked.

"As I informed you, I'm going to do a tasting thing," Ma Thanegi said, presenting me with a handwritten list of dishes while exposing her lower row of teeth in what was either a smile or a grimace. Her most distinguishing feature was an extremely pronounced underbite, which she accentuated with bright red lipstick. "I'm going to order a lot of salads and then a lot of noodles that Tony probably hasn't had yet."

Ma Thanegi was the expert, but I had to regain control of the situation or she was going to food-fuck us. Hours before, when I discovered she wanted to order thirty-seven dishes, I'd delicately explained the gist of how we worked and that to do the food justice we needed to not bite off more than Tony or the cameras could chew. The blunt truth was that I basically had to film all the food three times: first in a wide shot while Tony ate it at the table; after he left, we'd film preparation in the kitchen, then back out at the table, this time getting insert beauty shots, which required lens changes and a hand model, often Josh or me.

For an important meal scene like this, we had to film absolutely *everything*. Every ingredient, every step in the cooking process, every finished dish, because with Tony you never knew—until weeks later in the edit—what element he was going to want to talk about in his voice-over. And trust me, you did *not* want to be the one to tell him, "I'm sorry, I don't have that shot."

Filming in the kitchen after Tony ate the meal presented its own set of challenges. Over the years there'd been enough instances of "Oh no, we've run out of that dish," after a busy lunch or dinner rush that I'd enacted a policy of pre-ordering seven of whatever one dish might be eaten on camera. One for Tony, one for the kitchen prep, one for food inserts, double the number for fuckups, and add one more for safety. If I didn't know what he was going to eat, I'd have to order all the possibilities multiplied by seven. My strategic food-hoarding didn't always go over well in countries where resources could be scarce, and there were a number of times I'd inadvertently triggered a food riot. Worst of all, Tony getting food-fucked, a.k.a. overfed—a constant and very real concern—resulted in additional "digestion time" needing to be factored into the production schedule. Glancing over the scribbled laundry list Ma Thanegi had handed me, it appeared she was failing to grasp that it was in everyone's best interest to keep the menu as straightforward as possible.

"This is just too much for us to cover," I said, wiping the sweat from my forehead and forcing what I hoped was a convincing smile. "Normally we only film one or two things."

"No, no, no!" Ma Thanegi practically shouted. "As I informed you, that's not the proper way of eating in Myanmar, there must be a full table!"

"FIFTEEN MINUTES TO TONY, FIFTEEN MINUTES TO TONY," the walkie screeched in my ear. Our intrepid host's impending arrival elevated the already fever-pitched atmosphere in the restaurant to full-on panic. "I'm getting interference on my microphone," Todd yelled. Music from the temple had started up again. Zach was still adjusting lights, and it looked like Mo's camera was being denied access to the kitchen. When it came to Tony and the far-flung and ever-changing locations in which we filmed the show, nothing went according to plan.

"We'll be ready to start soon," I said. "How about we compromise on three to six dishes?"

Cursing food under my breath, I headed to the street to intercept Tony's arrival and clear my head with a pre-shoot smoke. Doing the math, I realized that, including duplicates for safety, I would have to order and film 259 dishes if Ma Thanegi had her way. With a sigh I turned around to get a cigarette, only to find Tony standing behind me. "*Ack!*" I involuntarily choked. "I mean, hi, Tony. Just a little food delay, we'll be ready to go soon."

"FIVE MINUTES TO TONY, FIVE MINUTES TO TONY," the walkie taunted.

"Why didn't you tell me we were filming with, like, the *most* hated woman in all of Burma?" Tony asked, lighting a cigarette. "You set me up with a fucking apologist for the regime!"

"Umm . . . huh?" I said. "Where did you hear that?"

"I bothered to take like twenty seconds and google her," Tony said. "She backstabbed all her former democracy buddies in exchange for early release from prison . . . It has to be acknowledged, or all the other people we filmed with who spent time in prison and didn't squeal will be furious!"

"But we promised no politics . . . " I trailed off while affixing Tony's microphone. Well, this was unfortunate . . . Screwing up the food and then missing this detail about Ma Thanegi was pretty inexcusable. Even though one of Tony's mottos, "Prior preparation prevents piss-poor performance," was drilled into my head, the show had been very much a fly-by-the-seat-of-your-pants operation. Make-or-break scenarios often happened in real time, requiring lightning-quick decisions and the ability to adapt to countless ever-changing variables. We were making a show for CNN now, and I'd been playing the television production equivalent of Russian roulette. Even though Ma Thanegi was apparently a "traitor to freedom," she'd offered her help when I needed it, and as a thank-you I'd put her in danger. I felt awful, and at the moment I wasn't sure who Tony hated more, Ma

Thanegi for crimes against democracy or me for crimes against TV. As I watched him charge toward the table, I estimated there was a fifty-fifty chance of the scene landing like the *Hindenburg*.

"Thank you so much for doing this," Tony said, sitting down.

"It's my pleasure," Ma Thanegi said, lower teeth glinting white against the red of her lipstick. She barked some orders at the wait staff and straight away, food started hitting the table.

"I want you to try the pennywort salad, give me your plate," she said. "It's very medicinal."

"Mmm, that's delicious," Tony said.

"This is tomato salad, and this one is samosa salad, and what is this that we have here?" Ma Thanegi said, raising her glasses to examine the dish in her hand. "That's either the ginger salad or tea leaf salad."

"Salad is a loosely used term here," Tony observed.

"We make anything into a salad, just chop it up. This is a salad of, um, tummy. And this is wild citrus salad with a very bumpy rind. And let's see," Ma Thanegi said, lifting a plate of greens up to her face for inspection. "Yes, this is string bean salad." She waved toward the waiter, who placed several more salads on the table. "This is grilled eggplant salad, and this is fish cake salad."

Shit. Ma Thanegi had gone rogue. My head was spinning with the number of dishes piling up on the table. Several bowls of steaming noodles arrived, and Ma Thanegi began shouting in Burmese. The waiter retreated into the kitchen, noodles in hand, and I sighed with relief.

"I told them to bring the salad first and then we'll have the noodles," she explained to Tony.

At this rate it was going to take all three cameras the rest of the day to get food prep, plating, *and* insert shots. We were on Ma Thanegi's turf, but I had to do something.

"I'm sorry to interrupt," I said. "But we should probably . . . "

Tony shot a frightening look in my direction, clearly telegraphing it wasn't a good time to speak up. Okay, message received, backing off.

"This salad is made from all parts of the chicken—the feet, the neck, and everything, and so it's all the chewy stuff, the skin, chop, chop, chop," she said.

"This is so good," Tony said. He'd been eating like a bird, courteously taking one peck from each plate.

If the list Ma Thanegi presented me before the scene was accurate, she'd ordered tea leaf salad, pennywort salad, long bean salad, kaffir lime salad, tomato salad, samosa salad with chickpeas, baked eggplant salad, fish cake salad, pork head salad and kaffir lime leaf, vermicelli chicken soup, shwe taung noodle salad, Putao noodle with soy bean sugar cane paste, and pickled tamarind noodle salad with dried prawn powder. But looking at the carnage on the table, it seemed like there'd been more.

"Well, that all suited me very nicely," Tony said. "If I didn't have dinner tonight, I'd eat more. I'm amazed by the variety. Actually, this is the most variety that I've seen at a restaurant since I got here. It's pretty extraordinary."

"We love to eat and don't forget, for fifty years we were under two dictatorships especially under socialist regime, not a lot of things to do . . . " she said with . . . was it a hint of regret?

"Yeah, socialists are very ambivalent about food," Tony said.

"No, it was just that there was no private enterprises allowed," Ma Thanegi said. "So it was like there was nothing to do but—"

"—but eat," Tony said. "Well, I'm grateful and honored that you did this."

"No, I'm honored," Ma Thanegi said, baring her lower teeth. "Very honored."

"Wide," Tony said. "Wide" was Tony's code word, meaning as far as he was concerned the conversation—and the scene—was done.

"Okay, thanks, everyone, take five then reconfigure for food," I said to the crew. Following Tony toward his waiting car, I crossed my fingers that he'd mellowed in regard to the earlier misunderstanding. All said, the scene had gone well, no lines had been crossed, and the food was certainly pretty. Blubbering apologies didn't go over well; it was best to stick to the basics. "Are there any dishes in particular we should cover?"

"Film everything," Tony said. Everything?! He must have known that would sentence me to food prison for at least the next twelve hours.

"So we can use the scene then?" I asked, trying to find the bright side. "Ma Thanegi ended up being okay?"

"We'll assassinate her in voice-over," Tony said.

"FRANKLY, I'M A LITTLE DISAPPOINTED," Tony said. "You had led me to believe there was going to be a colonial-era dining car with liveried waiters serving scones and Welsh rabbit almandine. But my spirits are buoyed seeing your look of utter misery and confusion."

Tony hated "transport beats"—the beauty shots that showed Tony en route from point A to point B—about as much as he enjoyed making my life a waking nightmare whenever I insisted on filming them. Regardless of the personal demoralization, I fervently believed that, this being a travel show, the spaces in between were worth the risk. And with the stakes so high for the new series, I needed something special. The Night Express to Bagan, a classic sleeper in the Darjeeling Limited tradition, seemed like a two-birds-with-one-stone solution. The British colonial–era train offered a textural and immersive way to film Tony taking in the countryside while also getting us 600 kilometers north to Bagan, Burma's ancient capital. It was perfect. If I could pull it off.

When we arrived at the station, a worried-looking representative from the Ministry of Rail Transportation and Ethnic Minorities regretfully informed us that the first-class sleeping coach had "lost a wheel." Fifteen minutes later, news came that the dining car—the main reason I was confident we could get a scene out of the trip—had suffered the same fate. It was looking more and more likely that putting all my eggs in what was turning out to be a rickety basket of vanishing train wheels might have been a colossal error in judgment.

In the interest of full disclosure, it wasn't a total surprise that moving our crew of twelve people and twenty-something cases of film equipment halfway across the country by rail involved an element of risk. I'd been warned that due to advanced age and poor maintenance, Burmese trains lacked punctuality, reliability, and were prone to "slip on the railway." Lurid photographs of smoldering wreckage and burn victims from last week's derailment that killed twenty-five and injured twice as many more were plastered across every front page. But there was no going back now.

A green flag waved, and the bell rang. With a hiss and *ca-clack*, the Night Express to Bagan lurched into motion. Creaking and shuddering out of the station for the ten-plus-hour overnight trip, I assumed my position behind Zach's camera.

"Tony, how do you feel finally being here?" I asked.

"I feel jet-lagged," Tony said.

Since arriving I'd really been hoping to get him to comment about his lifelong desire to come to Burma. We called these riffs "content" and Tony hated them, but he was just so good. When in the right mood, he could fucking talk, elevate the mundane into high art. Extreme, subtle, sentimental, amused, apoplectic, or sarcastic, his reactions spanned the gamut, and it was ideal when the content flowed naturally, but sometimes he needed a little help. The challenge was to keep Tony interested and stimulated. The way I saw it, if he wasn't inspired, or interested, that wasn't only my problem, it was my fault. Even though he never did anything but complain about my harassing him, I believed that deep down he was glad I tried so hard. Being oppositional was one of Tony's core personality traits, but his attitude toward the camera had been even more aggressive than usual this trip. I had a feeling that beneath the tough exterior something else must be going on. Or was the show just not living up to Tony's expectations?

"Well . . . this is the true old English experience," Philippe said. Tony's good friend and former boss from Les Halles just happened to be in Burma on a transcendental search for Buddha and would be joining us for the rest of the shoot. Thanks to Philippe's lilting French accent, relentless optimism, genuine curiosity, and classic good looks, for the last two days people had mistaken him for the TV star. "I wonder how old this car is," Philippe said. "Could be the fifties, maybe the forties?"

"It's steamy in here," Tony said. "The fan's not working . . . "

Despite the lack of a first-class sleeping coach, dining car, and any enthusiasm from Tony, it was hard to deny the train had character.

Clunking along at a snail's pace over ancient tracks, it appeared untouched since Burma's military junta seized power after World War II. Wide-open guillotine-style picture windows were flanked by threadbare curtains swaying in time with the rhythmic *clickety-clack, clickety-clack* of the wheels. A regiment of small key lime green fans were mounted to the ceiling. Those that worked oscillated in unison, though their whirring did little to move the heavy tropical air. We were the only foreigners among a mix of Burmese travelers, families, one or two businessmen, and Buddhist monks clad in vermillion robes.

From behind the camera, I tried again. "So Tony, perhaps you'd like to comment on the train ride?"

"I'd rather have a fucking water buffalo with a barbed penis chasing me across a rice paddy," Tony said.

Breaking free from Yangon, the landscape opened up. Low-slung wood and corrugated tin shanties, power lines, and cars soon gave way to endlessly verdant countryside interrupted by the occasional dirt road or thatched roof. The temperature cooled off, and the air developed a sweet, spring-like quality. Out the window I noticed everyone stopped what they were doing to watch the train pass by. As kilometers slowly clattered behind us, the sky lit up neon pink, orange, and yellow. Mist rising from rice paddies incandesced with surreal color.

"Wow. It's just sensational," Philippe said, gazing across the horizon. "What a beautiful part of the planet to be at dusk."

Unlike Philippe, Tony didn't strike me as particularly impressed. He'd spent much of the day ignoring our surroundings while bemoaning the lack of internet, railing against vegetarians, and trashing the documentary he had watched on the flight over. I tried to console myself that with b-roll and voice-over I'd be able to salvage *something* from the ashes of my precious train scene. The crew had been on their feet for at least seven hours, so once the sun set it seemed like a good time for a break. The camera guys ravaged our emergency supply of energy bars, chips, and an assortment of unripe fruit while

I collapsed into a chair and lit a cigarette. Darly, one of our camera assistants, pointed to a "No Smoking" sign above my head.

Before I could respond, the train took a terrific jolt as it pitched forward and began rapidly picking up speed. Lights flickered and the air pressure dropped, sucking curtains out of any windows that hadn't slammed shut. The carriages started shaking and undulating; metal twisted, producing alarming squeals and claps. All of a sudden we were going *fast*. Really *fast*. The train rocked and rolled back and forth while at the same time seesawing up and down. Loose film gear and our bags tumbled onto the floor, where cans of beer and camera lenses rolled around in every direction. Josh and Patrick grabbed whatever they could, trying to prevent anything else from following the case of water that had launched out the window.

"It's getting bouncy," Tony said. "Bouncy not like in a fun bouncy-castle kind of way, bouncy as in a pulverize-my-spine, turn-my-kidneys-to-gel kind of a way."

This was what we'd been waiting for. The train wheels screamed for the engineer to slow down and I shouted, "Battle stations!"

Within moments the cameras were rolling, with Zach, Mo, and Todd operating with one hand, grasping on to whatever they could with the other.

"Wheels have been falling off left and right. Now I understand why!" Philippe said, white-knuckling his armrest. "We must be going what? About forty, fifty miles per hour at this point?"

"Meh," Tony said, reclining his seat. "I could sleep like this." Which is exactly what he did, seemingly immune to the violent wrenching of the train as it shuttled along at an ever more frightening pace.

"Tony clearly got the best seat in the house," Philippe said. "I'm hitting the ceiling every two seconds and he doesn't even move!"

"Dude, it's the pilot," Zach said. "We came all the way here so Tony could sleep through this?"

I let go of the overhead luggage rack, trying not to lose my footing. Steadying myself against the yawing train, I leaned over and poked Tony with my walkie-talkie. "Wake up!" I said over the noise.

Getting no response, I went for a Hail Mary pass. "Tony, you're missing out. This is so *Parts Unknown*."

His eyes instantly opened wide, then narrowed. "I got a part unknown for you right here," Tony said, giving me the finger. Not the reaction I was hoping for, but at least he was awake.

"The other part that remains unknown is whether or not we're going to make it alive," Philippe said. "I mean this thing is going to derail at some point."

Despite every indication the train was going to fly off the tracks and accordion up like a pile of crushed aluminum cans, somehow it hadn't. Even better, the whole death-defying adventure was shaping up to be the best travel beat we'd ever filmed. One of the amazing things about making the show was that whenever things went wrong, plan B had a magical way of working out even better.

"This is Shwedagar," Patrick said as the train slowed down and clanked into the next station. "Time to reconfigure for the night."

The first-class sleeping coach had been swapped for one consisting of non-communicating berths, meaning movement between them was only possible when the train was stopped. This presented a number of logistical hurdles given we were expressing straight through until the morning. I worked out a plan to split up the crew, with Josh and me each supervising one member of the camera team. But of course, as always, nothing went according to plan. At the last moment Tony and Zach conspired to mutiny, exiling Josh, Patrick, and me to a shared compartment.

"But we need to film a night beat!" I protested. "And a morning breakfast beat!"

"Don't worry, we'll cover it," Zach said. Seeing the look on my face, he added, "I promise . . . have some faith."

Having faith was a tall order when it came to Tony spontaneously delivering transport beat *content*, but there wasn't time to argue. The bell rang; we were pulling out of the station. Fuck it. The universe had smiled on me thus far, and I could use an evening off. I settled in with Josh and Patrick, and soon we'd put a sizable dent in one of the six cases of jungle-temperature beer stowed in our cabin.

My eighties playlist blared at full volume on battery-powered speakers, Depeche Mode, New Order, Erasure, and Talking Heads barely audible above the rattle and clank of the train hurtling through dark countryside.

The full moon glinted off flooded rice paddies, and the occasional stupa sparkling with strings of electric lights whizzed by. We burst out laughing each time the train would take a sickening plunge and everything that wasn't bolted down levitated. Once I resigned myself to dying in a train wreck, I started really enjoying the real-life roller coaster ride. The beer helped.

"Thank you, guys," I said, offering a toast. "This is turning out to be one hell of an experience."

Around the time we finished the second case of beer, the train had slowed to a crawl, and I seized the opportunity to take a much-needed piss. Though I was quite drunk, or maybe because of it, I calculated relieving myself while hanging out of a moving train was preferable to our shadowy and malodorous bathroom. No sooner had I stepped into the doorframe than a palm frond whacked me in the face, and my glasses went spiraling into the jungle.

"Fuck, where the hell did that come from?!" I shouted. "Josh, spot me." When I was done, we traded places, and I took the lookout squinting into the dark, blurry void.

"Ahhhh . . . *yeeeeaaahhh* . . . that's soooo good," Josh said.

"Josh! I see lights ahead! I think we're coming up to a crossing!" I shouted midway into what was shaping up to be a *Guinness World Record* contender of a piss. "Put it away!!!"

"Oh god!" Josh yelled. "I'm trying! Oh god, I can't stop!"

A wall of motorbike headlights illuminated our train car wobbling past, treating men, women, and children perched on the handlebars to a full-frontal view of Josh spraying back and forth.

"I'm so sorry!" he cried. "I can't stop! I'm so sorry!"

I slept poorly that night, occasionally waking up midair before crashing back down onto the mattress. The next thing I remember was the shunting and screech of the train slowing down. Sunshine filtered through the gently swaying tatter of curtains. Outside, jungle rice paddies had given way to a vast stretch of arid yellow grassland.

The train hissed and ground to a halt. We were surrounded by a rush of food vendors dressed in brightly colored fabrics selling fried fish, bean curd, and samosas from trays and baskets balanced on their heads.

I hopped out of bed and made my way through the crowd gathered around the train. When I found the rest of the crew, they were already filming Tony and Philippe looking for breakfast.

"How was your night?" I asked when the cameras cut.

"Fantastic," Philippe said. "Eight hours solid."

"I was bouncing around like a pachinko ball," said a less than enthusiastic Tony. "It was just like bang, bang, bang, bang. I literally got whacked into the side once, it woke me right out of . . . well, I wouldn't say a dead sleep. So do we have any idea when our mystery train arrives?"

"I'm told another hour and a half," I said.

"That's not fourteen hours," Tony said, checking his Rolex.

"It's looking closer to eighteen . . . " I conceded.

"Ten, fourteen, eighteen. Who's counting? We could have literally flown to Hong Kong, had dinner at the Peninsula, and then flown to Bagan in the time this train has taken . . . or is taking."

Nineteen and a half hours after departing Yangon, the Night Express to Bagan reached its final destination. We limped off the train a bit worse for wear: grumpy, hungover, exhausted, and injured. Zach was coughing up brake dust, Patrick's hair was matted with what looked like the same dried puke on Josh's shirt. I was squinting to see without glasses and rubbing at a palm-shaped welt on my cheek while Tony grasped his lower back.

"All right, Bagan, here we come!" Philippe said, springing onto the platform like an adolescent gazelle. "*Mingalaba!*"

A BILLOW OF MARS RED dust swirled skyward, dwarfing our van as it navigated a rutted dirt road. We passed horse carts, farmers working their fields, and villagers carrying yokes laden with buckets of water. It was a sleepy agrarian scene set against a gothic backdrop of pyramid-sized temples and stupas stretching to infinity. Bagan had once been the capital of a mighty ancient kingdom and was said to be one of the most impressive archaeological sites in the world, rivaling the likes of Machu Picchu and Angkor Wat. International sanctions and tourism boycotts had thus far left the crimson-tinged landscape spectacularly untrampled. With the recent changes in the country, though, cranes stood sentinel on the fringes, silent for the moment and poised to begin constructing hotels for tourists that were soon to come.

Early morning light revealed the scars from a millennium of earthquakes and neglect. Some of the grand and mysterious edifices were partially covered by shrubs, others rose dramatically from stands of palm and tamarind. Livestock grazed in what would surely one day be a parking lot. There was an eerie feeling of emptiness to the place, only heightened by the lone tour bus that bumped through. Other than the farmers and a handful of aggressive children selling trinkets, we had the whole vastness of Bagan to our cameras.

Taking it all in, though I couldn't put my finger on it, I knew something had shifted. The move from the Travel Channel to CNN meant the show had a new gravitas. A giant leap toward what Tony had always wanted it to be. That ambition seemed to match his brooding, almost guilt-tinged outlook on his own celebrity, that it didn't really mean a damn thing unless he made it mean something. So, yeah, that probably was why he'd been so insufferable since we'd arrived. Here we were, poised to introduce the world to a country few outsiders had seen in nearly fifty years. Surely Tony felt the weight of what he was trying to do. And to a certain extent, its successful execution was entirely in my hands.

"FIVE MINUTES TO TONY, FIVE MINUTES TO TONY," the walkie chattered. The clock was winding down fast on this shoot. The cameras were ready to go when Tony and Philippe arrived. We removed our shoes and began climbing the crumbling stairs of a large bell-shaped stupa mounted on a decaying wedding cake base. Grass poked out of fissures, and small chunks of red clay broke off under foot, tumbling down the fifty-five-degree incline, which only

got steeper the higher we went. Arriving out of breath at a platform near the top, we were rewarded with a stunning panorama of the temple-strewn valley. A couple hundred feet of elevation demanded a whole new appreciation of the landscape. The Irrawaddy River glistened in the distance while a low line of golden mist clung to the horizon, silhouetting countless intricately shaped stupas and rising hot air balloons.

"Oh, this is stunning," Philippe said, his eyes wide with amazement. "This is so beautiful. So much like an ode to human, you know, beliefs and adoration and worshipping and—"

"Slave labor," Tony said. "I don't want to sound like a Debbie Downer here, but I'm thinking, you build this many temples—thousands of them—in a relatively short period of time, chances are, you know, somebody was working for less than minimum wage. Let's put it that way."

"Nevertheless, this is truly extraordinary," Philippe said. "Totally unique, I've never seen anything like this."

"Yeah, pretty awesome," Tony said. "Makes me almost wish I was a spiritual kind of a guy."

Tony had spoken to remarkable people who freely discussed politics, their experiences, and expectations for the future. We were going home with a strong story set in a beautiful, fascinating, visually arresting country opening up to the outside world. I should have been happy, but I wasn't. We were missing something. There was no question the move to CNN meant the stakes were higher. So much was riding on bringing back a kick-ass pilot episode for the new series, I needed Tony to express that he'd been genuinely moved or changed by the trip. I wanted Tony to be present this time. Fuck, I wanted to be present. The usual drill was weeks or months from now when the experience felt more like a dream than reality, the whole thing at a comfortable distance, Tony would write some poignant voice-over and then I'd know I'd actually been to Burma. But I didn't want to wait for the edit to know I'd been somewhere amazing this time. I gave it one last try.

"Umm . . . so . . . how do you feel being here?" I asked.

"I feel hungry," Tony said. "Like I'm waiting for my fucking chicken curry breakfast."

My heart sank. When Tony connected . . . well, it was the most amazing rush, my reward for a job well done. I felt like I'd moved mountains to put him in front of perhaps the most spectacular vista we'd ever filmed and it still wasn't enough . . . Prepared to throw in the towel, I had a thought. Could the problem be Tony was suffering from the same self-imposed pilot episode anxiety as me?

"Let's get some deep thoughts," I said, going for broke. "Deep thoughts" was production code for Tony silently looking out over a landscape. Maybe without the pressure to talk there was a chance he'd finally be able to get out of his own head. If that was the issue. It was worth a try. As Zach and Todd backed off to reset, Tony sat down on the ledge and gazed over the landscape backlit by the rising sun. A distant jangling of cow bells and the occasional bleat of a goat along with wisps from the perfume of a wood fire drifted on the morning breeze.

"Well . . . actually . . . I'm amazed being here," Tony said, breaking the silence. ". . . I mean . . . generally speaking we've been to a lot of places where people aren't happy to see cameras . . . whereas just about everybody here has been really, for lack of a better word, open and friendly. Which is really weird considering just last year and to some extent still, they're living in a place where for fifty years all that most people remember is an incredibly oppressive government. It's really extraordinary."

I couldn't believe what I was hearing! It appeared somehow I was getting what I wanted—what the show needed—and at the absolute last possible moment no less. I held my breath, worried that even exhaling would disrupt whatever magic we'd struck.

"You know I look at this as an essay," Tony said. "I spend a little over a week in Myanmar, Burma, this is what I saw, this is what it felt like. But something that we very much have to consider is that at the end of this week, we're all going back to New York. Where I can have myself a nice Frappuccino, and edit this show any way I want, right? But what we have to consider is whoever helped us off camera, whoever we hung out with, whoever we saw, whoever was nice to us, whoever associated with us during our time here, the point is, we don't pay the price for that show. Everybody who helped us could very well pay that price, so that's something we really got to balance especially when you know . . . we're not journalists."

Tony paused and looked back out over Bagan. His hand fidgeted. "What happens to the people that we leave behind?"

Chapter Three

APPETIZER

I WAS THIRTY-EIGHT WHEN TONY DIED, BUT I FELT LIKE I'D ALREADY LIVED nine lives and had the premature gray hair to prove it. For better or worse over the preceding decade and a half, I'd organized my life around Tony and the job.

All I have to do is close my eyes, and there he is, looking every bit the globe-trotting TV star. Both old and young at the same time, full head of curly gray hair, cigarette in his mouth, standing tall at six-foot-four, sunbaked, half-hidden behind a pair of solid black Steve McQueen Persols. Tony always seemed in a hurry, like he might disappear at any second. He'd only ever smoke about half a cigarette before stamping it out. I asked him once why he did that. "Old habit from my restaurant days," he said. "Gotta get back to the kitchen and see what's fucked up."

My relationship with Tony was complicated. Tony was hard to be around, and painful to be away from. He was intellectually stimulating beyond compare, and his energy would suck you dry. Frustrating, difficult, and even terrifying at times, but always fascinating, bigger than life. Taking a drag of his cigarette he'd say, "You gotta make sacrifices to do this." Now, without Tony, life as I knew it was over. It was starting to sink in that I had no idea who I was outside of the show.

TELEVISION IS AN AMAZING MACHINE. TV has the power to transport you far, far away. Away from the dreary everyday to somewhere better. More colorful. Believing the miracle invention to be evil, my misguided parents forbade me as a kid the comfort of TV's artificial bluish glow. But that didn't stop me. I would steal it late at night or whenever I was left home alone. I couldn't get enough. TV felt like dreaming awake, a place you could go to get away, at least for a little while.

Real life had bullies, and chores, and difficult, thorny problems. TV, on the other hand, had friends, candy, new cars, air-conditioning, and what looked like love. TV was easy to digest, and it made sense; the rules were clear. No chance of missing the point. The musical score told me exactly when to be scared, when to be happy, when something important was about to be said. A comforting laugh track made it clear I was in on the joke.

Sure, I could sense its one-dimensionality—flat, unrealistic sets and cheaply made characters. Wonder Bread family values, high-fructose morality, irradiated comedy for my viewing safety. But no one in the TV seemed to mind. And at the time, neither did I.

I wanted so bad to be there—to be on TV, to be in the TV. So, of course, I got a job in TV. I didn't need to watch TV anymore, because I was living it, high as a kite on the indefinable magic of the medium to transport and erase. There was some sacrifice here and there—lost friends, failed relationships, a warped worldview, an unhealthy amount of stress, and a good dose of psychological isolation—but the rewards turned out even better than I could have imagined. I had done the impossible, fulfilled my dream, and stepped through the screen into a more colorful, exciting, ready-for-prime-time dimension of travel, opulent hotels, awards ceremonies, and extraordinary adventures. My life became a collection of picture-perfect postcards, all thanks to the magic of television. And it was wonderful. For a while.

The irony, of course, was that the dreary life I had so eagerly sought to escape as a child was in reality more like Mayberry than anything on TV. My father bought a video camera when my younger sister was born. Cutting-edge technology in 1983, it was a monstrosity that came in several pieces, camera on the shoulder with the recorder tethered by wire and worn over the shoulder on a strap. It recorded what looked like a pretty magical and idyllic childhood in the woods. And for the most part it was. Except for school.

In addition to my impressive roster of learning disabilities, some of my best talents included crippling social anxiety and an uncanny ability to attract bullies. My teachers used to say I brought it on myself, and ultimately I'd have to agree with them. I knew how to push buttons, and I antagonized my peers to get attention. Though awful at the time, looking back, my greatest elementary school achievement may have been inspiring the entire fourth grade to write a group letter complaining about me. When Mrs. Bennaquade read it aloud in front of the class, I burst out crying.

"Are those real or crocodile tears?" she said with mock sympathy.

My social and academic struggles in school gave me a very strong distrust of institutions and made me want to take them apart. I became adept at instigating other people to do things that would then cause situations to spiral out of hand. It was my way to gain some power and control, and it was a skill that would end up serving me well in my chosen career.

One day I found myself standing with Tony behind a pier-side San Francisco burger joint while the directors of photography made final adjustments to the lighting inside.

"What's the best way for a kid to deal with a bully?" I asked. Even though Tony could be one at times, I knew nothing bothered him more than bullies. One of the best things about the show, if not *the* best thing about the show, was how Tony used his platform for good. From Mexican cooks to Palestinian shop owners, Tony championed the marginalized and gave a voice to the voiceless, stuck up for the little guy.

"In high school a friend of mine was getting pushed around by this jock," Tony said. "I went out and got an after-school job, saved up enough money to buy an ounce of weed. In the meantime, I'd gone to the library and learned how to pick a lock. So I broke into the jock's locker, planted the weed, then made an anonymous report to the police claiming the jock was dealing drugs. The cops searched his locker, found the dope, and the jock got sent off to juvie. Ruined his life. That's how you deal with a bully."

I was simultaneously impressed, a little terrified, and touched by Tony's story.

"I was bullied a lot," I volunteered. "One of the most embarrassing times was in elementary school when my math teacher was late to class. We were all lined up in the hallway waiting for her to arrive when Jenny O'Degan, smallest girl in the grade, punched me in the face. The rest of the class erupted into hoots of laughter and cheers. I was crying and they all high-fived Jenny."

"Where does she live?" Tony asked, taking a drag of his cigarette.

"Umm, I'm not sure," I said, surprised by the question. "I haven't really kept in touch, I think she's in Seattle now."

"All right, here's what we're gonna do," Tony said. "We're going to add Seattle to the book tour this summer. We'll look her up, find her address, send her gold-plated VIP tickets so she and seven of her best friends show up. Then at the end of the show, I'll call her up on stage, and you drop a bucket of festering pig's blood on her. You know, the *Carrie* thing. Then we watch everyone in the audience laugh. I know where to get pig blood in Seattle."

What Tony said meant a lot. He knew exactly when to make grand gestures, the kind of displays of warmth and caring that inspired a level of devotion that made me gladly put the show at the very center of my life, consequences be damned.

ONE OF THE SECRETS TO Tony's success was a fearless risk-all attitude that was at times indistinguishable from self-sabotage. It was a strategy that had yielded him a best-selling memoir and TV series seemingly out of nowhere. But after season two of *A Cook's Tour*, it appeared fate had called Tony's bluff. When the Food Network decided to cut international destinations in favor of domestic barbeque, Tony shocked everyone by quitting rather than star in a show he didn't want to make. He would often say, "Everyone on TV is afraid of not being on TV," but not Tony.

Chris and Lydia, who'd produced *A Cook's Tour*, spent a year or so trying to pitch a travel and food show with Tony but PBS and A&E along with everyone else declined. Just when Tony had made peace with his TV career being over, the Travel Channel ponied up the money to shoot three pilot episodes. All of a sudden he was back on TV. Titled *No Reservations*, this time the show took the ideas behind *A Cook's Tour* a step further, with episodes twice the length, a larger budget, and a more ambitious travel itinerary.

When Chris and Lydia started Zero Point Zero to make *No Reservations* in 2005, they hired me as post producer. It was my job to work with the editors after the crew returned from filming to convert roughly sixty to eighty hours of raw tape into one cohesive forty-two-minute episode.

It was great to be back with the team, but there was a problem. Watching that footage, I knew I wouldn't be happy stuck in an edit room. I had to find a way to be a part of making it happen. If other people could get paid to live what looked like the adventure of a lifetime, why couldn't I? ZPZ had an informal atmosphere, and it became something of a recurring joke that every Friday I'd go into Chris and Lydia's office and tell them that I wanted to travel. Eventually, maybe just to shut me up, they gave me a shot.

My first trip with Tony was to Moscow in 2006. I stood there waiting for him at JFK, feeling like I had won Willy Wonka's golden ticket. And in a way I had. Several days later I withdrew two weeks' salary from my personal checking account to balance the production budget so nobody would know I'd been pickpocketed in Red Square. Thus began a pattern of extreme ups and downs that would continue as long as I worked with Tony.

I was a wide-eyed twenty-six-year-old and joyously threw myself into the job 150 percent, fully committed to proving my worth. As the junior producer, my responsibilities included everything from managing our visa applications to pitching story ideas. I oversaw the booking of hotels, ground transportation, and flights. Once in-country, I was responsible for the petty cash, securing releases, keeping us on schedule, and making sure the crew was fed. Compared to later days when our shoots more resembled a film set with grips and dollies and a lighting truck, back then logistics were much simpler. For the Russia episode there was just one van, seven cases of equipment, a producer, cameraman, me, and Zamir, our fixer.

Zamir had arranged the two *Cook's Tour* Russia episodes, in the process proving himself an extremely entertaining on-camera companion. If Zamir wasn't a professional hustler, he might as well have been the world's amateur champion. Always scheming, running a side hustle, or pitching some get-rich-quick racket, often Zamir did all three at once. Zamir had intrigued Tony with his tall tales of underworld Soviet espionage and connections to shady figures in the Russian underworld. Zamir possessed a magic ability to open doors to locations and secure access to people usually off-limits to outsiders, let alone TV cameras. This time Zamir had used his connections to arrange a scene with Victor Cherkashin, the notoriously reclusive former KGB spy master and one of the most influential players during the Cold War. We spent the day with Victor at his country house outside Moscow. He and Tony wandered among birch trees collecting mushrooms while discussing counterespionage, double agents, and recruitment techniques.

The trip to Moscow exceeded my expectations; it wasn't easy, but it was far more thrilling than I could have imagined. Life was never dull when Tony was around. He must have been happy enough with my work because I became a regular part of the road crew. Back then I never could have imagined I'd ultimately work on roughly a hundred episodes; I pretty much took life one shoot at a time. After Russia there was a magical trip to Singapore, then Tuscany, where we all stayed together in a rented villa. One evening as we sat drinking wine watching the surrounding vineyards glow in a brilliant orange sunset, I worked up the courage to ask Tony to sign my copy of *Kitchen Confidential*. He gladly obliged and drew a kitchen knife along with the inscription, "To Tom, with many thanks for three, count 'em THREE flawless shows! Here's to many more. You make television fun again."

MUTED ORANGE AND BROWN LEAVES pinwheeled silently down from trees lining the Dâmbovița River. There was an uncanny quiet broken only by the odd crying baby or trundling of wheels over otherwise empty and uneven cobblestone streets.

I stood watching Todd film b-roll of neglected Beaux-Arts, Renaissance, Neoclassical, Gothic, and Rococo piles. Romantic Second Empire domes fish-scaled in faded blue slate showed patches of rafters like the protruding ribs of a decomposing whale. Bucharest, Romania's capital city, possessed an aura of nineteenth-century stateliness that was rudely interrupted by the occasional Soviet-era housing block. Small knots of emaciated dogs wandered about, seemingly less interested in the architecture than they were in Todd and me.

Both the grim housing blocks and the plague of roving mongrels were the result of dictator Nicolae Ceaușescu's urban redevelopment programs. Romania's violent 1989 revolution had resulted in Ceaușescu's execution along with the end of Communist rule, but Bucharest—along with much of the country—had yet to fully recover. The city once known as "little Paris" more closely resembled postwar Vienna. A beautiful woman with a dirty face.

I pulled the van door closed as more dogs emerged from the woodwork. "Umm . . . Todd?" I called over the walkie, hoping he was wearing his earpiece. We'd been warned about the dogs and how last month a Japanese tourist had been taking pictures when he was ripped limb from limb by a pack of strays. "Todd, I think you might want to get in the van," I tried again. Todd remained fixed to his eyepiece, oblivious to both my transmissions and the growling canine semicircle closing in around him.

It was late October 2007, almost exactly one year after my trip to Moscow, and I'd been given a trial run to see if I could handle being in charge of, well, everything, including—for the first time— prodding Tony for "content." Whether by pushing him to make an insightful observation or to wax poetic to the camera, I would discover it was easier said than done.

But I had an ace in the hole. Good ol' TV gold Russian Zamir was fixing my episode. He had a claim on all destinations formerly behind the Iron Curtain and had pitched Romania for his next adventure with Tony. But from pretty much the first moment we landed in-country, things started to go wrong.

One scene after another, the itinerary, locations, and even the menus turned out to be completely different than promised. Eventually it became apparent that the Romanian Tourism Bureau, with whom Zamir had cultivated a relationship, was blocking access to the sort of natural, working-class locations that were the show's bread and butter, instead attempting to steer us toward stage-managed government-approved duds. We'd show up expecting a natural scene at a family home only to find ourselves at an educational farm museum with the entire family lined up in fake traditional costumes. Zamir was drinking heavily and seemed oblivious to the problems, as well as perpetually confused about locations and people with which he was supposedly familiar. It was becoming clear Zamir was a little . . . unhinged. Not in an "I've had too much vodka" sort of way. Unhinged in a "trying to sell a decommissioned Russian nuclear submarine while dressed in a battleship Potemkin outfit" sort of way. Looking back, the show really went off the rails around the time we boarded a train to Transylvania.

"Zamir, are you wearing a crucifix?" I asked in surprise. "Aren't you Jewish?"

"It's the insurance policy against threat of vampire's blood sucking," Zamir said. "I have a basket of garlics if you are in need of the protection."

Our destination, the central Romanian province of Transylvania, was, of course, memorably described as the home of Count Dracula by Bram Stoker. The vampire legend was inspired by the life and times of a real fifteenth-century prince named Vlad Tepes, known for impaling his enemies and countrymen alike. As it turned out, Zamir actually seemed to believe in the undead—as well as Transylvania's untapped investment potential for Dracula-themed tourism opportunities.

"Jeez, Zamir," Tony said. "You're banging the Dracula thing pretty hard. Dracula motels, Dracula gift shops, Dracula theme parks, Dracula, Dracula, Dracula . . . What's next, are you going to pitch me on Count Snackula's Diner?"

Disembarking at Brasov, we traveled the rest of the way to our hotel by van along narrow roads twisting through thick Transylvanian forest. Out the window a slate gray October sky blended with wisps of fog curling down from the steep, snowcapped peaks of the Carpathian Mountains. Just after dark we arrived at the House of Dracula Hotel, a faux castle constructed of what looked to be highly flammable polystyrene blocks. It was decorated in a style reminiscent of Medieval Times meets Madame Tussauds, and Dracula-themed all year, although we had the luck of arriving on Halloween.

Being it was my favorite holiday, when Zamir had informed us there was a costume party at the hotel, I'd eagerly insisted we attend. Tony positioned a fake plastic knife on his head and painted a trickle of blood dripping down his face while Zamir squeezed into a pirate costume and I put on my homemade reindeer outfit complete with floppy antlers. We arrived in the ballroom, cameras rolling, to find ourselves in the midst of a tour group of retirees from Nevada. Despite being *promised* the party wasn't for tourists, I really should have known better. Dynel-wrapped vampires toasted fake-blood cocktails with septuagenarian sexy witches. It was basically Tony's worst nightmare. He described the atmosphere as something akin to "A Carnival Cruise to Geriatric Funkytown."

The whole sordid affair was as horribly off-brand as it was hilarious, and I continued to prod an extremely reluctant—and increasingly incensed—Tony for content.

"Oh my god, you just won't stop! You're like a fucking monkey jamming a fork into a light socket," Tony said. "You get zapped, but you keep doing it over and over again."

Meanwhile, on the other side of the room, Zamir was dancing the funky chicken and making new friends. "This is the best fake blood cocktail I've had in my life," he said, sipping from a goblet of bright red liquid. "Tomski, sit down with us. I would like to introduce you to the organizers of tonight's party. This is Uncle Dudu and his niece Miss Transylvania."

"Great party," I lied.

"From the most gorgeous girls from all over the country we make our selection of Miss Transylvania," Dudu beamed. They certainly made for an odd pair. Dudu was short, fat, bald, spoke in a high-pitched nasal voice, and was dressed in a white lace frock he explained was a "Little Bo-Peep" costume. Miss Transylvania, on the other hand, was stunning. She was wearing an emerald green ball gown and tiara that held back long brown hair, showing off her slender neck and delicate features.

"Will you excuse Uncle Dudu and I for just a moment to discuss some business?" Zamir asked, leaving me sitting alone with Miss Transylvania in an awkward silence. She was staring at me with an unblinking intensity. I hated meeting strangers, especially good-looking ones.

"They say you are a wealthy and important American television director," Miss Transylvania said, sliding a little closer to me.

"No, no. Actually, this is my first job," I said with a nervous laugh. "Umm . . . how old are you, by the way?"

Miss Transylvania smiled shyly and put her hand on my leg. "You look like my favorite actor, Cliff Owen."

"I have to get back to the shoot," I said, nearly knocking the table over as I hastily stood up.

ZAMIR CALLED IT AN EARLY night, but everyone, including Tony, ventured together into the shadows of the Translyvanian forest until we found a spot that offered a stunning mountain panorama. A distant howling floated on the night air, surely belonging to a dog but lupine enough to inspire a tingle of fear. Beneath the moon's brilliant glow we drank beer, smoked, laughed about the absurdity of the party, and Tony told ghost stories.

After a couple of beers I excused myself from the group and wandered off looking for a good spot to take a piss. Buoyed up by the mountain air mentholated with pine, I breathed in the moment and smiled. Soon I came across a small clearing, where I nearly tripped over a shovel. It was stuck in the ground next to a pile of dirt and a large hole. As I tried to make sense of what looked suspiciously like a freshly dug grave, I heard a rustling from the darkness. I stood frozen as the crunching, scraping sound came closer and closer. My mind raced with images of a wolf or a mummy, or worst of all whoever had dug the hole, but instead Miss Transylvania emerged from the darkness, her face pure white in the moonlight.

"Oh, it's you!" I said, relieved. "Look at this, I just found a fucking grave!"

"Why are you trying to escape me, my dearest deer?" she said, presumably making reference to my costume as she moved closer and leaned toward me.

"What are you doing?" I cried, recoiling in terror, convinced she was about to extend her fangs and bite my neck.

"Wah! You almost make me fall in the grave!" she said reproachfully. "I only want to kiss you."

"I think I need to go back to my friends," I said.

"No!" Miss Transylvania pouted and started backing toward the hole. "Kiss me or I will fall into the grave."

"Be careful!" I said.

"Kiss me," she said, continuing to back away, apparently confident in her charms.

"Seriously! I'm not going to stop you!"

"You must kiss me before I fall into th—" With a shriek and thump, Miss Transylvania fell backward into the grave.

Romania alternated between amazing, bizarre, serious, chaotic, fantastic, surreal, and tragicomic. By the end of the episode, Zamir was so hopped up on booze and pain killers he was barely coherent and unable to do much of anything. Worse, Tony had run out of patience, and it was dawning on me that losing control of the shoot was probably not a good business model.

A fitting end to the trip, on the last day Zamir took me aside for a private conversation.

"Tomski, I'm sorry . . . " Zamir said, a note of sympathy creeping around in his voice. "Unfortunately, you have committed what is considered a *serious* crime in Romania . . . Miss Transylvania is pregnant . . . and she is underage. Uncle Dudu is furious . . . I'm afraid this is going to be very expensive for you."

I rolled my eyes. "Zamir . . . I'm gay."

"Oh . . . shit . . . " Zamir said, seemingly disappointed. I lit a cigarette and shook my head.

THE ROMANIA EDIT WAS BITTERSWEET. I wasn't on the schedule going
forward, and based on how the shoot had gone, I didn't expect that
to change. If this was going to be both my first and last episode, I
reasoned, I'd better make it as good as possible. Jesse, the editor,
and I worked pretty much night and day, seven days a week. We
took a pretty simple approach and opted to just show it how it was.
Romania had been a perfect storm. Despite Zamir's fall from grace,
it being my first show, the Romanian Tourism Bureau meddling so
aggressively, and the campy nature of a Dracula-themed downward
spiral, everything somehow came together. Truth had been stranger
than fiction, and it was hilarious. At least I hoped it was. After the
first cut went to Tony, I got called into Chris and Lydia's office.

"Pack your bags," Chris said. "You're going to Colombia."

I could have jumped for joy. Apparently Tony had decided I'd be
sticking around.

"I was dreading watching that first cut assuming it was going to
be some plodding attempt to pretend Romania had been a normal
episode," Tony later explained. "Finally I worked up the nerve, put
in the DVD, and my jaw dropped. Jesus, you were relentless, going
right for the jugular again and again! Your hate for the place comes
through brilliantly! A strong point of view is *always* a good thing!
Bravo!"

Despite what happened there, I hadn't hated Romania at all,
just the opposite. But this was no time to argue. Turning out what
Tony instantly declared a "comedy classic" had cemented my role
as director.

I didn't expect what happened next, though in retrospect I
should have seen it coming. A massive scandal erupted when the
Romania episode was broadcast, generating the most comments ever
on the Travel Channel website. Romania's largest newspaper wrote

a scathing article casting Tony as Public Enemy Number One, and both the network and ZPZ had to issue statements.

I'd learned a valuable lesson. Romania showed me, for the first time, that people actually watched the show, and—much to my surprise—seemed to take it seriously. I did some soul searching, thought about what I wanted to do with my career. I reasoned that while I was traveling the world having fun, I had a responsibility to do better. Punching down was a bully move regardless of how funny, true, or deserving it might be.

On the next shoot in Colombia, I bent over backward to avoid the same mistakes. However, I was unprepared for how famous Tony was in Latin America. I found myself turning down overtures from captains of industry, offers of yachts, and invitations to estates. I even managed to demur repeated requests from the first lady to fly on the presidential jet to a private island. Colombia turned out to be a fantastic trip, and we succeeded in finding the real "roots" scenes we missed out on in Romania. Our last night, Tony hosted a wrap party in his luxurious Cartagena hotel room and screened the Romania episode. I beamed with pride watching Tony smile and laugh uproariously nearly the whole time.

THERE WAS ANOTHER IMPORTANT LESSON to come out of Romania, one with perhaps the farthest-reaching implications. Back in Transylvania, furious at me for subjecting him to the Halloween party, Tony had offered a bargain. He'd consider the score settled if I let Zach get a shot of me chained up in the "breakfast nook of the damned." Of course, for some reason there was a fully stocked medieval dungeon just past the dining room buffet.

From the beginning, I recognized in myself a willingness—a desire, even—to do *whatever* it took to make a good show and make Tony happy. And this being my first time directing, I had more control, responsibility, and more opportunity to succeed as well as provoke, fail, and humiliate myself. So I climbed into the stocks, and everything was fine . . . until Tony entered the room.

"Wait! This wasn't part of the deal!" I said, desperately trying to wriggle free. I could tell by the look on his face this wasn't going to end well. It turned out that, unlike the rest of the hotel, the heavy wooden stocks were very realistic, and I was trapped. Tony was wearing a black suit and, just like in *Reservoir Dogs*, he removed his jacket and rolled up his sleeves.

"Ooohhh, this is a good one," Tony said, perusing a rack of torture implements on the wall, including denailing tongs and a morning star. Out of the corner of my eye I could see him pick up a terrifying pitchfork-like thing with a row of sharp metal spikes on the end. "Do you speak Spanish? Have you ever heard the words *papi chulo*?"

"You've had too much to drink," I said. "And that's a real weapon!"

"Here we go, one . . . two . . . three . . . " Tony whacked me with the pitchfork so hard the end broke off. The cameraman and producer—somehow oblivious to my cries of pain—doubled over laughing. "You know, I think we've learned something here today," Tony said, turning to the camera. "Making cheeseball television does not come without cost."

I think more than a punishment, the real lesson Tony wanted to impart was my understanding—however briefly—of what he felt, to truly appreciate the dehumanizing indignity and torture of being on camera.

Whether intentionally or not, Tony had also demonstrated that a certain amount of suffering was part of the magic recipe. I wasn't sure which one of us had opened Pandora's Box, but there was no going back, and Romania marked a significant turn in our relationship.

As I would learn, the more shameful the situation, the more entertaining, as well as painful for the both of us. It was a bizarre pattern of mutually assured torture that would last throughout the course of our relationship. Over the next twenty-five episodes of *No Reservations*, twenty *Layovers*, and thirty-nine *Parts Unknowns*, the stakes escalated while we played our increasingly intense game of tit for tat.

The ignoble usually found its way to us whether we liked it or not. However, I figured since the cow was already out of the barn, I was justified in instigating the occasional miniature escalation, especially if it was good for the show. I got away with some stunts, others I didn't.

Allow me to unburden my conscience. I'd knowingly withheld information relating to a karaoke machine on skis that would be accompanying us on the ice fishing scene in Manchuria as well as a troupe of Greek circle dancers at the sheep roast on the island of Crete. There was a disastrous Haitian voodoo ceremony and Tony eating an endangered Vietnamese Java mouse-deer. Those were both accidents, but definitely my fault. In Amsterdam we conspired for the bar to break into Dutch folk song in unison, which totally freaked Tony out because he'd just got really stoned. Tony requested a vintage Ferrari to drive along the Amalfi Coast, but I rented him a Smart Car instead. I didn't just know about the pink stretch limo transport beat in Tijuana, I'd actively arranged it. Same goes for the monkey jockeys that raced on greyhounds. I hired a Punjabi dance troupe to pose as waiters then break into a Bollywood number halfway through Tony's meal. In Penang I swapped his trishaw for one bedecked in plastic flowers and spinning Christmas lights that Tony described as looking like Liberace's coffin. Adding insult to treachery, I chose to end that shoot day at the one hawker center in Georgetown hosting a seniors' country-western line-dancing night. For a scene in Korea where Tony was competing in a video game competition, I tricked him into choosing Little Red Riding Hood as an avatar. Her only power was love, and Tony was quickly smited by fire-breathing dragons. I once paid off a priest to deliver a narratively useful sermon, and in Sri Lanka I built a fake restaurant. I'd even been carrying an inflatable rubber chicken in my bag waiting for just the right moment. The only thing worse than risking personal disaster was a mediocre episode. Although our methods may have been somewhat unorthodox, it almost always made for great TV.

Chapter Four

HEART OF DARKNESS

CASUALLY ATTIRED IN A KHAKI LINEN SHIRT, CLARK DESERT BOOTS, AND his trademark Persol sunglasses, Tony made trekking through war-torn Congo look effortless.

"This is useful information, pretty much the best news I've heard all day," he said at the conclusion of our morning security briefing. "I didn't know you had a morbid fear of snakes and serpents, Tom. You know they prefer to bite the head off the penis, so if you were to expose yourself when walking through the underbrush, they'll probably go for that first."

We'd just been informed that highly venomous black mamba snakes were actually gray in color as well as a significant threat in the Democratic Republic of Congo, and Tony's biggest takeaway was that after ten years he'd finally discovered my fear of snakes. I'd grown accustomed to suppressing a myriad of inconvenient phobias while on shoots, but I absolutely drew the line at snakes. And now, in addition to "health and safety" concerns, such as the ever-present threat of armed rebel groups, I had to worry about Tony weaponizing his newfound information. Which is why I was somewhere down the Congo River worrying about rubber snakes.

TO CALL DOING A SHOW in the Congo Tony's "obsessive dream proj-ect" was a gross understatement. He always said you tend to see your life as a book or movie, and for Tony that story—if there had to be just one—was Joseph Conrad's 1902 novella *Heart of Darkness*. The book, set in the Belgian Congo, and its cinematic reinterpretation *Apocalypse Now*, about the Vietnam War, had been recurring motifs throughout Tony's work right from the beginning. Pretty much every river trip we ever filmed contained a Kurtz reference or some kind of homage to the theme of descending into madness deep in the jungle.

"Congo should be Africa's richest country; instead it's one of the world's great historical injustices," Tony said. "Nobody even knows there was a fucking holocaust here. Ten million people—half the country—killed. If the Congolese didn't meet quota, the Belgians would cut off a hand to inspire productivity among the workforce. That's the thing about *Heart of Darkness*, 'agents' like Conrad were working for King Leopold, raiding, slaughtering, enslaving the pop-ulation for ivory and rubber. It was unbelievably brutal, and it was all just business as usual."

Much to Tony's delight CNN was all too happy to finance the big-ticket destinations on his bucket list, and so far in the first season of *Parts Unknown* we were checking off a good number. But filming in the Democratic Republic of Congo—one of the most danger-ous and politically unstable countries in Africa, if not the entire world—was going to be a challenge. For nearly two decades, count-less armed rebel groups and splinter factions backed by neighboring countries had been waging a brutal civil war against federal author-ity in the resource-rich Eastern DRC. Five million people had been killed and four million more displaced, making Congo the bloodiest conflict since World War II. The current instability stemmed from a period of political assassination and dictators, which in turn was a legacy of the unimaginably ruthless Belgian colonial rule.

As with any episode, the first step was to find the right local fixer. But everyone we spoke to said it couldn't be done. One photojour-nalist with a camera? Risky but doable. Full-on *Parts Unknown*–sized film crew and accompanying infrastructure including half a million dollars' worth of film gear? No way in hell. So impossible that an undertaking of this style was not only inadvisable, nobody had even attempted it, at least since the 1990s when rebels burned, raped, and pillaged their way across the country.

"Hell yeah, we can do that!" said a gravelly voice at the other end of a long-distance phone call. "Just stay away from the cannibals. When I filmed that shit a crowd of five hundred began stoning me. I barely made it out alive. But this is why you should hire me: I have a really good handle on how to operate here. You'll be in safe hands, by Congo standards at least." Originally from upstate New York, Dan had chosen to spend his mid-thirties embedded with alternating Congolese military and rebel groups while filming a documentary about the heaviest fighting the Congo had seen in years. Dan's time in Congo had left him with shrapnel wounds, a little hearing loss from an anti-aircraft round, some insect eggs growing in his foot, and a gallows sense of humor. I wasn't certain where he fell on the spectrum between brave and foolhardy, but in spite of some personality quirks, it was clear he was no idiot. As I would learn, Dan and his friend, collaborator, and right-hand man, Horeb, were probably the only people alive who had just the right combination of skills to get our show through the Congo.

But before we could retrace Conrad's journey down the Congo River, we had to get there. The fastest way to do it, and really the only way, given our time constraints, was to fly into Rwanda, enter Congo through Goma—at the epicenter of the fighting—then fly to Kisangani and hook up with the Congo River there. Despite finished shows giving the impression we were in the farthest flung corners of the globe, with all the gear and a crew that could approach twenty-five with local hires included, the production wasn't as mobile as you might think, and we often tried to make it look farther out from an airport and nice hotel than we were. Thing was, the Congo wasn't just far out. It might as well have been the other side of the moon.

This shoot was going to have to be different; there'd be no thirty cases of film equipment or two-hour setups for a food insert shot. We were going to rough it on this one—smaller, leaner, with an alternate crew of burly survivalists, just two cameramen, a producer, and me. I wasn't quite sure where I fit in with the rest of the team, but I'd got us through some tough locations before and I had, perhaps, the unhealthy habit of putting the show above my own well-being or sanity. It was a trait Tony appreciated. The way I looked at it was, yes, there were sacrifices, risks, and Tony could be difficult—often making crazy, unrealistic demands—but I'd been given one hell of a golden ticket, and I was going to make the most of the opportunity. So I bought a fancy pair of snake-proof boots and packed my suitcase. Crazy or not, we were going to the Congo.

Landing in Rwanda, I watched nervously as machine-gun-bearing soldiers in fatigues rifled through our luggage looking for prohibited items. Walkie-talkies were at the top of the list, and I was smuggling fifteen of them in my suitcase. "Walkies are a big no-no," Dan had warned. "Just one can be used to command a battalion of four hundred rebels, so governments here are all hard-core about that shit." I found this an impressive statistic, as I had trouble using them to command just two cameramen. There was a commotion when one of the soldiers found the producer Moose's huge stash of high-protein energy bars. Worried about food options in the Congo, before leaving New York, Moose had gone to his local camping retailer and filled a shopping cart with every last energy bar and freeze-dried field ration in the store. The cashier had asked with a somewhat worried expression, "Is there something you know that I don't?" Apparently, plastic bags were also prohibited in Rwanda, and the ban was taken seriously. We waited while each of the energy bars was opened and tossed into a government-issue burlap sack before the whole sticky mess got stuffed back in Moose's bag.

"Welcome to the jungle!" Dan said on the other side of customs. With a cigarette in his mouth, baseball cap, and rumpled Hawaiian shirt, Dan looked younger than he sounded over the phone. In addition to the usual fixer responsibilities, we were counting on Dan to get us through checkpoints, as well as keeping us from getting robbed, jailed, or worse.

"This episode is gonna be killer!" He grinned. "Figuratively speaking."

Checking in to the Gorillas Golf Hotel—a generic establishment catering to business travelers—we met Dez, the team leader of our new "risk management consultants." Along with Warren and Stew, the field medic, they were a group of confidence-inspiring ex–British military types. After the gear was unpacked and Tony arrived, we gathered in the hotel's fluorescent-lit conference room to go over a security briefing.

"You gents have picked one hell of a place to make a TV show," Dez said in a pleasant Kiwi accent. "As you well know, the Congo is in the midst of a very ugly war. The Eastern DRC is considered high-risk for hijackings, robbery, military and police roadblocks, as well as disease outbreaks. Additionally, as of last week, peace talks with M23 rebels who hold territory to the north and west of Goma appear to have collapsed. Unconfirmed reports suggest the M23 have moved closer to the city and could invade as they did last November. There are a number of warning signs that point to a possible escal—"

"Should I be wearing one of those cool Geraldo Rivera journalist safari jackets?" Tony asked enthusiastically. "Do they make those for men? I hear Christiane Amanpour has hers personally tailored at Yves Saint Laurent in Paris."

"We'll be monitoring the situation," Dez said, clearing his throat. "But in terms of likelihood and probability, crime and logistics are the biggest hazards. We have a large footprint, which exacerbates the potential for harassment, intimidation, and demand for bribes by government officials, the army, and police, all of whom are highly prone to corruption and have a reputation for substance abuse. Interactions with anyone thought to be under the influence of drugs or alcohol should be treated with a high degree of caution and a cool head. Panic breeds panic. Unfortunately, there aren't any 'good guys' in this conflict."

"Welcome to my world," Dan said. "About fifteen different 'soldiers' extorted cash from me at gunpoint just on the scout, and some drunk FARDCs started fucking with me because I approached a 'checkpoint' too late at night . . . I can't count how many times I've been robbed, arrested, officially and non-officially, and shot at. This is life in Congo, man."

WE SET OUT AT DAYBREAK for Goma. Our five beat-up Land Cruisers convoyed through steep green mountains, in and out of cloudbanks and highland villages. Animals, children, pedestrians, and street vendors were all well rehearsed at stepping out of the way of our trucks at the last possible second. We encountered the aftermath of a massive tractor-trailer wreck, but the roads were well paved, and thanks to the ban on plastic, Rwanda was spectacularly clean.

On the four-hour drive, there was plenty of time to question the wisdom of bringing our semi–food show to an active red zone where the population was starving, and most people lived off less than a dollar a day. Out the window, Rwanda's terraced farms of plantains, cassava, and corn whizzed by in a blur. I'd read that in contrast the Congolese didn't farm. If you had a patch of land with stuff worth killing for, someone would kill you for it. Our security briefing the night before had been a stark reminder of where we were headed. In most places there was at least some sort of rule of law, and you knew who might do you harm. But the Congo was in ruins: much of the country was a patchwork of lawless rebel-controlled territories.

Thinking it through logically it really demanded the question, *Why the fuck were we going to the Congo?* Was it just about satisfying one of Tony's biggest obsessions? Or was it a way for him to use the show to shine a light on something bigger? When I asked Tony why he wanted to go to the Congo, he said, "Don't worry about why, did he tell you why in *Apocalypse Now*? No. He wanted a mission. He got one." Although I didn't voice my concerns, I found Tony's answer unsatisfying. I well knew Tony liked to make people think, keep them guessing, his storytelling style a reflection of unsatisfying real-life complexities. But this wasn't a show sum-up, this was our lives we were talking about. There just had to be a better reason we were going to an active war zone.

"Get ready to say goodbye to civilization," Dez called over the walkie as we approached the border. Entering Congo, there was no mistaking Goma was a battlefield. Alongside NGO trucks we navigated a maze of semi-passable roads, barbed wire, bombed-out buildings, and UN armored tanks, while choppers hovered overhead.

Checking in to the hotel, I made sure Tony was connected to the internet and asked if he had any b-roll shot requests before we headed out. "Women doing all the work, bathing and washing, the struggle to stay clean and alive," he said. "The big takeaway is beauty and misery." I left Tony to his iPad and went to join the crew loading up the trucks.

"Above all this country is a dog-eat-dog world," Dan was saying in the way of a pre-shoot pep talk. "We will need to do surgical strikes. Get in and out quick before it gets too hairy. It's fucking heartbreaking, it's also reality. The city is built on and with lava, dirt, dust, trash, sorrow, and intensity . . . "

To break the tension, Jerry—one of our directors of photography famous for his affable and soothing demeanor—offered a group fist bump and said, "Superpowers unite, take the form of . . . Television Crew!"

As we hit the streets with cameras rolling, shouts of "*Mazunga!*" greeted us everywhere we went. Due to the endless fighting and various rebel groups roving the jungle just outside of town, Goma was overcrowded with refugees, and now with the looming threat of another invasion by the M23, society felt like it was on the verge of collapse. Downtown we filmed two men playing guitar; it was a moment of peace amid the crowding, yelling, bustle, and chaos of people struggling to stay alive in a garbage-strewn landscape.

Horeb, Dan's right-hand man, was always with us. A native Congolese, Horeb had a gentle demeanor that stood out in stark contrast to the aggressive, hard-edgedness of, well, almost everything else. A youthful forty-five, he spoke eight languages and was constantly dealing with some sort of mini catastrophe like the multitude of people who came screaming at the cameras, demanding paperwork or money, or both.

"Why were those guys so angry?" I asked after what felt like a particularly aggressive interaction.

"They say people with cameras come, take pictures, nothing changes," Horeb said. "I told them you are the good guys."

Horeb's words caught me off guard. Were we actually the good guys? At the moment it certainly didn't feel like it. Working in more troubled parts of the world highlighted an uncomfortable aspect of the job. We weren't here to dig wells or bring health care to the Congo. When your objective is to get footage that illustrates a story—in this case how much destruction and tragedy exists in a place—it puts you in the awkward position of witnessing human suffering as a goal. After asking to photograph someone in desperate conditions, I returned to a nice hotel, while they did not.

"It's the worst for women," Horeb said. "Rape happens all the time in Congo. It's okay to rape if you give a chicken to the woman's family. I do this job because I want my country to be better for my children when they grow up."

While we were filming Goma's lava-ravaged cathedral to illustrate the devastation from a 2001 volcanic eruption, street children started pelting us with rocks. Mo, our other director of photography—who wore multiple cameras like some people wore jewelry—kept recording while we jumped back in the truck. "What the fuck was that?" I asked as we drove away, Mo's camera still rolling on a man chasing off the kids with a big stick.

"There is so much anger, even from the children," Horeb said. "Everyone is tired of the war. More than five million dead, hundreds of thousands of refugees because of this war."

What started at dusk as tropical rain had distorted into an unbroken roar by the time our trucks arrived back at the hotel. We joined Tony on the veranda for some beers under the protection of a leaking roof. When not filming standard food and travel stuff, what the show did best was talk to people when their world wasn't burning down. The Congo, however, was on fire.

"These bottles are worth more than the beer inside," Dan said. He was holding a half-full Primus up to the light while watching the carbonation expire. "They're reused and re-transported over all the Congo's shitty roads. Many of these bottles have probably seen several wars in their lifetime."

Despite Dan's tough exterior, I got the sense being surrounded by so much pain and suffering weighed heavily on him. "There aren't any easy answers," he said. "Many Congolese are forced into these rebel groups. They're all fighting over ores like coltan, it's some shit in every cell phone. There's trillions of dollars' worth of it here. So the fighting isn't going to end any time soon."

"SHIT, MAN, I JUST GOT a call from the driver heading to Kisangani with our supplies. He got fucking held up for all his cash!" Dan said, finishing a cigarette. "Aren't ya glad we're flying?"

Weeks before, while planning how to get the 400 miles from Goma to Kisangani—our closest rendezvous point with the Congo River—it had become clear the overland route was not an option. The Congo's once well-developed network of highways had been all but reclaimed by jungle or destroyed by war and, as warned, was a hunting ground for bandits. But flying didn't seem much more appealing. In the Congo, commercial airliners were known for going down on a somewhat regular basis. "Look at it this way," Dan said. "Planes here crash in the jungle all the time. Would you rather be in a Boeing going five hundred miles per hour or a bush plane going fifty miles per hour?" To someone like me, with a morbid fear of flying, it sounded like a sensible, if unsettling, argument.

Dan knew a charter outfit that operated some cinematic and historically significant aircraft. "My bush pilot buddy Wiyo told me he's flown JFK's private jet and Elvis's old tour plane," Dan said. "Dude has some crazy stories." At least if we were going to die in a plane crash, it was going to make a good scene.

Approaching the airport, Mo got shots out the car window of UN guard posts and abandoned 707s. Once we arrived, the crew started to unload and set up gear while Dan, Dez, and I went to investigate the airworthiness of our plane. Seeing the comical antique shoebox of an aircraft for the first time, I thought, there's no way in hell Elvis or JFK would be caught dead in this thing. It looked like a less aerodynamic version of a 1960s Winnebago with two propeller engines and an unusual stubby double-finned tail.

"SC-7 Skyvan," Dez said, kicking the tire. "Same type my mates Sledge and Nobby were killed in. It's a good crate."

"This was the plane used to transport Queen Victoria's wardrobe on her tour of Africa," said a proud young man in pilot's uniform.

"Meet Wiyo," Dan said. "Don't worry, he went to aviation school in Florida."

"So, Wiyo, Dan tells me you've got some interesting stories about flying," I said, making small talk.

"Oh, yes," Wiyo said with a broad smile. "I was landing one time and a poisonous snake dropped out of the console above my head. Make a move and it bites, I die. Don't move, I crash the plane. What to do . . . ?"

"FIVE MINUTES TO TONY, FIVE MINUTES TO TONY," crackled over the walkie, and I was actually glad for the distraction this time.

"So, what's your evil plan?" Tony asked me as he arrived.

"Well, I thought we'd do a little 'pre-game' talk before taking off. The weather is turning," I said, eyeing the darkening sky. "And I'm told this was formerly Queen Victoria's 'Flying Wardrobe.'"

"I think you mean Queen Elizabeth," Tony corrected, looking doubtfully at the airplane. "Though she must have been very young at the time."

Seeing Tony was in a frolicsome mood and Mo had the camera ready to go, I asked, "So, what are we doing today?"

"We're flying to Kisangani; this is the preferred route," he said. "The alternative is how many hours?"

"Four and a half days."

"Yeah . . . well, we could drive for four and a half days over what could only notionally be called roads, or we could . . . fly this."

A huge bolt of lightning and boom of thunder shook the runway. "Uh oh . . . " Tony said with a slightly nervous laugh. "Well, I'm a fatalist. I don't worry about individual aircraft. I figure your number's up, your number's up. And today's not my day."

As if on cue, there was another flash of lightning and peel of thunder. "Well, let's get this thing airborne," Tony said. "You're anticipating a smooth flight today?"

"No," Wiyo said, looking up at menacing storm clouds. "As you can see, the weather is deteriorating now."

"So, a little bumpy?" Tony asked.

"I'm wondering if we should wait until after the storm," I said.

"Yeah—" Wiyo began.

"I'm sorry. Are you the pilot?" Tony interrupted. "If the man says we're ready to take off, then I put my faith in him."

"You didn't even let him finish!" Turning to Wiyo, I asked, "Are we good to go or should we wait?"

"Yeah," Wiyo responded.

"Okay, then let's go," Tony said, boarding the airplane. "There's no room for yellowbellies on Queen Victoria's Flying Wardrobe!"

At this point all sorts of things were running through my head, like I was pretty sure Wiyo had been trying to say it wasn't a good time to take off. And I was losing control of the situation because Tony was in a hurry. And our plane must be overloaded with gear, and this was the worst day *ever* for my seat belt to be broken, and I didn't want the headline to read, "Anthony Bourdain and Unnamed Film Crew Perish in Flying Wardrobe," and what had happened to Dez's friends Sledge and Nobby? Fortunately, by the time the crew loaded up, a torrential downpour with accompanying crashes of thunder enveloped the airport, and it was clear we weren't going to beat the storm. "Beer o'clock," Dan said, as we all ran to the terminal for cover. A frighteningly huge crack of thunder made everybody jump as sheets of rain came down sideways, the power went out, and staying in Goma was starting to seem like an attractive option.

"So what groups are in between us and Kisangani?" Tony asked.

"We'll start off going over M23," Dan said, opening a beer. "But we won't get enough altitude to get out of firing range."

"Right, so if somebody's a little high and wants to pop off a few rounds at us, there's that?" Tony said with a laugh.

"Pretty much. Then once we pass them, we'll go over the FDLR."

"And those are the former Interahamwe, genocidal Hutus?"

Dan nodded. "After that we go over the FARDC."

"Which is the, uhhh, not particularly nice government forces?"

"Exactly. Then about fifteen or twenty Mai Mai groups."

"And you get along with those guys?"

"Yeah, they're cool . . . except for when they eat people."

"Now, let's not be judgmental. We respect all lifestyle choices on this show," Tony said. "Okay, shut the camera off. You've had enough of my tarmac snark."

The weather cleared enough for a DC-10 cargo jet to land, and we reboarded. As the engines spooled up and our flying death trap accelerated down the runway, Tony closed his eyes to take a nap while my hair turned white. Once airborne, water started leaking through the ceiling, but Dez was more concerned that Dan was smoking. Several hours later, approaching Kisangani, Mo strapped on a harness to get some aerial shots of the river. Wiyo opened the rear cargo hatch and the cabin depressurized, sucking out a flutter of production receipts. Despite my having absolutely convinced myself that our plane was going to crash in a vast uncharted jungle full of cannibalistic rebels, we landed safely.

"THE PLACE HAS A MYSTERIOUS vibe," Dan said as we drove into town. Kisangani was once the Congo's second largest city, and we passed Belgian colonial houses, administrative offices, hotels, and tall apartment buildings; many of them were choked with trees and vines, giving the impression of being dragged back into the jungle against their will. Compared to Goma, however, the local population was quite friendly.

Tony was in a strange mood and eager for his first look at the Congo River. I was starting to get the idea we weren't just about to embark on the dramatic climax of the Congo episode; as far as Tony was concerned, this river trip was going to be the climax of his travel career. No pressure.

Standing on the bank, we watched commuters traverse back and forth across the water on hollowed-out tree-trunk canoes called pirogues. Larger wooden boats arrived crowded with passengers while goods were loaded and unloaded via narrow planks. Women and kids transported large yellow containers of water on their heads. Squealing livestock was tossed overboard and rounded up. Between concrete staircases leading to nowhere—the orphaned remains of what must have once been a network of piers—women did laundry, men washed motorbikes, and kids splashed in the water.

"So, this is Kisangani . . . Known in *Heart of Darkness* as the 'Inner Station,'" Tony said to the camera with a wistful expression. "It's what Conrad saw here that inspired the book and, of course, *Apocalypse Now*. It's been a lifelong dream to retrace Conrad's steps. Now here I am."

To clarify, we weren't *actually* retracing Conrad's steps, instead kind of doing the geographic opposite. "Inner Station" was where Conrad's protagonist Marlow had *concluded* his arduous river journey of psychological isolation that so captivated Tony. In fact, probably the very spot we were standing at that moment was the setting for his encounter with the infamous Kurtz, an ivory trader gone mad, worshiped by the local population as some kind of god. Much like Marlow, Tony saw Kurtz as an alluring and enigmatic figure. Was he monster, demagogue, or prophet? Kurtz had gone to the Congo with "good intentions," but ended up decorating his house with severed human heads. Kurtz, what the book represented, as well as Tony's infatuation with it, were all somewhat . . . ambiguous and open to interpretation. Conrad quit after his first trip as steamboat captain on the Congo River, the horrors of what he witnessed having left him in a deep depression. Now 123 years later, it was our turn to embark on a river journey toward our own indefinite narrative conclusion.

AT FIRST LIGHT WE HEADED down to the river to check out the boat and deal with all the things that would inevitably go wrong. For starters, an unfortunate coat of gleaming white paint on the picture boat was just being completed. "You've gotta be fucking kidding me!" Mo said, kicking the nearest tree. "White is the absolute *worst* possible color for filming in equatorial sun!"

On the bright side, "*La Vie Est Un Combat*," which translated to "Life Is a Fight," had been painted on the wheelhouse. The top deck, where we'd be sleeping, ran nearly the full length of the thirty-meter-long vessel. Beneath was a large space that would serve as galley, dining room, and storage for our gear. Nearly walking right into an irregular sized ceiling support beam dangerously lower than the others, I made a mental note to affix some brightly colored gaffer tape as a warning. Our ship was no Belgian Colonial steamer or Vietnam War–style patrol boat, but she came with a crew of five trusty local sailors, had a bespoke charm, and reeked of fresh paint.

With two hours until Tony's arrival, I went over our supply list one last time while Moose coordinated with the security team, camera crew, and production assistants to load up the gear. For one night on the river we were bringing a charcoal cooker, fuel, generator, machete, case of light bulbs, fourteen mattresses and mosquito nets, umbrellas, oil lanterns, the remainder of our bottled water, cutting boards, forks, knives, coffee cups, plates, frying pans, pots, two dozen eggs, bananas, pineapples, bread, spatula, seven handles of Johnnie Walker, five crates of beer, a baby goat, a duck, and twelve chickens. There was also personal luggage, film equipment, a medical kit, a satellite phone, emergency MiFi to keep Tony connected to the internet, and Moose's burlap sack of energy bars. In my backpack were essential props: a copy of *Heart of Darkness*, a 1902 map of the Congo found on eBay, and several tins of Spam. Though it might not sound like it, for us, this was traveling light.

"Good news," Dan said, hanging up the phone. "Between the hotel and our connections, we managed to get everything Tony wanted. Just not the tomatoes." I wasn't sure what was worse, that we hadn't found tomatoes or that we'd somehow managed to source everything else on the impossible eleventh-hour shopping list.

"I'll make coq au vin," Tony said last night at dinner. "If we're gonna endure a fetid, humid, mosquito-ridden night of sleeping on the boat while parasites hatch in our kidneys, we might as well eat a good meal." Tony often did surprising things; they just didn't usually involve him cooking on camera. Despite having spent twenty-eight years working in a kitchen—or maybe because of it—he usually made a point of leaving the food preparation to the local experts. On the rare occasions when Tony did participate, he usually had a good reason. The coq au vin, I estimated, was an insurance policy on his other unexpected pronouncement. "Each of you are going to kill your own chicken . . . on camera."

I'd ordered the death of enough animals over the years in the course of making the show, but I'd *never* killed anything myself before. I didn't like spiders, but that didn't stop me from scooping them up with a cup and putting them outside when I crossed paths with one. Why was Tony intentionally manufacturing conflict and stakes with this chicken menace? Was the shoot not living up to his expectations?

I took a deep breath and resolved to put the whole thing out of my mind. Knowing Tony's fickle nature, it probably wouldn't happen anyway. And right now, I had other pressing concerns, like the kerfuffle from inside the boat when Jerry whacked his head on that troublesome low beam. And on shore a well-upholstered man with a gold watch, neatly pressed slacks, and a badge (never a good sign) was arguing with Moose and Horeb.

"Dude claims to be a 'port official,'" Dan said. "He's fucking pissed we didn't pay his office some imaginary 'fuel surcharge,' and is demanding five thousand dollars or we'll have to cease operations immediately."

"Well, that sounds like it could be an issue . . . " I said, worrying about the schedule. We had to make it at least eighty clicks downriver before nightfall, as moving on the water after dark was extremely dangerous.

"It's a cultural tradition for everyone here to cause problems and block other people's shit," Dan said, lighting a cigarette. "Don't stress, Horeb will get him down to twenty dollars."

"FIVE MINUTES TO TONY, FIVE MINUTES TO TONY," the walkie squawked. Fuck! Tony was already en route from the hotel and we weren't done loading, and the extortion situation had yet to be resolved, forget being ready to film. As soon as I saw Tony step out of his Land Cruiser, I could tell something was a little off. He was uncharacteristically decked out in two tribal necklaces, an endangered leopard skin purse, and, most worrisome, he appeared ebullient. Coming right over, Tony said, "Cameras not ready yet? Too bad, because it's been my life's ambition to come to the Congo.

Boom, bumper! I'm just enjoying torturing you, Tom. I'm brimming with content. So, I'm ready any time."

Mo materialized out of nowhere, camera in hand, and said, "I'm firing."

"Did you maggots load the chickens? And you are fully briefed and squared away as far as plucking and gutting of said chickens?" Tony asked, looking in my direction. "I will take your guffaw and expression of utter disgust as meaning yes. Well, I'm psyched. My dream has finally come true. Or kind of, almost, about to be. I shall dub this boat *The Captain Willard*."

While the remainder of the gear was loaded, Tony boarded for an inspection and promptly whacked his head on the low beam despite a large neon-green gaffer tape "X." Unharmed, he waved toward the offending support and said, "Have this unnecessary hazard removed immediately. Anything else I should be aware of?"

"Well, there's a little paperwork issue," I said.

"Oh, no . . . Blocked by officials? This could be months," Tony said, looking concerned. We watched as more of our local crew got involved and additional "port officials" joined the mess of wild gesticulations and yelling. At one point Dan's voice rose above the rest. "I don't fucking care what it takes, we need this boat to move *NOW*!" Some amount of money presumably greater than twenty dollars changed hands, and passage was granted.

As we left Kisangani, the Congo River opened up ahead of us like a superhighway. Much as in Conrad's day, it had again become the main route of transportation, but other than a pirogue or two and a few scows like ours, traffic was scarce. Small thatched villages were occasionally visible, but mostly the banks remained clad in an unbroken wall of green.

Going below deck, I found Tony ominously singing, "Time to kill chickens, weed out the chickens," while using a large amount of our fast-dwindling supply of bottled drinking water to rinse the onions and potatoes he'd been cutting. Without looking up, he said, "Getting close to killy time, Tom. These decks will soon be awash with blood. Summon the crew. I want this on tape."

"I'm not killing a chicken," I said, my voice getting a touch shrill. "They're cute."

"We'll see how cute they are when you're wrist-deep in their guts. Flapping their wings, the little severed head gazing up at you." Switching to mock chicken falsetto, Tony squeaked, *"Why me, Tom? Why?"*

If Tony could make a joke that resulted in you doubled over laughing or, conversely, scared shitless, well, let's just say getting big reactions out of people was one of Tony's joys. But engineering an improvised sadistic chicken killing ritual was a new level of . . . I don't know what. Was any of this rational? Was I losing my mind? One thing was clear: I was definitely losing control of the situation. With everyone present and Mo rolling, Tony proclaimed, "Gentlemen, we're in? We've got a chicken for each of you. Mo, Jerry, Moose?"

I watched in dismay while my fellow crew members fervently chorused, "Let's do this," "Hell yeah, I'm in," and, "Just another day in the Congo."

"This will not be my first time at the rodeo," Tony said. "I'll tell you right up front it's extremely unpleasant. There will be no joy in this. But, Tom, in the interest of togetherness, I'm really impressed you've chosen to go along with this. After all these years on the show, basically exploiting the miracle of human toil, and food production, and animals' lives. I think it's only fair you learn on a cellular level, in a deep way, where your food comes from."

Over the last couple of days Tony's references had increasingly switched from *Heart of Darkness* to *Apocalypse Now*. In our security briefing when Dez cautioned about the dangers of getting off the boat—snakes, armed militia, bandits, parasites, etc.—Tony had interrupted with a quote from the movie: "Never get off the boat, unless you're going all the way, man." But from where I was standing, any potential shore-based hazards seemed worth the risk compared to what was happening on board the boat. With or without my consent, the whole grisly scene was shaping up to be like some corporate retreat held in the Seventh Circle of Dante's Hell. There was no question the farther we got from a cell phone signal, the further we were descending into madness. The basket of chickens arrived clucking in terror, and Dan went first. "I'm not gonna hurt you, I'm gonna kill you," he said, sawing off the chicken's head. "Wow, this knife is dull!"

Still somewhat in a state of denial that this was actually happening, I began backing away and said, "I'm just going to make myself useful opening these bottles of wine."

"Nah, you're just gonna kill a chicken," Tony said, cutting through his chicken's neck with some difficulty. Plucking a bloody feather from his cheek, he said, "Tom, you might want to observe how it's done, so you don't cause the poultry any unnecessary suffering. Jerry, let's go." Jerry put down his camera and—being a farm boy from Iowa—nonchalantly popped off the chicken's head like it was a bottle cap.

"Clean kill, Jerry, clean kill," Dan said, having adopted the role of execution commentator.

Holding the bloody severed chicken head, its beak still slowly opening and closing, Jerry asked, "What do we do with these?"

Tony looked proud, and I decided my best course of action was to slip overboard unnoticed, or at least disappear for a bit. I turned around to sneak away and slammed my head into the low beam so hard I fell back flat against the floor. My first thought was, maybe if I'm paralyzed, I won't have to kill a chicken! Regrettably, I was uninjured.

"It's batter up, Tom," Tony said.

"Please, I really don't want to do this," I said.

"If we don't kill those chickens, we'll starve to death," Tony said, thrusting the bloody knife in my direction. "You want to eat a raw onion for dinner?"

As much as I didn't want to kill a chicken, I also didn't want to look like a chicken in front of Tony. I know none of this makes any sense, but such refined notions as logic had been left a long way upriver. Besides, both cameras were pointed in my direction—which in case you didn't know has a way of making people do stupid things—so I took a deep breath and resigned myself to participating in Tony's bizarre blood rite. I reached down and grabbed the chicken, who stopped struggling and stared up at me. As Tony had prophesied, I could tell the chicken was thinking, *"Why me, Tom?"* Hovering, Tony said, "Don't be gentle, you're not going out on a date. C'mon, just do it!" I looked away and plunged the knife into the chicken's neck and sawed and sawed as hard as I could. Over the ringing in my ears and the horrified screams of the other chickens, I could hear voices shouting, "Hold it higher so I can get a better a shot!" and *"Kill! Kill! Kill!"* The Congolese boat guys were all watching the spectacle and must have been wondering what the hell was going on. When I looked down, it seemed like the knife was barely penetrating, let alone going all the way through, and the chicken was still looking up into my eyes, and there was blood.

"Saw harder!" Dan laughed maniacally.

I was really trying, back and forth with the knife, and the chicken was still looking at me. "Do it faster!" Tony commanded. "You're making him suffer!" And that's when the panic set in. "Stop it, stop it!" I yelled through tears. I felt myself let go of the knife, and I ran to the other side of the boat. Had it been an axe or even something sharp, it would have been bad enough. But that fucking knife was so dull, and I just couldn't stand the thought of the poor chicken not seeing another sunrise.

When the red mist cleared, I felt pretty pathetic for freaking out over a chicken, considering I was in a country where horrific acts of cruelty and violence were facts of life. Worst of all, I'd failed the test. I was too chicken to kill the chicken, too chicken to say no, then too chicken to finish the job. The sad truth is I was the chicken all along. I'd managed to hold it together very well on the Congo shoot thus far—and for the last ten years of working on the show—but Tony had finally broken me. He had a way of always getting what he wanted. Perhaps as a consolation prize Tony put a smudge of blood on my forehead and said, "Now you can join our treehouse."

THOUGH SOMEWHAT MACABRE AND PERVERSE, the whole day had been pretty lighthearted, at least as far as Tony was concerned. But as the last bluish remainders of twilight faded away, fate was about to ensure nobody got off the boat unscathed.

"We're in a hurry," Tony said, organizing his *mise en place*. "I need my secret blend of herbs and spices and these bottles of wine opened." Jerry and Dez went to the stern and fired up the generator rigged to a string of bulbs around Tony's work area. Trying to focus over the din of two clattering outboard engines and now a clanking, sputtering generator, Tony placed the first chicken on the cutting board, raised his knife, and the lights cut out, plunging us into complete darkness. "*Jeee-zuuus,*" Tony said, drawing out the syllables for dramatic emphasis. "I need some fucking light so I can see what the fuck I'm doing!" I felt around along the floor to my backpack and found a headlamp. Moose did the same, and soon a few beams of illumination cut through the inky void. Dez went to investigate why the generator was still whirring away but not providing power. Within a minute or so, the bulbs flickered on to reveal a pissed-off looking Tony. "This knife is as dull as a soup spoon," he said, going to work butchering the chickens. "Get me the machete, and I need another pot." Before either could be found, the lights wavered, dimmed, and failed again. "*Fuuuuck,*" he moaned. As power returned, I was faced with an even more pissed-off Tony, arms folded. Wiping some blood off his Rolex to check the time, he said, "Tom, if we're going to eat at all, you need to *unfuck* this situation!"

Like it was my fault the generator wasn't cooperating with Tony's "Full Metal Julia Child" fantasy of effortlessly preparing a jungle-style coq au vin. "Well, it *is* a documentary. I'm just 'letting it happen.' Isn't that what you're always telling me to do?" is what I wanted to say. Instead I tried to sound like I knew anything about electricity and offered, "Maybe there's too many bulbs going; how many do we have on?"

"There's only a draw of two hundred forty watts," Mo shouted from behind his camera. "It's the shitty generator!"

"Where's that empty pot I asked for?" Tony demanded as the lights flared out, then on.

"Hey, this is Congo, man." Dan chuckled at the absurdity of our predicament.

"This is gonna be starvation is what it's gonna be," Tony said. He ineffectually hack, hack, hacked away at a chicken foot. "I'm never gonna get through with this fucking knife! And open the wine, *please*. Somebody!" Thankfully, Dan had been a sous chef in a previous life and went to work assisting with the food prep. "Dan, I want you to take the onions and put them on the fire and stir it until such time as they're clear," Tony said as the boat plummeted into blackness. "You're fucking loving this, Tom." His voice loomed up from the abyss. "More interested in getting the shot of me looking desperate and miserable than helping me out even a little by like doing anything about food."

Clearly such refined notions as logic had been left a long way upriver, but I was still operating under the assumption it was my job to make sure the food got filmed. In fact, I'd just been thinking about all the elements needed to edit this scene to Wagner's "Ride of the Valkyries." When the lights came back up, I said, "Jerry, maybe you should get some coverage of the generator drama."

"NO!" Tony yelled, slamming down his knife. "Maybe we should figure out how to cook fucking dinner, unless you don't want to eat anything. Okay? So, let us dedicate all our attention to that. While all this might be high comedy, I've had a peanut butter and jelly sandwich today and I would like to eat, especially since we've gone through all this fucking misery with these fucking chickens. I think it would be right, and only respectful of the chicken you so cruelly tortured and left slowly dying, to actually eat them."

I heard a sound sort of like glass breaking when Tony said that. It was all in my head, of course, but something inside me *had* just snapped. It wasn't just the Congo and the chicken or even the stress of the first couple shoots for CNN. A flood of stress and resentment and a bunch of other feelings, some of which had nothing to do with the job, things I'd bottled up since—well, forever—were all hitting me at the same time. I decided it might be prudent to take a temporary leave of absence. Yes. Best I step back and let nature take its course, maybe even enjoy the show.

By this time, a nearly apoplectic Chef Tony had resorted to yanking out spines and guts with bare hands, the entrails wrapping around his arms as he attempted to toss them overboard. "Shit! I busted a gizzard," he cussed. "Can I please get the motherfucking pot?" The lights, now flashing on and off like in a horror movie, revealed everyone running around in a full-on panic. Dez, Stew, and Warren were still desperately working on the electricity issue, assisted by Jerry, who was rushing back and forth between the scene and the generator when he whacked his head into the low beam of death for the second, then third time. Dan was drinking scotch and trying to light the charcoal cooker. Horeb was tearing apart the stores looking for Tony's missing pot. Moose was searching for backup batteries when he stepped through a broken floorboard and twisted his ankle. Tony was waving his knife, yelling, "Will one of you useless puddles of reptile vomit open the fucking wine?!" I was watching the escalating dumpster fire while hiding behind Mo for protection. Each time the bulbs flickered back on, I could see we were attracting an increasingly large swarm of every manner of jungle insect. "Where are the tomatoes?!" Tony shouted frantically while swatting at the Oldsmobile-sized moths fluttering around his head. "Dude! Don't do that!" Dan warned. "There's poison on the wings. If you crush one, your whole face will swell up like a casaba melon!" Mo was recording everything, and when it occurred to me this was perhaps the most surreal stand-and-stir ever filmed, certainly the most bizarre for CNN, I almost laughed. Almost.

"We've got the genny sorted," Dez called over the walkie. "Power situation is right as rain." At which point the lights cut out again. When they blinked back on, Dan was standing in front of me pouring a big red plastic Solo cup full of Johnnie Walker.

"We don't have a corkscrew," he said, taking a shot.

"What is the condition of the onions?" Tony barked, wiping sweat from his brow. "If they scorch for even thirty seconds in that thin-ass horrid North Korean–made pot, the acrid flavor will permeate the entire batch!"

Glancing over at the smoldering onions and embers coming from the fire—fanned as it was by the movement of the boat—I realized we'd been charging ahead at full speed in complete darkness and shouted, "Shit! Why is the boat still moving?!"

Our lives, the captain, and his ship had all been in jeopardy because nobody had given the order to drop anchor. It was sort of ridiculous, I'd been too busy playing with the camera, *manufacturing* drama with some chickens, to pay attention to the *real* danger.

As we slowed and drew close to the shore, Mo pivoted around to get a shot of the captain shining a searchlight along the shore. "Is he looking for crocs?" Mo asked.

"I think most of them have been eaten," Dez responded. "He's gonna swim in now to tie up the boat."

I held my breath while the captain jumped into the dark, potentially alligator- and snake-infested water. Fortunately, nothing ate him.

Now that we were stopped, the breeze was gone, and it got hotter and even buggier. Like insanely buggier. Despite spraying clouds of DDT, we were all getting eaten alive but afraid to swat anything away because of the poisonous moths. Several hours later, dinner was finally ready. The prospect of eating was less than appetizing for a myriad of reasons, but at least the mood seemed to lighten a bit as everyone sat down around the table.

"Tom, I want you to fold the dinner napkins into origami swans," Tony said. "And why is there no decorative centerpiece on the table?"

"That's a little colonialist of you," Dan said, chasing his coq au vin with a glass of scotch.

"Listen, this is a tough environment," Tony shot back. "You gotta keep things organized, keep things clean, have a plan. Prior preparation prevents piss-poor performance. Also dying."

While attempting to choke down a zinc-flavored onion, my mind drifted toward Kurtz. Maybe there'd been a method to the madness all along? Was Tony's point that—as in *Heart of Darkness* and *Apocalypse Now*—deep in the jungle everyone goes a little bit crazy? That we all have a Kurtz somewhere within us? We'd arrived in the Congo with good intentions, and ended up doing something as vulgar as playing with our food in a country of starving people . . . on TV.

Later, lying in bed counting the holes in my mosquito net, I found myself again wondering why and how I'd ended up in a place like the Congo. My method for coping was the same it had always been: focus on the objective. By looking through the camera or immersing myself in the success of the operation, I could almost trick myself into believing what I was seeing was on TV instead of real, blurring the lines between reality and how it was all going to play out in the edit. The camera functioned as both a protective agent and survival strategy . . . but in the process it could make me lose perspective—and empathy. The people we filmed, the things we saw, my own health and safety only had value in the context of the show. Ultimately, I'd been willing to do whatever it took to make sure Tony's experience lived up to his grand narrative, regardless of the cost.

Despite everything the Congolese had been through, Horeb and so many others worked incredibly hard for what they believed in, and here I was just playing some stupid game with a camera. We'd go home with the footage, and I'd probably find a way to fix it in the edit with Tony's voice-over. It was easier not to think too hard about how our new friends would be staying behind in their country and continue fighting just to survive.

TWO DAYS LATER, WE WERE at the end of the shoot, hot, dirty, and exhausted, stopped dead in our tracks during another series of protracted negotiations. This time the operators of a large metal auto barge were refusing to take us across the water until they received "back pay." After two hours, the situation didn't seem to be progressing. I stepped away to find somewhere to take a piss. Alone in the dense underbrush, I heard a rustling. I spun around expecting to see Tony with a rubber snake; instead I was confronted by a soldier, AK-47 over his shoulder. He looked like a teenager, and his eyes were as red as his beret. He stood there staring at me while tracing a finger along the trigger of his gun. His blissed-out state of mind reminded me of college when my friend Waz got so fucked up he genuinely believed he was a daisy. But as the soldier kept his unnerving grin trained on me, I couldn't imagine this kid's delusions having anything to do with flowers. I took a deep breath and smiled while backing away. "Keep calm, panic breeds panic," I repeated to myself.

When I got back to the group, I instructed Moose to pay the ferry operators whatever they wanted; it was time to go home.

Like many travelers who find themselves in a moral inferno, we'd begun in search of Tony's childhood heart of darkness adventure fantasy. What we'd found was something different . . . Maybe Tony could still say something that would justify why we'd risked life, limb, and sanity to go to the middle of the freakin' Congo. I needed to know if it meant something to Tony. That I wasn't disposable. I wanted to know if it had all been worth it. Or even if he thought it hadn't.

Fortunately, the Travel Minute—a network promo where Tony sums up his visit—often served the unintended purpose of providing a rare window into how he really felt. Whatever he was about to say, it was going to be as close as I would get to the denouement I was so desperate for. I held my breath while a sunbaked, somewhat frazzled, and thoroughly exhausted Tony sat down in front of Mo's camera one last time.

"There's that great line in the beginning of *Apocalypse Now*," he said. "You know, 'I wanted a mission, and for my sins, they gave me one.' I've wanted to come to the Congo for as long as I've been telling stories or making television. I've been a student of its history. Uh, it's a place that's always fascinated me in . . . in sort of an awful and mesmerizing way. And I knew it was going to be a frustration shooting here, I mean, it's a dangerous place. You're at the mercy of many, many, many unpredictable things . . . I wanted to come here . . . And I did."

Chapter Five

SIGNS YOU'RE IN A CULT

I SPENT THE WEEKS AFTER TONY'S SUICIDE IN A STATE OF SEMI-STUNNED autopilot. As hard as it was, and nearly impossible to focus on work, I was thankful to be busy and glad for the distraction. It seemed distasteful to consider legal obligations at a time like this; however, there were realities to deal with. For starters, the company owed more episodes to fulfill the contract with CNN. Chris and Lydia called a meeting, and it was decided that we would produce two final episodes of *Parts Unknown*: "Tony's Impact" and a "Crew Special."

"I call 'Crew Special,'" I said without thinking. I didn't have to think. The "Crew Special" as I envisioned it would be a behind-the-scenes look at some of the madness as well as a tribute to Tony from the people who'd made the show. I was hoping to start to process some of the chaos going on inside my head, and I instinctively knew it would give me the opportunity to talk to all the core members of the team, help answer some of the questions I'd been wrestling with since even before Tony's death. I knew it wasn't going to be easy given that we were all still in a state of shock and grief.

Meanwhile, something unexpected was happening. Tony was being lauded as inspirational, and had come to embody respect, compassion, authenticity, tolerance, empathy, adventure, humility, and humanism. Fuck, Tony was practically being ordained a saint. It seemed like I couldn't open an email or web page without being exposed to the outpouring of grief. How did he have such a deep impact on such a large number of people? Over the course of years spent making the show, whoever may or may not have been watching had become something of an intangible concept. Truth told, I'd forgotten it was a TV show; Tony was the only audience that mattered.

In *Kitchen Confidential*, a chapter is devoted to Tony's mentor, Bigfoot, whom he describes as,

> Cunning, manipulative, brilliant, mercurial, physically intimidating—even terrifying—a bully, a yenta, a sadist and a mensch: Bigfoot is all those things. He's also the most stand-up guy I ever worked for. He inspires a strange and consuming loyalty. I try, in my kitchen, to be just like him. I want my cooks to have me inside their heads just like Bigfoot remains in mine. I want them to think that, like Bigfoot, when I look into their eyes, I see right into their very souls.

I think it would be fair to say that Tony had succeeded, and then some. On my last shoot, while in Indonesia, I'd had a revelation.

"We need to get you a pair of Persols. Those drugstore Ray-Bans aren't going to cut it around Tony," I said to Alex, a cameraman who didn't travel with us on every shoot.

"*Oh my god*," Alex said. "You guys are in a cult."

"Ha, ha, nice try," I said. But later that night in my hotel room I sat up googling *Signs you might be in a cult*. "Zealous commitment to the Leader, who is the ultimate authority." Hmmm . . . Check . . . "Socialize with fellow Cult members only." Well, yes. Check. "The group has been conditioned to be paranoid about the outside world." Okay . . . Check. "The Leader relies on shame cycles." *Double* check on that one. "Separation from the family unit." "Encouraged to dress similarly." "Dissenting opinion is crushed." Check. Check. Check. Shit. Alex was right.

I guess the signs had been there all along, and I didn't even notice. Three years before Indonesia, we had been in Korea. The shoot was a bit of a disaster, and it was a godsend to have Helen—Tony's badass "Director of Special Operations"—along for the shoot. We'd start each day greeting each other with "Funny story . . . " referring to whatever nonsense we were currently dealing with, like reminding the fixers that we needed to film in the kitchen for the fourteenth time, or that just like every scene we film, yes, we needed the gear van to be accessible when filming today.

We were all set for the hwe-shik scene, a tradition in Korea that is essentially a company-sanctioned night out to get hammered with the boss. The only problem was the businessmen we had lined up had thought better of participating and backed out at the last minute. This scene was arguably the cornerstone of the entire episode, and we had nobody to film with. There were now fifty-five minutes until Tony's arrival, assuming he wasn't early. It was officially time to panic. In a desperate last-minute effort to find replacement salary men willing to get wasted on camera, the crew fanned out across the restaurant and neighborhood, accosting anyone in suit and tie and asking, "Do you speak English and want to be on TV?" Miraculously, at the last moment Helen found a group already a few rounds of soju deep, who were kind enough to save our asses and let a CNN camera crew join them on a full-fledged drinking binge. The poor guys were really going to regret this tomorrow morning.

The evening ended up going pretty well until the very end. Tony had signaled he was done, but there was one more important shot we needed, so I asked him to play ball and take another drink of soju. Out of nowhere Tony went from zero to sixty, and in front of everybody, he began hurling a tirade of particularly vitriolic and cutting insults in my direction. As he stormed out of the scene to head back to the hotel, I noticed the local Korean crew had all covered their faces with their hands to spare me the embarrassment.

In the traumatized silence of the van ride back to the hotel, Zach spoke first. "Man . . . Tony can be such a fucking dick sometimes."

"It's not his fault," I said after a long pause. "He has a very stressful job."

"OMG. You guys have Stockholm syndrome," Helen said from the back of the van.

I googled it, and she was right. The next day I confronted Tony about the unprovoked nastiness. He instantly became gentler. Putting his arm around my shoulder, he said, "Tom, you're not only so good at your job, you're a good person. If I need something or I'm in trouble, you're really one of the first people I'd call. I'm there for you. I'd show up at your funeral and hunt down any fake mourners and kill them." Then the next day he unexpectedly turned on me again.

In a weird way, making the show felt like going to war, without the guns. Well, mostly there weren't guns, although sometimes there were. Is there such a thing as vacation-of-a-lifetime PTSD where your main tormentor is also your hero, mentor, and boss? After having had these intense experiences of being in the trenches together with Tony and with the crew, sharing these adrenaline-inducing, life-altering experiences, going back to my regular life felt like the real trauma. It was all some Gordian knot of irreconcilable contradictions, basically a giant mind-fuck.

Everything centered around wanting to please Tony. And it wasn't just me and the crew. It was also the fans and the restaurants, and the hotels and the airlines and the network and the advertisers and the people on Etsy that made all those "Saint Anthony the Opinionated" prayer candles.

"Do you think you were in a cult?" I asked Todd, who'd been shooting the show since the start of *No Reservations*. He chuckled at my question.

"Well, it's hard to say, because I think I signed a nondisclosure agreement, so I really can't talk about the cults other than saying— I forgot what it was I was going to say. You see? I've been brainwashed . . . "

Tony became extremely close with those who'd been on the show the longest. It felt validating to be a part of a small, elite group, surrounded by people I respected. He called us the "A-Team" and/or his LRRPs (Long-Range Reconnaissance Patrol), comparing our deployment in the field to Captain Willard's mission in *Apocalypse Now*. "He was wrapped too tight for an office job, man."

In order to maintain the intense, small, in-club loyalty, Tony gave us a license to kill. Creatively speaking, of course. Everyone who worked the show looked up to our "fearless leader" adoringly, and we operated more like a fraternal organization than a standard TV production. It was very hard to get in; once you got in, it was very hard to get out; and once you were out, you were dead. Or might as well be.

The rules for working on Tony's shows were not to be found on the pages of any HR manual. There were behaviors perfectly acceptable in polite society that were unforgivable deal-breakers for Tony. Stingy tipper, vegan, mediocre, tea drinker, late, or a fan of Jimmy Buffett's music, you're off the show. Conversely, horribly embarrassing, self-destructive acts that would be more than reason enough for termination at any other place of employment might be perfectly acceptable conduct among Tony's "band of misfits." Binge drinking, grand theft auto, perjury, or psychological blackmail, no problem. Threatening to leave an "upper-decker" in the network producer's toilet, now that deserves a promotion!

Tony's leadership techniques were CIA caliber: duplicitous, unforgivable, possibly criminal, and usually extremely effective. Tony recruited informants, disseminated fake information, and stoked inter-team rivalries, pitting director against director, camera against camera, to motivate everyone to do our best work.

Doctor Tony held liberal views on the dispensation of prescription medication and was a staunch advocate of flying pills. "Toss back a few of these bad boys with some scotch before takeoff, and you wake up in Asia. Really, it's the only way to fly." One morning at the airport Tony asked the crew how we were planning to "manage" the flight. Everyone broke out their stashes for a game of "pill poker," swapping a rainbow assortment of sleeping pills, pain meds, and antianxiety meds. "I'll see your Xanax and raise you two diazepam for one Klonopin . . . " Washing down a fistful of pills with a breakfast beer, I couldn't help but notice the wholesome family at the next table staring at us with a look of horror and disgust on their faces that was . . . memorable. Those delightful little pills did wonders for my fear of flying, and it was smooth sailing until the time I accidentally consumed the wrong cocktail. I hazily recall an erudite conversation with the woman seated next to me. She was a Rhodes Scholar and seemed genuinely interested in whatever it was I did for a living. The next thing I remember was *THUMP* as the plane touched down at JFK. The seat next to me was empty. I was later informed that, among other indiscretions, I'd apparently rummaged through *every* overhead bin in the cabin looking for my checked suitcase. It was more the fear of waking up zip-tied to the bulkhead than the shame and embarrassment of liver failure at 35,000 feet that eventually convinced me to quit the magic flying pills.

There were some close calls, like the time in Cambodia when we met a rickshaw driver who hooked us up with pot. In order to prevent getting stoned and accidentally smuggling drugs across an international border, a weed-loving DP who shall remain nameless made sure to always keep our stash in the same pocket of his camera bag. After landing at JFK, while we were waiting at the carousel for our luggage, a beagle wearing a Customs and Border Protection uniform complete with badge beelined straight to our pile of luggage, including the pot camera bag. Oh fuck, had we forgot to flush what was left of the drugs? Everyone slowly backed away, leaving our producer, Marcy, who hadn't been aware of the business dealings with the rickshaw driver. The CBP beagle's handler was an avuncular looking customs officer who, seeing the Pollyannaish look on Marcy's face, must have mentally ruled out drug smuggling, money laundering, and terrorism, because he asked, "Young lady, do you have any food in your suitcase?" Marcy regularly brought home all sorts of goodies, everything from a smoked reindeer leg to peculiarly flavored novelty potato chips. Travel professional that she was, Marcy put on her best smile, batted her eyelashes, and said, "Good evening, officer, what a cute doggy you have. Umm . . . food? No, I don't think I have any food." Ignoring his beagle, who was all over our luggage, the customs officer instead watched Marcy sheepishly open her personal suitcase. I'd been slowly edging back toward our gear and craned my neck to see what Marcy had been smuggling this time. The inside of her bag looked like a convenience store. There was a stash of Kampot peppers, several bags of nuts from a street vendor, as well as a tattered two-liter soda bottle refilled with local moonshine.

With an apologetic smile, the customs officer confiscated the contraband and gave Marcy a gentle warning. "Now, miss, next time you really must observe the regulations. Remember they're for your own safety as well as the safety of others." Then he left, struggling to gracefully drag his beagle away from the camera bag while Marcy curtseyed and waved goodbye.

I wasn't so lucky a couple years later. Deep in the Dominican Republic's interior, my production vehicle got stopped at a checkpoint. I hadn't realized police in the Caribbean dressed in fatigues and rode around in tanks. I also should have known that the DR was one of those countries where they film *Locked Up Abroad*. As in being caught with drugs meant the likelihood of some serious jail time as well as a career-ruining scandal. So, when the military police found pot in the camera bag, it didn't matter that it wasn't mine. The situation eventually got resolved thanks to a very generous bribe, but not before I was designated collateral and held hostage while the driver took my ATM card and left to withdraw several thousand dollars from my checking account. The next morning, I saw Tony at breakfast. Traumatized and desperate to confess, I told him how the night before I had been led into the jungle and forced to lie facedown in a freshly dug hole. I told him I'd noticed a shovel, desperately trying not to wonder what the hole was for. I continued to explain to the seemingly unimpressed Tony how I'd *really* gotten scared when the unstable kid with the machine gun started to shake and cry because it was taking so long for the driver to return with the bribe.

Tony finally looked up from his iPad and said, "Getting fleeced in the Caribbean is a rite of passage." Then he went back to whatever it was he was reading.

"BY THE WAY, I WAS in a cult," Josh, who was producing the "Crew Special" with me, said when I interviewed him. "No, but honestly, it was very much a cult and I'm not afraid to say that, because that's kind of what it was. I like to think of it as cutthroat affection."

"Cutthroat affection" was a poetic way to describe the capricious man who both fought tooth and nail to get me on the Emmy nomination year after year, as well as threatened to attach jumper cables and a car battery to my testicles in Vietnam.

"You're off the show" might as well have been one of Tony's catch phrases. Most often he said it as a joke, but the line between a truth and a joke . . . well, it's complicated. There was a culture of Wild West mob justice, and with Judge Tony on the bench, let's just say that was not a courtroom in which you wanted to find yourself.

One of the things that made being a part of the crew perhaps a little dangerous was Tony's willingness to cut off his nose to spite his face. Punishments for "violations of the code," as Tony called them, often outweighed the crime. Sometimes, getting fired was getting off too easy. Instead he preferred creative punishments that sent as strong a message to everyone else as they did to the intended target.

Tony once devised a unique strategy for resolving a personnel issue in the editorial department. It was decided one of the four editors who worked on the show was obstructionist and wasn't pulling his weight. So Tony sent each of the editors an expensive meat basket, with a note thanking them for their work. All of them except the problem editor. Tony knew people talked at the water cooler, and it was only a matter of time until "Did you get the meat basket from Tony?" came up. Let's just say the message was received loud and clear.

"It was a cult that I would happily join again," said Nari, a close friend and producer since the *No Reservations* days. "Like, give me the Kool-Aid. Where's the Kool-Aid? I'll drink it. I'll drink gallons of it. You kind of have to have that mentality. The show was very difficult at times, given certain circumstances, but it is—for all of us, and I can say this without a doubt—the greatest thing we've ever done and we will ever do. It was such an honor and privilege just to be near him and to work with him and really become a part of his family. We were family."

I think we all felt that way. It was one big dysfunctional family, but a family nonetheless. We were a group of like-minded people with a shared compulsive need for stimulation and a relentless drive to produce work of ever higher caliber. We got paid to travel all over the world, partaking in an astounding range of experiences, and we got to do it together, year after year. It really was the best job in the world. Sure, making the show was a huge amount of work. Physically, emotionally, psychologically, temporally. It was not fun, by any standard definition. But it never felt like a job; it was a lifestyle, a calling. Best of all, at the center of it was Tony.

AS I CONTINUED CONDUCTING INTERVIEWS for the "Crew Special," I was surprised to learn that Tony had been far from a monolith. In general, everyone spoke of overarching personality traits, but Tony seemed to have the uncanny ability to adapt himself to whoever he was interacting with. Within maybe five minutes of meeting, he could size someone up and figure out how to make the puppet dance. It was a talent for sure, and perhaps part of how he was able to connect with his single-serving TV friends.

My relationship with him was markedly different from almost everyone I spoke with. Tony seemed to instinctively know how to get the best work—and provoke the most loyalty—out of everyone. For one crew member that might mean showering him with compliments; for another it might mean playing it low-key. For me, it meant a full immersion experience, a combination of adrenaline, stimulation, and fear. I had a front-row seat to join him on an existential psychodrama, where the boundaries between work and play were blurry at best. Where did reality end and television begin? Our relationship with the camera and each other brought out the best and worst in both of us, and at times it could be hard to know which was which.

While I ran around wearing a look of harried intensity Tony's chef friend Andy Ricker said, "Tom, do you ever get to relax and enjoy yourself? Man, you're in Thailand!" Tony answered for me, saying, "Andy, shut up. We like him just the way he is."

Tony's leadership philosophy, "Only pat the baby when it's sleeping," was a calculated approach from his days in the kitchen that meant you were unlikely to hear praise for having done a good job. If he looked happy after a scene I'd worked hard to put together and I made the mistake of asking, "So, how'd that go, Tony?" he'd say something like, "It was fine. Mostly. Nothing to write home about." The harder he was on me, the more desperate I was for a little bit of positive feedback or approval. Then when Tony said, "You're like a son to me," or called me part of the "A-Team," or at the end of a good shoot when he'd say, "I'll miss you most of all, Scarecrow," I'd feel worse than I had before. Whenever I tried to thank Tony, tell him how much it meant to me, he'd say, "Jesus, Tom, okay, I get it, I get it, you're happy and all emotional and shit. Enough already. You're ruining the mood."

THE LAYOVER PUT OUR RELATIONSHIP to the test. Over the summer of 2011 and 2012—in between regularly scheduled seasons of *No Reservations*—I was Tony's constant travel companion for about thirty days straight. A spin-off series for the Travel Channel, *The Layover* focused on what a traveler could actually do should they find themselves with a twenty-four- to forty-eight-hour layover in a given city. "God, if I was really saddled with a twenty-four-hour layover, the last thing I'd do is leave the airport. I'd sleep!" Tony complained. He hated doing such accessible programming, and dubbed it the twenty-four-hour "fuckover." He only agreed to do it because the series was basically a scam to burn through the number of episodes contractually owed to the Travel Channel. Here's how it worked: We'd land in one city to rendezvous with a crew already set up and ready to go, then shoot for about two insanely packed sixteen-plus-hour days before departing for the next location, where the process would start all over again. Each alternating crew in each location stayed on for another week to fill out the rest of the episode after Tony and I departed.

Every episode of *The Layover* had a producer who knew how all the pieces fit together and who would take their show through the edit. As the series director I was essentially the "Tony handler," a task that by this time had become my speciality. This isn't to say the experience wasn't without its speed bumps. Namely, in the second season, when I may have gone a *touch* too far by exploiting one of Tony's phobias for purposes of entertainment. He often referred to a hilarious and crippling fear of mimes, and for the longest time I assumed it was just part of his shtick. Until we went to France.

Tony stood framed in a picture-perfect postcard. Pastel green leaves rustled in the breeze, children laughed, an opulent Beaux Arts fountain murmured, while a mime wearing a red-and-white-striped shirt, carrying a tramp suitcase and umbrella, face covered in greasepaint, emerged from behind a tree. It was Paris, and Tony had just wanted to stroll through the park, which a month before, as we were planning the trip, had sounded boring. "Surprising" him with a mime had seemed like a great idea. But now all I could think about was how much Tony *hated* mimes and clowns, and if I got caught, there was no predicting what he'd do.

"You know . . . the first time I came to Paris, my dad brought me to a park just like this," Tony said. He smiled with a hint of nostalgia watching the children play. "It's a treasured memory."

Fuck! Tony was delivering exceedingly rare sentimental content direct to camera! *"Kill the mime, kill the mime!"* I whispered into the walkie. One of our production assistants grabbed the mime by his suspenders and pulled him behind a bush.

"Okay, let's hit the road," Tony said.

Dammit. Typical. Tony had a habit of shutting down when he sensed the camera was set with a good close-up. "Umm, okay, Tony, just stand here for another minute while we back off and get a wide shot," I said. Then I squeaked into the walkie, praying Tony wouldn't overhear, *"Cue the mime!"* I could almost hear the *Jaws* soundtrack as the mime jauntily tiptoed closer and closer. I was playing with fire; the entire farce required Tony believing the mime was an unlucky chance encounter.

"My father got me a wood boat to sail in the fountain," Tony said. "I've been thinking about him a lot . . . those were good times."

"*Kill the mime! Kill the mime!*" I said. Just in time, our heroic production assistant tackled the striped bogie lurking in the background of the shot. But no sooner were the cameras back on Tony than his inspiration evaporated. "Got your wides? Great, let's go," Tony said, without waiting for an answer.

It was now or never. "*Cue the mime, now! Now! NOW!*" I ordered. The mime leaped out from behind a flower bed and put Tony in an invisible box. Our Paris fixers hadn't arranged just any old back-alley mime; this mime was Marcel Marceau's protégé, so the invisible box was inescapable. It was hilarious, and Tony was a good sport, even when his hand became "glued" to the mime and he couldn't let go. There was no question the interaction was hilarious, and best of all, I appeared to have gotten away with it! My sordid act of television-related treason complete, Tony sat on the edge of the fountain. He had a strange look on his face, and I watched him for a moment before going over. "Everything okay?" I asked.

"Fifty years of coming to Paris," Tony said, staring right through me. "And I've never been mimed." After a long pause, he turned in my direction, his face drained of color and hand twitching. "I was raped by a clown as a kid," he said.

The cigarette fell from my hand as Tony silently got up and walked toward his waiting car. Raped by a clown? Tony was fucking with me; he had to be playing the game, right? Somehow he'd figured out the mime was a setup—it was the only logical explanation—and he was fighting fire with fire . . .

Twenty-three days later Tony and I landed in Philadelphia. It had been a busy summer. Since Paris we'd been to São Paulo, Seattle, Toronto, Dublin, Taipei, New Orleans, and Chicago. Seven cities crisscrossed around the world in just over three weeks, and we were exhausted.

While in Chicago we'd planned to film at a hot dog place, but the restaurant had violated our strict no social media policy by posting on Twitter before we filmed. After double checking with the office to confirm the restaurant was aware of our rules, Tony replied to the tweet saying, "This is how to not end up on television. #SceneCanceled." The Chicago NBC affiliate picked up on the story; Tony was portrayed as a callous and wealthy celebrity chef picking on humble restaurant owners, who—unfortunately for the optics—also happened to be North Korean refugees struggling to make it in the States. Eventually it was revealed the office had in fact neglected to inform Budacki's not to tweet, and most damning, Tony had been knowingly lied to.

I had nothing to do with the hot dog cover-up, but Budacki-gate, as it became known, continued to escalate. Soon almost everything Tony said seemed to revolve around themes of trust and betrayal. Meanwhile, I was becoming increasingly paranoid, with the Paris mime incident eating away at me for weeks. "Everyone fucks up," Tony said. "It's lying about it I can't forgive. Heads will roll for this." Was he talking about Budacki-gate or the mime, or both? I had a terrible sinking suspicion he was giving me every opportunity to admit I was responsible for the mime. But I just couldn't.

We had dinner at the hotel our last night in Philadelphia, and as was often the case at dinner, Tony ordered a massive bone-in rib eye, medium raw. He didn't seem to notice when the food arrived; he just sat there with that same thousand-mile stare from Paris. Tracing a finger along the blade of his oversize steak knife, Tony said, "You know, Tom, trust is a funny thing. Very easily given, very easily lost, and almost impossible to earn back." *Fuck.* He had to know about the mime. I was far too frightened and confused to think clearly, let alone admit what I had done. Fortunately, *The Layover* was almost over for the season. Best to let things cool down, I reassured myself.

The next morning I checked to make sure the coast was clear then darted across the hotel lobby. As I lifted my suitcase into a taxi eager to get to 30th Street Station, Tony pulled up in his car and said, "Tom, there you are. Come with me, I'll give you a ride back to the city." Shit . . . Just me and Tony in his car for the next couple of hours. I thought about making a run for it, but I knew he'd catch me. Much of the drive was spent in brooding silence, but all the while my internal monologue was screaming back and forth.

"He knows, he knows, that's why you're in the car. Honesty is the best policy, just come clean! . . . Cool it, I got away with it, he doesn't know anything . . . Tony totally knows, he knows everything! . . . What if he doesn't? Don't be stupid, people are losing their jobs over a freaking hot dog, and I flagrantly used a childhood trauma for purposes of comedy! Don't! Say! Anything!"

The Meadowlands—that vast, featureless swamp in northern New Jersey where the Sopranos were always doing something sinister—signaled we were nearing New York. This was my last chance. I was pretty sure I was going down one way or the other, so I might as well go down with as much honor as I could salvage. After what I'd done, making it geographically convenient for Tony to dispose of my body was the least I could do.

"Tony, I have something I need to tell you," I said, getting emotional. If I thought Tony looked upset before, I was unprepared for the intensity that consumed his face as he took his eyes from the road and looked right at me. I swallowed and braced for impact. "In . . . in Paris . . . the mime . . . It was my idea, I arranged it." It took a moment for Tony's expression to change. First he went blank, then he started to laugh.

"What's so funny?" I asked hesitantly.

"I thought you were going to tell me something serious!" he said. "This reminds me of my godson. You know, I thought he was just some misanthropic teenager who spent all his time in his room jerking off while playing video games. But turns out the whole time he was actually running a highly sophisticated drug ring selling pot to all the rich kids at school." Tony paused, waiting for me to catch up. "You know, I really *shoooould* be mad at the kid, but . . . honestly, I was sorta proud."

It took a little bit of time for me to understand what Tony was saying. I was incredibly relieved to be off the hook, but was he suggesting he thought of me as a juvenile misanthrope and was impressed I'd pulled off something so sophisticated as instructing the fixer to hire a street performer? I'm pretty sure that's exactly what Tony was saying. This was fantastic news! Given our unique relationship, it was clearly advantageous to come off as a bit stupider than I really was. Unless of course this was a ploy to lure me into a state of false security . . .

"Did a clown really rape you?" I asked when I regained my composure.

"Looks like there's traffic on the George Washington," Tony said, swerving off the highway without signaling. "I'll show you a shortcut to the bridge, we go right past where I grew up."

Chapter Six

KILL YOUR DARLINGS

"SOMEDAY THIS WAR IS GONNA END," JESSE SAID, REPEATING ONE OF Tony's favorite quotes. I smiled tightly. As hard as it was to believe, *Parts Unknown* was winding down. Two months after Tony's death, it was the end of the line—whether I was ready for it or not. In addition to the "Crew Special," I was wrapping up the Indonesia edit. Footage from the uncompleted episode in France wasn't going to be used, which made our Indonesia shoot the last episode Tony filmed that would make it to air. This was going to be our last chance to make Tony proud.

I was glad Jesse was editing Indonesia; we had quite a history. We'd both started on the show at the same time way back on *A Cook's Tour* when I was a tape logger. We'd worked together regularly since my first episodes of *No Reservations* in 2005, and Jesse had edited Romania, infusing it with his trademark sense of humor, all but securing my role as director. Now here we were in the surreal position of cutting a posthumous episode of *Parts Unknown*. It was humbling, after all I'd learned from Tony over the years, and I was still having trouble figuring out how to end the show.

Tony's absence loomed large; it was his creative vision that drove much of the editing process. Even more than my time in the field, I felt like I'd really got to know Tony through *our* edit collaborations and battles over the years. It was the part of the process where he really shined, and arguably where I learned the most from him during our time together.

"BE INCREASINGLY SURREAL," TONY SAID. "Make this show as hallucinogenic as possible. I want images from Haitian art, crosses, skulls, dicks, babies, limbs intercut with the dreamlike surreality of the actual environment."

By 2010 the show was starting to repeat locations, and Tony had wanted to stretch his legs, tell some different stories. He'd insisted, then finally demanded, we go to Haiti, and ultimately the Travel Channel had begrudgingly approved the trip. We arrived several months after the massive 7.0 earthquake that had left a quarter million people dead. This would be the first time the show had *purposefully* ventured to a truly "high-risk environment." I don't think any of us quite realized what we'd signed up for until landing in Port-au-Prince. The city was gone. In its place was a patchwork of grief, mass graves, countless makeshift refugee camps, collapsed and twisted concrete stitched together by a network of partially blocked roads. Thousands were still missing, survivors were dealing with a cholera outbreak, and foreign aid and attention were flagging. Driving at night, the only light came from an occasional passing car or burning oil drum, indication of an improvised roadblock. Our head of security, Damien, never had his hand far from a gun secreted in the glove box.

The shoot had been emotionally intense, but two months later back in New York, the edit was coming together well—really well— until the network did what seemed like their best to ruin it: "Lose Tony eating second helping. Doesn't make him look good in a food shortage" and "Is there any tourism still available?" More worrisome, there were demands for more clarity in the voice-over, more linear explanation, a neat sum-up at the end and generally less artistry in the storytelling. Eric, the editor, and I were horrified, fearing the network might succeed in gutting our show. But Tony stepped in and pushed back, fiercely defending the cut.

"This episode is Emmy material. This is not *Frontline*. We want impressionistic . . . we are *showing*—*not* telling. This is not polemic. There is no happy conclusion or *any* conclusion to be reached that won't be out of date by airtime."

Tony ultimately prevailed, and he was right: the show won Zach and Todd a well-deserved Emmy for cinematography. It also set a precedent that raising the bar sometimes required traveling to more challenging locations. It also required knowing how and when to push back against the powers that be.

If I wasn't in the field shooting an episode or sleeping for a week straight when I got back home, you could probably find me working with the editors. I was always intimately involved in my edits; I had to be. The way I looked at it, if the show got left on the edit room floor, it didn't matter how hard we worked in the field. Edits may not have been as glamorous as the shoots, but they were just as high stakes and far more satisfying. In a strange way, through the edit I'd actually realize I had been there and sort of vicariously enjoy the trip in a way I hadn't been able to while filming. Television production—especially with Tony—was an "ends justifies the means" operation. It might have been the most horrible, painful, humiliating, awful shoot, but if it was a spectacular edit—a great end product—almost everything bad that happened in the field was forgotten.

Successfully guiding a show through the edit required long days screening raw footage, pulling sound bites, doing additional research, and creative collaboration with the editor. The real storytelling happened in the edit room. I always strived to add bells and whistles, make something that was beautiful, emotional, honest, or even just special to me personally. The ultimate goal was, of course, making a good show, and Tony was the ultimate judge of success.

The edit was the part of the creative process Tony enjoyed the most. Tony was as ingenious as he was demanding, and his feedback could be scorching.

"Rule one? Show, don't tell! It's intro to storytelling, for fuck's sake!" Tony said. "This cut has too much blah blah like a fucking museum tour when it should be a dynamic, breathtaking visual demonstration. Why are we not showing Zach's gaze? I know we have the footage!"

Tony was a big believer in the power of point of view. Finding people with a good point of view for Tony to interact with on camera allowed us to look at a place through someone else's eyes. It granted Tony and the show an insider's access and was part of the magic recipe. Usually, Tony's sidekick of choice was a chef returning to his ancestral homeland for the first time, or traveling Eastern Europe with Zamir. But this time we were visiting southern Spain with Zach, our director of photography. In a strange breaking-the-fourth-wall twist, Zach was both behind and in front of the camera with Tony, and apparently Jesse and I were ruining it in the edit.

"What is this show about?" Tony continued. "Whose point of view are we telling it from? Answer: We are telling the story from Zach—a cinematographer's point of view. What would Zach see? Make it beautiful, the way a cinematographer would see the world. Let the images do the talking. Make the ending 'about something,' a reminder, visually, of who is looking. Unfuck this edit and make it as excellent as it can be and should be."

Tony set a high bar. He asked a lot of everyone who worked on the show, and specifically the editors. They were an amazingly talented bunch held to a standard that would probably be considered unattainable or even abusive on other shows. Editors might have had the hardest job on the team, as a huge share of the pressure to constantly reinvent and elevate the show fell on their shoulders.

My professional experience was pretty much limited to making shows with Tony, but I had a dim understanding that our post-production workflow was a little unusual. We had nine weeks to edit each episode, which was apparently a lot compared to the industry standard of four and a half weeks. And nine weeks was based on everything going according to plan. Nothing ever went according to plan. Edits would continue on at roughly $10,000 a week until Tony was satisfied the episode was right, budget be damned. Looking back, I knew I was lucky, but I don't think I realized just how spoiled

I was to work on a show where quality not only came first, but it was also pretty much the *only* concern.

But nothing good comes easy, and navigating the potential editorial pitfalls was a long and bumpy road. Despite Tony's unique voice and style permeating every frame, he most often couldn't offer much in the way of specific direction until he saw the all-important first cut (our initial attempt to make sense of the sixty to eighty hours of raw footage). Tony's opinion of an episode would never recover from a bad first impression, so the more polished, the better. The editor would basically have to cut a refined first pass of the entire episode, even though it was almost inevitably going to be redone.

If Tony didn't like how an edit was going, he'd refuse to write the voice-over script. I should really say *rewrite* the script, as it was up to the editors or me to write the initial scratch narration. Tony's voice-over made up the literal backbone of the shows, and his rewrites essentially served as the seal of approval. But even if Tony liked a cut, he often didn't write to what had been edited or even the scratch voice-over script he'd been given. Tony wrote what he wanted to write. This meant reverse engineering the cut to fit what Tony provided was all but inevitable.

It was an admittedly inefficient backward workflow, but it was what Tony needed and therefore just the way things were done. It was also demoralizing for editorial department morale.

Tony, who wasn't the type to take prisoners, often seemed to have little if any sympathy for the editor's perspective. Part of the issue certainly stemmed from Tony being naturally suspicious of "pale, pasty-face types that actually choose to sit alone locked in a dark room in front of an editing board all day watching other people do things."

Since I moved through the production as well as the post-production worlds, I felt like I understood both sides, and I'd learned it was best to wear kid gloves when offering my edit feedback. Even more important was softening how Tony felt whenever possible. If he didn't like the way a cut was going, if he found himself unimpressed with the artistry in the storytelling? Well, let's just say Tony's

feedback was an art form in and of itself. My inbox contains countless three a.m. emails that go something like this:

> The end of the show is turgid and saccharine and schmaltzy to
> a fault. it's painfully, sophomorically WAY WAY WAY over the
> top. Currently the show is a pointlessly arty mish mosh of mixed
> metaphors. Don't bludgeon the obvious references/homage
> into the ground for fuck's sake. Please! It's bathos-soaked and
> delivered at the end of a meat mallet. So some SERIOUS surgery
> on Act Six. It utterly blows. As is its conventional season two,
> and the MUSIC is abominable—or inappropriate throughout. It
> sounds like an 80s Tom Cruise film. PLEASE. Un-fuck this show.
> **Sent from my iPad**

But for all his bluster, Tony was kind of a softie at heart and
didn't relish confrontation. Unfortunately for everyone, one of these
emails inadvertently made it to McIndio, the editor of the show with
which Tony was displeased. Faced with the realization that his feedback had pushed McIndio to the verge of a mental breakdown, Tony
invited him along on the Thailand shoot by way of apologizing.

"Jeez, these freaking editors," Tony said. "We need to get them
out in the sunshine, thicken their skin, and it'll also be good for
creativity."

Unfortunately, the "Editor Outreach Program" didn't go quite
as expected. Already well out of his comfort zone by the time he
touched down in Bangkok, on the van ride to the hotel, McIndio
spasmodically swatted at imaginary mosquitos while simultaneously
tabulating and cross-referencing numbers and letters on license
plates, convinced he was seeing patterns. Unfortunately, the situation pretty much deteriorated from there. "It was like a haunting,"
Tony said. "By the end of the shoot, he was walking around in con-
centric circles arguing with himself about prime numbers. Fuck me.
Some people are better off left in their cage."

Tony terminated the outreach program as well as most direct
contact with the editorial staff, leaving that task to people like me.

However, as much as Tony couldn't sympathize with the editor mindset, he also understood they held the keys to the many "strange and terrible tools" of filmmaking. Tony was fascinated by and dependent on whatever idiosyncratic brain chemistry made editors expert at communicating through cuts, sound design, and music rather than words, and as such, he had a great deal of respect for what they could do.

And it was impressive. The ability to shape the vast amount of raw footage into a cohesive narrative as well as put up with Tony without going "McIndio" required near superhuman abilities. Take for example Hunter, who joined the ranks shortly before the move to CNN. Hunter's first cuts somehow looked like finished shows, always cinematic, and he had a magic ability to present complicated and difficult subject matter both clearly and without being heavy-handed. He was low-key, low maintenance, and strangely normal for an editor. Hunter was also an absolute genius.

Knowing how much Tony hated sum-ups, Hunter had the idea to end our Laos episode with no talking or voice-over. It should be pointed out just how radical an idea this was. Network television observes near religious adherence to a belief that the audience needs a constant and reassuring voice reminding them of what they saw, what they were seeing currently, as well as what was coming up next. This holds especially true for the end of the show, where there was typically a relentless push for Tony to deliver some sort of satisfying platitude.

But Hunter pulled it off. No talking, no voice-over for five and a half minutes, just natural sound and music over footage of Tony at a local festival. Colorful paper lantern dragons along with countless floating candles are set adrift, transforming the entire Mekong River into an ethereal blaze of light as the soundtrack builds to a crescendo. It was beautiful and a record time without speaking, a true high-water mark.

"My god, he's some kind of wunderkind," Tony said. "Nobody's that perfect. He must murder hookers in his basement to vent his rage, it's the only logical explanation. Make sure Hunter doesn't get busted. He's too valuable to go to prison."

A NATURAL-BORN EXAGGERATOR WITH A superb taste for the absurd, Tony was the ultimate storyteller. Tony's way of looking at the world, his ability to transform the bland everyday into a fantastic reinterpretation of reality, only seemed to add more meaning and truth to the original event.

"Both versions of the scene will begin with the same shots of the train approaching the station. Keep my version straightforward, about food—with a passing reference to the hungry kids," Tony said, talking a mile a minute, pausing only to light a cigarette. "We want to leave almost no hint of how badly things spun out of control in my version, skim over the ugliness and culpability and shame and spare the viewer the awkwardness we felt."

Trying to focus over the sound of gunshots in the background, I struggled to keep up, scribbling down Tony's edit direction in my notebook. We were standing in a modest backyard in the Hezbollah-controlled Dahieh suburb of Beirut, waiting for the cameras to finish setting up a family meal scene. As was often the case, while shooting one show, I'd be overseeing another through the post-production process. And, as was also common, the edit—in this case Madagascar—had hit a speed bump.

"I'm sorry, I'm still just having trouble understanding the justification for multiple versions of the food riot," I said.

Tony rolled his eyes and sighed. "So, to clarify, the idea is at the end of the show, I ask Darren how *he* would tell what happened on the train. We then cut back to the train for Darren's version, which this time includes the starving children stripping me of my food. Much bleaker. Much less flattering. Unsparing. Dark. Brutal. Frightening even. Darren's version shows the reality on the ground in all its buzzkill awfulness."

The Darren Tony was referring to was Darren Aronofsky, director of such films as *Requiem for a Dream*, *Pi*, *Black Swan*, and *The Wrestler*, among others. He'd accompanied us to Madagascar, the island nation off the southeast tip of Africa that most people associate with animated lemurs. However, environmental apocalypse, crushing poverty, and human suffering were more representative of what I saw. That speed bump in the edit revolved around what we'd assumed would be a routine food stop while on a scenic train ride to the coast.

A couple hours into the trip, our train stopped at an isolated jungle station. Cameras rolled as Tony and Darren disembarked in search of food, and much to everyone's surprise the situation quickly began to spiral out of control. What started with a large crowd of local village children shouting and fighting over scraps of food, spare change, and even plastic recyclables soon devolved into a state of anarchy. The children slammed their fists against the train in what appeared to be acts of violent begging. The few tourists on board tossed empty bottles out of the window in fear. There was the sound of crying among the screaming. The samosas we'd arranged for Darren and Tony to eat were ripped from their hands by the mob of hungry kids, and we had to retreat to the train. The desperation and poverty had been heartbreaking, the whole thing a dramatic and deeply unsettling reality check.

"Darren's version ends with the two of us sitting in stunned silence on the train afterward," Tony said. "The contrast between our versions should be shocking."

"Yeah . . . but I'm worried the multiple perspective pulls us out of the moment," I said. "Doesn't it kind of needlessly distract from the very serious issues we bring up in the show and instead call attention to us?"

"*Exactly,*" Tony said. "What do we include, what do we choose to leave out? Either way it's our choice. It's about the moral quandary of travel and white privilege. The camera is a liar. Drawing attention to it calls into question our own reliability and shows our hands aren't clean. I want to show how manipulative even 'honest, tell it like it is' TV can be."

That was one of the great things about Tony. He never shied away from complicated topics or from presenting himself in an unflattering light. And Tony wasn't just honest about it, he often bent over backward to highlight just how manipulative the TV machine could be.

TONY WAS A BRILLIANT WRITER with an exceptional imagination, gifted with the ability to write like he spoke. Despite being the smartest and most literate person I've ever met—capable of wielding the English language like a pillow or a sword, sometimes in the same sentence—Tony didn't have much of a formal education. High school, one year at Vassar in which he said his most successful academic pursuit was scoring Quaalude prescriptions, and a Columbia writing workshop. He often talked about his writing teacher, who had taught him to "kill your darlings." This lesson became his most frequent creative direction. Tony repeatedly said, "The best piece of writing advice I can offer is to kill your baby. Lose what you think is your best line. It'll be better."

I remember Tony sitting in the recording booth reading voice-over when he trailed off mid-sentence. Looking up from the script, he asked, "What bong-smoking monkey wrote this? Did you sneak this in the script? It's so heavy-handed with the drawing people together. We need a *much* lighter touch. You're hammering all the stops on the organ like Elton John at a funeral. Subtlety. It's a freaking virtue! I don't mean just this specific line, I mean in general we're falling into a formulaic, heartwarming get-out. Next it'll be every fucking segment before commercials. You know ... We're going to have a group hug each episode, we keep this up. Is that what you want?"

He scowled at me over his reading glasses, one eyebrow raised high enough that I got the idea the question wasn't rhetorical. I pressed the talk-back button and said, "Well, it's just that I think we should say *something* nice, because the show has been a little sarcastic at times."

"I know. So it's particularly disingenuous and incongruous to turn around and get all schmaltzy at the end," Tony said.

Tony viewed an end-of-the-episode conclusion as a betrayal of what was inevitably a much bigger and more complex subject. He'd always rather leave the audience thinking, keep them guessing, wondering. While I understood—and mostly agreed with—Tony's knee-jerk reaction against feel-good happy endings with a neat and tidy message, I had less of an appetite for the unresolved. In fact, secretly, I was a bit of a sucker for a cotton-candy Hollywood ending. Over the years this led to many instances of head butting, and ultimately Tony would always win out. But sometimes he'd surprise me by unexpectedly insisting on a happy ending himself.

Without fail, Tony was completely unpredictable. One of his most important rules was the shows always had to be different each week. Manic depressively and schizophrenically different. Always pushing forward, doing the hard thing, even the stupid thing, as long as it was the different thing. Tony was a big believer in failing gloriously in an attempt to do something interesting, rather than succeeding at being mediocre. "If it's not interesting, we may as well be working a lunch counter," Tony said.

It had taken years, but by the time we began *Parts Unknown*, Tony had essentially assembled his dream production team. It was a Skunk Works where Tony encouraged wild and often inappropriate risk-taking, rewarded experimentation, creativity, and thinking differently, while at the same time publicly shaming traits like consistency and level-headed thinking. Tony advised to "watch movies, read everything you can. Be inspired by what others have done and learn from their mistakes. Stealing is fine as long as you can reasonably suggest it was just 'borrowing' in court."

He challenged the editors, camera people, directors, and producers to come up with crazy shit, to innovate, and he fiercely guarded our freedom to try new stuff and to have fun while doing so. The point wasn't to be sensational, it was to innovate by fucking with the format.

It was pretty extraordinary thinking about it. Tony helmed a show that had no business being on CNN—on paper at least—but along with the crew we'd all made it their number one–rated program. We might feature a gritty sociopolitical episode in Colombia one week, a sophisticated deconstruction of the world's best restaurant in Copenhagen the next, then an episode in Tokyo investigating rope bondage subculture, or a trip to Buenos Aires visually inspired by an obscure Wong Kar-Wai film. Watching the shows, you never knew what to expect, and that was the point.

Credit is due to CNN for allowing us the creative freedom to experiment as well as the platform and tools that allowed the show to become what it had always wanted to be. At times it must have seemed to them like one series-ruining idea after another. A couple weeks into the Korea edit, Jesse suggested we cut the episode in reverse.

"Stick with it," Tony said, instantly latching onto the idea. "Emphasize the reverse storytelling. I will back you up. But don't let anybody water it down. We begin at the end, no explanation. We tell the story backwards. Let the audience catch up."

Just like the editors, the directors of photography, Zach and Todd, were always experimenting, always pushing the boundaries of what was creatively as well as technically possible. Ditching our regular Sony F-55s for the Korea episode, they'd conceived of and jury-rigged an entirely new camera system, just for the Korea episode. It allowed for dynamic movement while operating miniature handheld lipstick-sized lenses capable of capturing broadcast-quality footage. The downside was everyone was tethered to what looked like a *Ghostbusters* proton-pack, all seventy-five vertebrae-compressing pounds of which was often strapped to me. We moved across Seoul, an unwieldy octopus of cables, cameramen, and delicate and finicky recording equipment. Really, it shouldn't have worked, but somehow it did. In the edit Jesse took full advantage of the frenetic in-your-face camerawork, cutting the episode split and triple-screen as well as backward. We even played the show's graphic open in reverse. The Korea episode was just a glorious, glorious mess. Which, as usual, our executive producer, Sandy, had to clean up.

"I've been on the phone with the network nonstop," she said. Sunken cheeks and a pale complexion were evidence of the difficulty of mediating between Tony-inspired creative terrorism and network realities. Sandy's job was as thankless as it was ludicrous. "The reference to eating dog vomit was helpful, thank you," she said. "But the network is putting their foot down about running the credits backwards at the top of the show. They're just too worried it will trigger people to switch the channel. I'm sorry, it's the one thing they won't approve."

TONY WAS CHAMPION OF THE misunderstood, stragglers, stalwarts, pioneers, lovable drunks, the marginalized—those left behind or left out or fallen by the wayside. Maybe it was because he knew what it was like to be an outsider. Growing up, Tony hadn't fit in; he'd always considered his time in the kitchen as being part of a pirate crew of misfits. Even though we made a TV show, Tony promoted the idea we weren't a part of the mainstream. We always pushed for diverse voices and did our best to shine a light on underrepresented cultures and gave them the last word. Tony always stood up for what he believed was right, and everyone who worked on the show took pride in the responsibility. This was perhaps one of the best things about the show, and it could also be one of the most controversial.

"Sooo . . . Sandy and I just got off a very long call with CNN," I said, regarding the Iran episode. "They actually accused it of being a 'piece of thinly veiled anti-American propaganda.'"

"You're kidding," Hunter said, sounding worried. " . . . Right?"

I was not kidding. And I shouldn't have been surprised that shooting a show in Iran had been wading into dangerous waters. Instead of the popular conception of Iranians being murderous exporters of terror, we met welcoming families, curious strangers, and young people hanging out on the streets at night in front of ice-cream shops. They smiled at the cameras; everyone was welcoming and liked Americans. Frankly, we'd all been utterly taken with the place and the people we met.

Of course, the country had problems. There was justified tension between our governments, and the rights and freedoms of Iranians were continually being repressed, among other issues. But our line of work had taught us there was a difference between people and their government. Iran was a once-in-a-lifetime sort of trip. We'd been given a real opportunity to tell a different story, and it was of the utmost importance we got it right. This episode had the potential to do what Tony had always aimed for and I was proudest of: challenge stereotypes while resisting the othering of people we met by treating them with dignity, respect, and approaching a complex situation with an open mind. The Iran episode also served as a reminder of what could happen to the people we leave behind.

Shortly before completion of the edit, we learned Jason Rezaian and his wife, Yeganeh Salehi, both journalists who'd appeared on camera with Tony, had been arrested and detained indefinitely without charges. They'd been the kindest, most optimistic people we'd met in Iran, and it was unclear if their arrest was a result of having filmed with us, and how the show might affect their situation. What we did know was that in Iran, the line of what was okay and not okay to speak about was constantly shifting. Care had to be taken that nothing said in the show might inadvertently make the situation worse. It was a concern not only for Jason and Yeganeh, but also all the other people who'd helped us or appeared on the show. It was going to be a delicate line to walk between the Iranian government, the network, and the truth. Thankfully, Hunter was editing the episode. His big heart and nuanced and intuitive editing style brought a level of depth to everything he cut.

"The show is so powerful, Hunter," I said when the edit was complete. "It makes me laugh, cry, and think. That's a pretty impressive spectrum of emotion for forty-two and a half minutes of TV. You never resort to any cheap tricks or pandering and yet there's not a dull moment or missed opportunity. With how awful and scary the world seems today—how hopeless these divides can feel—your show is proof that there is hope. The world just might not end after all! Thank you again for everything."

Several weeks later, I watched the show's premier broadcast. It was a poignant example of Iran's seemingly mutually exclusive contradictions, and also those of our work. It was a powerful reminder of why I stuck with the job and the meaningful purpose behind it, which often got lost in a whirlwind of adrenaline.

The episode ends with Tony drinking non-alcoholic beer and eating take-out pizza alongside a group of classic American muscle car enthusiasts in north Tehran. The scene looked like it could have taken place in LA. Hunter cut together shots of vintage Mustangs and Camaros doing burnouts along with laughter and portraits of the various people we'd filmed throughout the episode. Tony's voice-over said, "After ten weeks Yeganeh was finally released, but as

I read these lines, Jason remains a prisoner. His future, the reasons for their arrest are still unknown." The show made me tear up every time I saw it.

Later that night I received an email from Tony:

> Such a great episode! You and Hunter should be very, very proud. Really a great accomplishment. Maybe your best. Iranians saw it by the thousands and have expressed huge love. Maybe the best twitter Facebook reaction ever—and huge ratings. Thanks for all the careful, hard work.
>
> *Tony*
> **Sent from my iPad**

IN THIS WORLD OF EVER more rules and regulations, Tony was a rebel who constantly dared to say fuck it. Every hero needs a villain, and ironically for us, the bad guys were also the ones who paid the bills. Networks—in general—strive to remain inoffensive to the largest group of potential viewers and therefore advertisers. It's a sound financial strategy that Tony—a natural-born risk taker—blamed for the ubiquity of bland, derivative, watered down, and generally mediocre content. It was almost like Tony was genetically programmed to resist network TV mores. While in Inukjuak, an Inuit village in Arctic northern Quebec, for an episode of *No Reservations*, Tony forcibly squeezed his hand into an oversized furry mitten, then turned to the camera and said, "Feels like fisting a Samoyed."

To our delight, Tony's fisting comment was broadcast without being censored. That Tony had made a reference to inserting a fist into a dog's anus or vagina only came to the Travel Channel's attention when viewers wrote in complaining. After that, some poor intern was assigned the job of checking the script against urbandictionary.com.

CNN, on the other hand, was far more organized and had an entire department charged with upholding the typically conservative principles of network decency. It was called Standards and

Practices, or S & P for short. These corporate arbiters of morality decided what was acceptable to broadcast, keeping the airwaves free of potentially offensive language, visuals, or subject matter.

S & P had their work cut out for them when it came to Tony. Out of countless skirmishes our Thailand episode stands out. It was a rice whisky–soaked food stumble across Chiang Mai, punctuated by inappropriate behavior, dildos, green-screen animation, slurping down a bowl of particularly graphic raw blood soup, ladyboys, and frequent profanity.

"I want blood," Tony said. "Lots and lots of blood. And cursing. Go overboard. That way when the network cuts it back, we'll still have plenty left in the finished show."

Usually, Tony pushed the boundaries of what was permissible to air for an arguably artistic or even altruistic reason. But sometimes we just thought it sounded like fun to toss a bunch of monkey wrenches into the machine and see what we could get away with.

"Can we discuss the S & P notes on Thailand?" Sandy asked, dark circles under her eyes. Reviewing them quickly, I did my best to keep a straight face.

1:06:44	*God Damn whiskey (God Damn is pretty offensive to some people)*
1:10:16	*I'd rather have a big pile of nutsack*
1:11:45	*Discussion of the blood soup that has cow feces in, lots of "shits"*
1:12:30	*Funky ass-tasting stuff*
1:12:30	*I'd eat it out of Chris Christie's jock strap on a hot summer day*
1:12:56	*If you eat too much of this shit you'll go blind*
1:13:21	*I don't care if Justin Bieber took a dump in that soup, that was delicious*
1:13:24	*God Damn*
1:13:35	*If you ever stuck your tongue in the asshole of a really beautiful woman*
1:13:44	*Picture Angelina's ass tasting like that*

1:13:46	So here's to analingus. This is CNN.
1:15:52	Intestine has that farmer's daughter taste
1:16:26	Fuckin' noodles
1:19:17	Is that a dildo in that woman's mouth?
1:20:21	That's a fuckin' brilliant idea
1:21:23	"Lady Boy" puts her head between guy's legs
1:22:0	Prostitutes with their sunburned ex-pats (recognizable images)
1:22:30	We're drunkass walking to beat the clock
1:23:22	It's like Guy Fieri's scrotum
1:24:36	Drunk ass food
1:24:50	Fuckin'
1:26:10	God Damn that's good
1:29:21	Ooooo, more boners. You know what's weirder than shitting blood? Shitting someone else's blood.
1:33:51	Fuckin' delicious
1:40:50	Theoretically, if someone were to suck your dick, that could be really painful
1:40:54	#1 advice to young cooks, don't touch your peepee after working with these chilies
1:41:23	Paid for tomorrow with ring burn (ass burn)
1:41:47	Pick what I want to protect myself from, like chlamydia
1:45:45	Tony describes his toilet after having one of these meals. Pretty gross.

"I forgot to pass on one other note from our lawyer," Sandy said, sitting down at her desk with a deflating sigh. It was four p.m. and she was only just getting to her lunch. "There are two nipple slips. Those shots have to be replaced or blurred."

"Oh my god! The nipples are only visible for like three frames!" I cried, histrionically slapping my forehead to hide that I was trying not to laugh. I considered the whole game absolutely hilarious, though winning necessitated an appearance of genuine anguish.

I was Tony's emissary, and I didn't take the responsibility lightly. Starting the negotiations, I offered, "We can drop the 'shit' from 'If you eat too much of this shit you'll go blind,' *but* I want to keep all four 'shits' during the discussion of the blood soup with cow feces. They're literally eating shit. It's a technical reference. Also 'funky ass-tasting stuff' and 'drunk-ass food'? Are they serious? What's wrong with that? Same goes for all the times Tony says, 'god damn, that's good.'"

Sandy sighed while joylessly picking at her kale and walnut salad. "I'll push back to keep 'god damn,' but please try to cut it down to only one or two uses," she said.

"If we have to, we can lose 'ass burn,'" I said indignantly. "Same goes for 'touch your peepee with chilies,' 'painful dick sucking,' 'Guy Fieri's scrotum,' the Justin Bieber dump reference, the guy getting a fake blow job from the ladyboy, two of the three dildos, and all the 'fucks.'"

I saw Sandy brighten slightly. She must have thought for a brief moment I was going to be rational. With her defenses lowered, it was time to go for the kill.

"However, after discussing with Tony we feel it's vitally important to keep 'big pile of nutsack,' 'I'd eat that out of Chris Christie's jock strap on a hot summer's day,' 'Angelina Jolie's ass tastes like this,' 'farmer's daughter taste,' and most importantly Tony downing moonshine shots while toasting 'So here's to analingus. This is CNN.'"

Sandy uttered a quiet cough and put down her spork.

TONY DIED BEFORE WRITING OR recording any voice-over for the Indonesia episode. In a perverse way it meant he'd get that show he always wanted with no voice-over. But the episode just didn't feel right. I was used to Tony defining what was either right or wrong. It wasn't always the easiest feedback, but it was all I knew.

I was numb watching the footage, trying to figure out what to do. Even though Tony wasn't here, it felt like there was some small part of him still alive in the edit. Subconsciously, maybe, I could sense once we were finished, Tony would really be gone for good. It was a catch-22: a painful episode to work on, but even worse to think of it being finished. I wasn't ready to move on.

The endings were always the hardest part, and Indonesia was no exception. The last scene of the episode—the last scene I ever filmed with Tony—had been a funeral and cremation ceremony with the ashes scattered on the beach. Tony never would have chosen to use the funeral at the end of the show; given what had happened it was too "on the nose." Instead, he'd have advised to think outside the box. Jesse and I had experimented with a few options, but without Tony's voice-over, everything we tried just made an already complicated situation even more complex.

The best solution I'd come up with was to include a previously unused voice-over line Tony had recorded for the Greek Islands episode a few years back. "All good stories end on a beach. Why should this one be any different?" it went. Ending this way wasn't the way Tony would have done it, but the more conventional and comforting ending with an uplifting voice-over suggestion of hope before the credits was closer to the ending I wished Tony had had.

Tony on the Mekong River. Luang Prabang, Laos, 2016.

Tony and I after the scene. Bahia, Brazil, 2014. *Todd Liebler*

Parts Unknown crew and I enjoying a moment of laughter
while filming. Seoul, South Korea, 2014. *Helen Cho*

(Top left) A few palliatives to ease my fear of flying.
Somewhere over the Pacific, 2015. *Jeff Allen*

(Top right) Tony flipping off the camera. Jaffna, Sri Lanka, 2017.

(Bottom) Behind the scenes. Bali, Indonesia, 2018.

Filming the food scene with Ma Thanegi on the pilot episode of *Parts Unknown*. Yangon, Burma, 2012.

Josh, a.k.a. "Magical Giant," acting as food insert hand model after the scene with Ma Thanegi. Yangon, Burma, 2012.

Zach climbing up a doorway to get the shot while filming a walking beat. Yangon, Burma, 2012.

Tony, Zach, and Todd after the scene. Bagan, Burma, 2012.

Questioning the wisdom of my career choice. Night Express to Bagan, Burma, 2012. *Josh Ferrell*

Me in Congo. Our jeeps were marked "T.V." to identify ourselves as journalists while filming in conflict zones. Kisangani, DRC, 2013.

Erik "Moose" Osterholm

Tony in Congo. DRC, 2013.

"Queen Victoria's Flying Wardrobe." Goma Airport, DRC, 2013.

Tony watching the Weginia fishermen. Kisangani, DRC, 2013.

Tony preparing his "jungle-style coc au vin."
Somewhere down the Congo River, DRC, 2013.

Filming at a traditional tea house. Tripoli, Libya, 2013.

A destroyed market. Misrata, Libya, 2013.

Josh at Margaritaville. Ocho Rios, Jamaica, 2014.

Crew meal at Margaritaville. Ocho Rios, Jamaica, 2014.
Margaritaville Staff

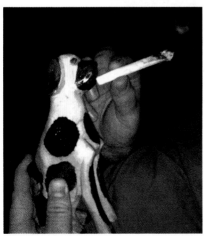

Mr. Papers behaving badly. Oracabessa, Jamaica, 2014.

Dr. Hoe's Rum Bar at James Bond Beach. Oracabessa, Jamaica, 2014.

Filming at Winnifred's Beach. Portland, Jamaica, 2014.

Tony's birthday:
rum cake on the beach.
Portland, Jamaica, 2014.

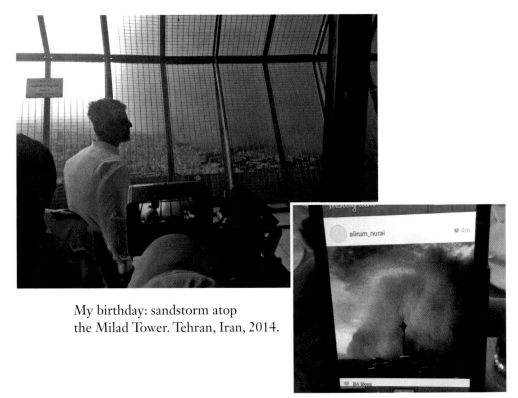

My birthday: sandstorm atop
the Milad Tower. Tehran, Iran, 2014.

Tony sitting by the Skrang River. Borneo, Malaysia, 2015.

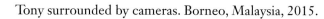

Tony surrounded by cameras. Borneo, Malaysia, 2015.

Tony and Asia Argento at the EUR. Rome, Italy, 2016.

The Angry Cousin restaurant. Rome, Italy, 2016. *Frank Vitale*

Massive ARRI cameras required for filming anamorphic. Rome, Italy, 2016.

Tony waiting nervously before the scene with President Obama. Hanoi, Vietnam, 2016.

President Obama arriving to film with Tony. Hanoi, Vietnam, 2016.

Meal scene with President Obama. Hanoi, Vietnam, 2016.

Crew photo with the president. Hanoi, Vietnam, 2016.
Pete Souza / White House

Tony's favorite: low plastic stool and bowl of noodles. Hanoi, Vietnam, 2016.

Pool scene. Bali, Indonesia, 2018.

Camera setup for beach meal with Lawrence.
Nusa Penida, Indonesia, 2018.

PART TWO

PART TWO

Chapter Seven

HIGH-RISK ENVIRONMENT

"WELCOME TO LIBYA!" REDA, OUR FIXER, CALLED OUT AS THE CREW AND
I exited the airport. After multiple false starts, dead ends, and years
of trying, we were finally here. It was January 2013, and following
what was perhaps the most unexpected and impressive victory of
the Arab Spring, for the first time in forty-two years Libya was free.

"Congratulations on the new series," came a familiar voice. It
was Damien, our lead security consultant. "All's quiet on the western
front thus far," he said, clicking his heels. Damien's presence indi-
cated our insurance carrier considered *Parts Unknown* episode 104
a higher than usual threat to our well-being. The fall of Muammar
Gaddafi, Libya's megalomaniacal dictator, had led to a power vac-
uum, allowing various militia groups and radical Islamist elements
to flourish in recent months. Beheadings and Westerners being
targeted had been playing on the news. High-risk environments
weren't my cup of tea, but this shoot was important to Tony, so of
course I had fully invested myself. Despite current events, Tripoli,
Libya's capital city, looked a lot like everywhere else. High-rises,
paved roads, traffic jams. From what I could see so far, at least, the

only evidence of fighting was several burned-out tanks left to rust along the airport road.

As we drove to the hotel, instead of soaking in the atmosphere or reveling in the excitement of being somewhere new, I was trying to rationalize two mutually exclusive realities. There were the obvious security concerns, and there was what Tony wanted. We didn't usually head into a shoot with hard and fast preconceptions, but this time Tony had made it *absolutely* clear he wasn't at all interested in depicting what was screwed up about Libya. The current security situation was an inconvenient reality that threatened to get in the way of the story Tony wanted to tell—had been wanting to tell—about regular people, kids mostly, fighting for and winning their freedom. It was an unusually sentimental and optimistic viewpoint.

Arriving at the Radisson Hotel, our van stopped at the perimeter gate, where they checked for car bombs. "CNN, CNN," our driver shouted. The stern face of the guard instantly brightened, and he waved us through with no inspection.

"We're having some issues communicating the concept of keeping a low profile," Damien explained.

"Libyans love CNN," Reda said. "They were the only ones here with cameras when Tripoli fell." Name-dropping CNN could do nothing to speed up the airport-style security at the hotel's front entrance, however. It took over forty-five minutes to get our gear through the x-ray machine.

"Libya is a *high-risk* environment," Damien said in a refined British accent that could be alternately charming, authoritative, disarming, sadistic, or irreverent. "The situation remains fluid, blah, blah, blah, proliferation of weapons following the 2011 uprising, etcetera, etcetera. Good, I'm glad we got that out of the way."

Wearing a tweed cap and vaguely anachronistic bootcut jeans, Damien didn't look or sound like a typical "security consultant." He had almost no hair, and what little there was—really only his eyebrows—matched the light color of his skin, rendering them almost invisible. The only contrast on his face was the hint of green in his yellow eyes, which were always scanning the room or whomever he was speaking with. Having spent years deployed to Afghanistan in the service of Her Majesty's Royal Marines, Damien now worked "cushy" media jobs like ours.

"Recent developments along the borders have my panties in something of a bunch," Damien said, delicately sipping a cup of tea. "There's concern about a 'spillover' effect here in Libya."

In the weeks preceding our arrival, everyone had been paying very close attention to rising tensions across the region. Ongoing French military intervention in neighboring Mali had increased the possibility of attacks targeting Western interests. The week before we arrived, just across the border in Algeria, hundreds of workers had been taken hostage when jihadists stormed a gas plant, resulting in the deaths of thirty-seven foreigners. Deadly riots were gripping Egypt, and there were reports that terrorist cells were operating in southern Libya. Benghazi, the country's second-largest city, had been suffering a recent string of attacks on Western diplomats, including the assassination of the US ambassador by al-Qaeda-linked extremists. International news reports were starting to refer to the situation in North Africa as a "cauldron of extremism." Though locations on our itinerary were considered secure and stable, regionally we were heading into what appeared to be a deteriorating security environment.

"Aye. It's right fucked," Bowler said. Bowler was also a former Royal Marine and Damien's right-hand man. Bowler's calm, even demeanor inspired confidence, and I'd grown to really like him. The trouble with Bowler was I often couldn't make out what he was saying, thanks to a thick Glaswegian accent. If Bowler talked fast, forget it. "Asye neight gang sith," he said.

"Exactly," Damien said. "Which is why Wally and Mick are here to be a couple extra sets of eyes." I'd worked a half dozen shows with Damien and Bowler over the years, but four security guys was a new record.

"Time to pull up the big-boy pants," Josh said.

"Indeed," Damien said.

While Josh wrapped up some logistics with Damien and Bowler, I found Reda in the hotel restaurant.

"Hold on, I need a pen," Reda said when he got off the phone. I watched him searching his bag, entertained by his failure to realize he had one behind his ear as well as several more stuck in his hair. I liked Reda and had got to know him well over the last couple months via Skype as we planned the shoot. He was quirky, always laughing and intensely proud of this country, a trait I highly valued in a fixer. When not missing, Reda's glasses were perpetually smudged, the frames mangled from having been stepped or sat on, or perhaps simply caught up in the chaos and disorganization that constantly swirled around him. But what Reda lacked in organization, he made up for when it came to creativity. Fixers were our lifeline to a country. Pretty much everything that made the shows what they were came through them, their contacts, knowledge, preferences, and prejudices.

"I am very appreciative of you understanding profoundly the good vibes, and not only bombing and fighting," he said. "It means so much, the story you want to tell about Libya."

Tony had been itching to come here since the revolution broke out, and we had what was shaping up to be a pretty good show. Reda had helped me organize an impressive roster of mostly average kids turned soldiers who fought for freedom and toppled a brutally repressive regime. But we still had a few kinks to iron out in order to finalize the logistics of the shoot.

"Any updates on the Misrata barbeque scene?" I asked.

"I swear to you two hundred dollars is more money than anyone has ever paid before for a goat in Libya," Reda said, rolling his eyes. "Hamid is blackmailing for a goat!"

"We should just pay the money," I said. Reda and Hamid—one of our most important sidekicks—had disliked each other since meeting on the scout, and it seemed the relationship hadn't improved. "We can't let the entire production grind to a halt over two hundred dollars. We've all worked way too hard for that."

LIBYA, SHOOT DAY ONE. I stopped to savor the moment. It was a beautiful day, bright sun, the crisp smell of sea air. I watched the camera crew load up the vans with equipment. This morning's itinerary was intentionally light: b-roll first, then a scene in the evening. This was the best way to get everyone comfortable working together, ease into it before shit started to hit the fan. Which it always did once we started filming with Tony. I checked my phone and saw a message from Damien. *"Collected Tony from the airport. He's in good spirits, wants to know his call time for this afternoon."* Let the countdown begin, I thought.

Hitting the streets, what struck me was how extremely friendly everyone was. "How are you? Very good Libya!!! Welcome to Libya!!!" they said. Tripoli's old city was a combination of traditional Libyan architecture with occasional colonial-era Italian buildings. The Libyan flag was painted on every surface possible. Almost as ubiquitous were murals honoring the martyrs who'd lost their lives in the fight to free Libya, most of whom barely looked fifteen.

"For the first time artist expression in Libya is free!" Reda said, referring to cartoonish graffiti depicting Gaddafi getting simultaneously punched in the face and kicked in the ass.

We rendezvoused with Tony at four p.m. for our first scene. As luck would have it, our first day was Magreb, the Prophet Muhammad's birthday, and there was supposed to be a fireworks show at Martyrs' Square.

"Did you shoot the graffiti making fun of Gaddafi?" Tony said, lighting a cigarette. "I love the ones where he looks like a sissy or a wimp. I saw one of him in prison uniform being brutally tortured on a medieval-style rack. That was some twisted shit."

"I want one of those on the wall in my apartment," Damien said.

"Copy that, I'll add it to the b-roll list," I said, anxious to keep us moving and make every minute count. "Okay, everyone, listen up! The plan is to walk through the medina and make our way to Martyrs' Square where the celebrations are supposed to be. Let's all stick together and make sure to stay out of frame. We'll follow Reda."

We began twisting through ancient, narrow, maze-like streets, populated mostly by kids. Some were playing with frighteningly realistic toy guns, others set off bottle rockets and cherry bombs, stamping them out with flip-flops when one dropped or threatened to misfire.

"There's a good alley right over there," I said to Tony. "Can you walk around that corner?"

"No," he said. "Let's just keep going."

As always, Tony hated being the center of attention, in public at least. And to be fair, walking beats were a spectacle. Reda was leading the way, followed by the security guys making a human V to split traffic. Then came the production assistants humping bags of film gear. Josh was right behind them snapping production stills; I was next trying to look forward to see where we were going and back at Tony at the same time. After me, the two assistant cameras spotted Zach and Todd, who were walking backward filming. Last was Tony, who had to pretend he wasn't being led by a stampede of thirteen people, half of whom were constantly shouting "CNN" every time we nearly knocked over a curious shop owner or stepped on an old lady. Low profile, we were not.

"Watch your back," Tony said the instant before Todd crashed into a wall.

"Damn it!" Todd barked at his AC. "When I'm walking backwards you've got to let me know if I'm about to hit something!"

Todd was strong, barrel-chested, and had been working on the show since the beginning of *No Reservations*. He was known internationally as "Mr. Clumsy Man" ever since he accidentally took out a padang restaurant's entire supply of food for the day. In the subsequent years he'd been responsible for countless camera-related mishaps. Off the top of my head I remember Todd breaking a UNESCO church in Mozambique, leveling a Santería shrine in Cuba, and getting punched for stepping on a devotee at an Uzbeki mosque. His foot went through the roof of a house in the favelas of Medellín, he caught fire in Hawaii, and wiped out a koto-roti restaurant in Sri Lanka. A generation of fuzzy yellow chicks were found in his bootprints at a village in the mountains of Laos, and he crushed a stroller in Bangkok. Thankfully, it was empty at the time. Todd broke our executive producer's wrist and may have been responsible for the extinction of a species of lemur in Madagascar. Allegedly.

Large animals—bulls, oxen, and water buffalo in particular—seemed to get enraged whenever Todd was around, even if he hadn't broken anything. I never figured that one out. But Todd could always be relied on in a pinch and had a good sense of humor about the wake of destruction that seemed to follow him around the world.

Zach, our other DP, sighed with disgust at the slowdown and scrambled off the ten-foot ledge he'd scaled. He was small and precise in an evil-genius-cat-meets-Inspector-Gadget sort of way, and at the moment he was dressed like Lawrence of Arabia to protect his fair skin from the sun. Before Steadicams were available to us, he'd developed a gyroscope device built from decommissioned military surplus. Zach really was a genius and could be impossibly rigid. He'd been around almost as long as Todd, and the pair couldn't be more different, which sometimes caused friction. But they complemented each other marvelously. Tony considered them his original A-Team.

"Let's keep moving," I said. "Todd, I'll spot you." We started walking again and, momentarily distracted by a six-year-old with what appeared to be an AK-47, I led Todd directly into a stone pillar. The impact caused part of his camera to fall off and hit the ground with a sickening clatter.

As we got closer to Martyrs' Square, the narrow streets filled with a mix of people. Women in full niqab, some wearing a headscarf, men in suits, others in long robes, and of course fatigues. There were more guns than I'd ever seen; they were practically a fashion statement. The crowd weaved through vegetable and trinket vendors set up in front of solemn murals and glossy makeup advertisements.

We arrived at sunset just as the call to prayer began. Martyrs' Square was vast, lined by a mix of grand mid-century and historic arcaded structures, and to my disappointment, it was mostly empty of people. Blinking Christmas lights decorated lampposts and palm trees. A few spectators stood on the periphery, and here and there some kids set off bottle rockets. A lone motorcycle bounced over cobblestones playing American pop music.

"I think we got enough of this," Zach said after a few minutes of filming Tony standing around looking bored.

I know it sounds strange considering we were in Libya, a place we'd worked so hard to get to, but keeping everyone engaged, especially Tony, was a concern. Gatherings or festivals such as this made for a welcome change to the typical sit-down meal scene, but they were much harder to pull off. If we didn't get the timing right or if Tony decided we were wasting our time, he'd get anxious to head back to the hotel.

"Perhaps you have some sort of expository thought for the camera?" I asked. Tony just glared at me. My hopes of salvaging *anything* from the day were looking increasingly dubious.

"Okay, let's get a big wide shot of Tony walking through the square," I said, trying to buy some time. We set up the shot, and Tony walked through the frame and off into infinity.

"He's not coming back," Zach said.

"Fuck!" I said and ran off to retrieve him. By the time we returned, the sun had fully set, and little by little a crowd was forming. Skater boys, Libyan hipsters, hip-hop kids, break dancers, and militia in fatigues with machine guns slung over their shoulders kept coming. Everyone was friendly; they wore huge smiles and made the victory symbol for the camera as they walked by. People in the crowd started setting off fireworks, lighting the night sky with a flurry of colorful sparks. I sent Todd, Josh, and Damien off to go get b-roll and kept Zach filming Tony.

The bursts grew to explosions, which soon transitioned into a battery of hearing damage–inducing artillery fire. Cars and motorcycles revved their engines, and burned rubber added to the smoky air, already heavy with the smell of cordite. A huge firework went off at a forty-five-degree angle, landed on the roof of a nearby building, and continued exploding. Other rockets misfired, shooting sideways directly into the crowd. Everyone cheered. The only problem was Tony wasn't talking. By now the ever-increasing volley of fireworks was coming from all directions. Revelers held boxes of Roman candles in their hands as they shot up into the night sky. Cars spun around doing donuts while tossing fireworks from their windows. There was a deafening *Ka-BANG-wfizz* as a Roman candle shot from somewhere and exploded just near our feet. Everyone scattered while Zach and I screamed. Tony didn't even flinch.

"That was good," Tony said, laughing.

I was worried the security guys would consider such close proximity to explosive projectiles a health and safety violation, but they were having fun like everyone else. Everyone but Zach, that is.

"Let's try and not get blown up . . . " he shouted. It was getting hard to hear over the nonstop barrage of ear-splitting whizzing, popping, and flash-banging explosions. Fire trucks and ambulances were stuck in gridlock traffic, the wail of their sirens mixing with blaring car alarms, laughter, and shouts from the increasingly rowdy throng all adding to the cacophony. I decided to check in with Josh over walkie to make sure Todd was getting everything.

"Affirmative," Josh said. "Great stuff here. Damien almost got hit by a firework, but he was able to use Todd as a human shield."

"Keep up the good work," I said.

I saw Zach was smiling and peered over his shoulder. In the monitor was a toddler on his father's shoulders; both of them were looking up, and fireworks exploded, momentarily illuminating an expression of awe.

"It's like the first fourth of July on steroids," Zach said, having come around. Tony was clearly enjoying himself as well, but still not saying anything. My train of thought was interrupted by a loud *ker-BLAAAM* as I got hit in the back by a fireball. When I turned around, Reda and the rest of the local crew were laughing. "Someone did that on purpose!" I shouted, really pissed off.

"Did you get the shot?" he asked Zach. "That's in the show."

"On the bright side, now that I've been hit, I know that they don't hurt," I said, checking to see if my jacket was singed.

"Yeah, just as long as you don't get shot in the eyes," Zach said.

It kept getting better and better. A live box of Roman candles tipped over, sending rockets bouncing off the pavement, skipping, hitting the steps, and shooting into the spectators. *Fizz, whap, crack, BAM.* People yelled and waved the Libyan flag from the backs of horn-blaring pickup trucks. Every part of this would be totally illegal back in the States, and it was going to make some great TV.

"Are you getting the car doing the donuts?" Tony asked, referring to a BMW drifting dangerously close to the crowd. Before Zach could answer, there was another explosion, and a bright red rocket hit Tony in the back of the head. "Ouch," he said, rubbing behind his ear. "That's gonna leave a mark."

"How does it feel to finally be in Libya?" I asked, trying again to get Tony to say something usable.

"Please stop," Tony said. "I got nothing to say, and you're harshing the buzz."

"It's just we're getting so much great footage and—"

"STOP!" Tony shouted. "Will someone *please* kill him?"

"This is fantastic!" Reda said, laughing. "There were fireworks under Gaddafi, but never a party like this! This is freedom for the first time in forty-two years!"

Reda was right. The energy was amazing, and we'd captured the historic feel. Even though Tony wasn't going to talk, it was still one hell of a first night. Someone sparked a joint and passed it to Tony. He took a hit and said, "How do you say . . . shakran?"

"You know shakran?" Reda said excitedly.

"Mastool," Tony said. At which point Reda doubled over laughing.

"What does mastool mean?" I asked.

"It means I'm totally wasted!" he said. "Mastool!"

SHOOT DAY TWO WE FILMED a scene at a traditional Libyan tea house with Tony and an expat journalist who'd grown up in Libya and returned post-revolution. They marveled at the "against-all-odds" victory, the kindness and optimism of the population, as well as the exuberance of the previous evening's fireworks-related celebrations. They also discussed the immense challenges facing the country. One of the biggest issues involved the militias who'd fought Gaddafi and weren't taking orders from the new central government. One detail in particular caught my ear. Recently there had been reports of militias rounding up and torturing gay men. While researching Libya before the trip I'd read that, along with things like alcohol, the official policy toward homosexuality was pretty much zero tolerance. A lot of places we went there was some sort of prohibition on being gay, so for shoots I just casually put it aside, as if you could take off being gay like taking off a sweater.

That evening we returned to Martyrs' Square for the second day of Muhammad's birthday celebrations, expecting a repeat of the previous evening. So it came as a surprise that there was barely anyone there, just a few lone cherry bombs in the distance. The mood had changed. It wasn't hostile per se, but certainly not the exuberant, friendly, frenzied welcoming atmosphere of the previous night. It seemed the second shoot day was far less remarkable than the first. That is, until I went to bed.

Around three a.m., I was woken up by a knock at my door. "Tom, it's Damien. We need to talk." Entering Damien's hotel room, I was confronted by Zach, Josh, and the security guys, all of whom were looking very worried.

"The British foreign office has issued a statement that they are aware of an imminent threat in Benghazi," Damien said. "Apparently there was an attack by jihadists that's not being reported in the news yet, and Westerners are being urged to leave immediately. There is now a very direct kidnap threat running right across from Algeria and Liberia down to the south of Libya, including the vicinity of Tripoli. The vibe at Martyrs' Square was clearly ominous, and you've had a number of sidekicks drop out. It's my feeling the local population knows something's up and don't want to be associated with us. We've been on the jungle drums and though it's not confirmed yet, our intel informs us two Western female journalists were abducted here in Tripoli."

"Holy fuck! What are we going to do?" Zach asked.

"Bowler will be taking watch tonight. In case anything happens, there's a plan to escape. Tony has been advised," Damien said. "Remember as we practiced in the HET course, in a kidnapping situation, control your emotions. It's likely your captors will be nervous, unstable, and anxious. Follow their instructions . . . if conscious."

Holy shit, I hadn't expected this. Over the years we'd been to some tough places with Damien, but this was the first time we'd been woken in the middle of the night and told our lives might be in danger. After I finished packing just in case, I sat on my bed, my mind racing with everything from mortal terror to contingency plans for the episode. Obviously, I wouldn't be getting any sleep, and I assumed Josh wouldn't either. I went over to his room.

"I stood for what must have been like an hour and a half with the lights off halfway between the bathroom and the bed," Josh said. "I was afraid to make a fucking move because I thought I heard something outside."

"Josh, it's going to be okay," I said. "Tony's invincible, remember?"

"I know," he said. "But that doesn't mean that side characters like us can't get picked off."

Fuck, Josh was right . . . This was the worst time to be stuck in a dry country.

SEVERAL HOURS LATER, TODD CAME down to breakfast well rested and saw the rest of the crew, dark circles under our eyes, silently drinking coffee.

"Ummm . . . did I miss something?" Todd asked.

"You didn't get woken up?" Tony said in surprise. "Gee, Todd, forgetting you is starting to be a regular thing." A couple weeks earlier while Josh and I prepared for the Libya shoot, Zach, Todd, and Tony had been deep in the Colombian jungle. While there, Damien had accidentally left Todd at a rest stop in FARC territory. Or so the story went. A similar thing had happened in Haiti when we switched hotels. We only realized Todd wasn't with us once we'd checked in to the new one. Todd was rightly starting to develop a complex about being left behind in hazardous environments.

"Apologies, Todd. I pledge to do my sincere best it doesn't happen again," Damien said. I wasn't sure if he was being sarcastic or not; it could be hard to tell. "Unless you prefer a pacifier, bottle, and a nap, let me get you up to speed," Damien continued. Yup. He was being sarcastic.

Despite the recurring Todd lapses, at this point we had a long-standing and trusting relationship. Since that first shoot together in Haiti when we'd all decided to stick it out through food riots and with a hurricane bearing down on us, Damien had accompanied us to Mexico at the peak of drug cartel kidnappings, and the worst thing that had happened was Tony flying off the handle when I "surprised" him with the pink stretch limo transport beat in Tijuana. The last season of *No Reservations*, Tony convinced the network to approve a shoot in Iraq. Due to the higher than usual risk, in addition to security accompanying us in the field, the insurance company required us to take what's called Hazardous Environment Training (HET). With Damien's flare for the dramatic, his course wasn't going to be anything less than a full-immersion experience. Due to more relaxed laws surrounding guns and explosive ordnance, Damien had opted to hold the training in rural Virginia.

"Welcome to Virginistan," he'd said as we arrived from New York.

Damien presented us with laminated press badges and written information including a faked Wikipedia printout as well as a stern warning to take the training course as seriously as we'd take our upcoming trip. Damien had devised a complete backstory of civil unrest and political overthrow. Virginistan even had its own currency, which we were to treat like real money. Basically, Damien had endeavored mightily to provide a realistic experience designed to prepare us for Iraq . . . and scare the hell out of us in the process.

Virginistan highlights included getting sunburnt while using a knitting needle to pick my way through a supposed minefield and an actor vomiting Dinty Moore stew to simulate the effects of shock. As the course progressed, there were medical training, live ammunition handling, checkpoint exercises, kidnapping scenarios, and fake blood. Despite what I'd been told, unfortunately the fake blood stains did not wash out. Regardless, I had to say, Damien put on one heck of a good show.

When we finally deployed to Iraq, we were definitely more prepared. Everyone survived, but there were a few intense moments—like when we inadvertently stopped to take a piss break in Mosul, a well-known red zone. And the time when a kidnapping false alarm resulted from Tony's driver not speaking enough English to follow instructions. One of Damien's team misread the situation, and, fearing a hostage situation, nearly gave the driver the "good news" (Tony speak for snapping the driver's neck). When I saw Tony after the little "misunderstanding," as it became known, he was visibly shaken. "It was just like fucking Virginistan!" Tony said in between drags of his cigarette.

Now, here we were again. But this was no simulation.

"If we knew before we came to Libya what the situation was going to be, we would've told you not to come," Damien said.

"Do we need to leave?" I asked. "Is it that bad?"

"The unfortunate thing for you is I'm not here to tell you what to do. Ultimately you, as the director of the show, are responsible for your crew," Damien said in an ominously deliberate voice. "I've given you the best information I can. You'll have to make the call."

"I can't make that decision for everyone," I said, shooting a worried glance at Josh, who looked as nervous as I did. "We should take a vote each day and decide as a group."

"All right," Tony said, breaking the silence. "Libya was a high-risk environment, we all knew that when we signed up. Who's in? Who wants to keep going for another day?" Todd and I raised our hands. A moment later Josh and Zach followed suit.

"Very well," Damien said. "In that case I'll have to insist on a few changes in the way we operate. The production will need to move faster, be in and out of each location quickly."

"What exactly do you mean by quickly?" I asked.

"We'll evaluate on a case-by-case basis. But I estimate around one hour maximum," Damien said.

"One hour?!" I practically choked. On a normal day, setup and lighting alone usually took about two hours, then another one to two hours with Tony, and some time afterward to film food prep. An average food scene required approximately five-plus hours. These days it took us an hour just to get out of the van. Literally. So I couldn't imagine being in and out in that time.

"I understand this style of working presents some challenges to your flow," Damien said. "But in order to mitigate risk, I feel it's a necessary precaution if we want to keep operating. I'll be timing you today to see how it goes. Also, to reduce our exposure, we're going to shake up the schedule and not let locations know in advance we're coming."

"The restaurants will be furious!" I said.

"You all are a very resourceful bunch," Damien said. "I trust you'll find a way."

Coordinating sidekicks, locations, and timings was going to take a feat to pull off. He was spot on about one thing, though: we were very resourceful.

"I DON'T KNOW WHY YOUR guys are telling you that," Jomana said. She was CNN's Libya expert. Although I didn't feel right telling the crew to stay, I did have the power to pull the plug if it seemed prudent, and I wanted another opinion. "Government officials are claiming the UK warning is unfounded. Yes . . . I've heard about the kidnapping of the Western journalists, but it's not true. These are rumors designed to stir up tensions and cause fear in order to undermine Libya's stability. It's the same thing with the supposed attack in Benghazi. Nothing has happened there."

The night before when I'd updated the office on our situation, they immediately checked in with the CNN International desk. CNN was aware of the warnings but still felt Tripoli was stable. The information I was getting from both CNN and now Jomana painted such a different picture. I needed to find Damien, but before I did, Zach popped out from behind a large potted fern.

"Dude, we got to get the fuck out of here. This is not what we signed up for! Did you see how freaked out Damien looked? I've never seen him like that before!"

"I know," I said. "I'm far from happy about what's going on. But I just talked to our contact at CNN and I got a *very* different story. I don't know, but it seems like Damien might be jumping the gun . . . "

My gut was telling me to trust Jomana over Damien, but I wasn't exactly impartial. We had a TV show to make, and bailing on the second day of the shoot wasn't a good look. This was only the fourth episode of *Parts Unknown*. If we pulled the plug for what turned out to be no reason . . . well, there was no going back now. At least not without a credible threat. When I found Damien, he was looking down at his phone and laughing.

"What's so funny?" I asked.

"Oh, just looking at some pictures," Damien said, smiling. "From my annual pilgrimage to the Nevada desert." Damien was referring to his Burning Man trips. Apparently desert raves were how he chose to blow off steam in between assignments.

"Here I am corralling the ponies," he said and flashed me the picture. Unfortunately, there was no way to unsee what I'd just been shown. Indelibly imprinted on my mind was an image of a late middle-aged tent orgy, the participants naked on all fours, each ball-gagged and sporting what looked like matching sparkly silver batons with extra-long tassels. The batons had been inserted somewhere I didn't think the manufacturer had intended them to go. Unless they weren't batons . . . In contrast to the ponies, Damien was fully erect, a whip in each hand. He was covered from head to toe in silver paint, and only silver paint. "The ponies were disobedient," he said reproachfully. "They left me no choice but to teach them a very firm lesson."

"Right. Um, I spoke to Jomana from CNN," I said, cutting to the chase. "She's been in touch with her sources, and had a different take on the situation . . . " When I finished explaining to Damien what I'd learned, I could tell he was not happy about having his authority challenged.

"With all due respect to Jomana, she is in Tunisia," he said coldly. I didn't know who to believe. It was like both Jomana and Damien had been given the same information, and each was twisting it in the complete opposite direction. But I thought there wasn't much chance they were both lying. I couldn't figure out exactly what was going on and had no choice but to speculate.

ON THE VAN RIDE TO our lunch scene—the first attempt at *Parts Unknown* guerilla edition—I thought about all the things that could go wrong. The camera guys didn't work well under this kind of time pressure. The restaurant didn't know we were coming. What if they said, "No, come back tomorrow?" What if the sidekick didn't show up thanks to the last-minute schedule change? We were going to have to get everything as we went—no coming back later for exteriors, food prep, or inserts—because at any moment Damien might shout, "Get in the vans!" And what if Damien was right about the threat to our safety? But most terrifying of all, Tony was sitting next to me. He hadn't traveled with the crew to location in seven years, and I wasn't sure what would happen if he had to watch us set up. Reminders of the artifice of making TV had been known to throw Tony off his game and could have negative creative implications.

"I'm starting the clock," Damien said as we arrived. It was showtime. Tumbling out of the van, I was met by a strong breeze blowing off the Mediterranean and the smell of fresh fish. Reda went inside to secure permission, the camera guys started unloading gear, while I met Omar the sidekick. Straight away I got a good vibe. He'd been a travel agent before the revolution, when he took up arms to fight Gaddafi.

"You and Tony stand out front, choose your fish, then go inside and eat," I said, dramatically abbreviating my usual pre-shoot sidekick pep talk. "Be yourself while we film, it's simple!"

"That's the best way to do it!" Omar said.

"The restaurant said yes!" Reda reported. Everything was going according to plan so far. Surprisingly.

"What do they do? They just grill that?" Tony asked, walking up to the diverse array of sea creatures spread out over ice in front of the restaurant.

"Yeah, they open it and grill it," Omar said. "Some garlic, some sauce. It's really awesome. One of the best foods in Libya."

Okay, the scene had definitely begun, ready or not. Zach and Todd had started filming, but they were in each other's shots and yelling about who should move. The crew vans and piles of equipment were lying out in the background, and our driver was talking up the taxi stand, probably explaining we worked for CNN. We obviously weren't keeping a low profile. Damien was watching disapprovingly.

"Let's get one of these fish. Some shrimps. Calamari too," Omar said.

"Okay, some snapper, how about four of these," Tony said pointing at various fish, his eyes wide with hunger. "Some wild dorado, one of these in the sauce, harime, and oh, octopus, I like that too. And the calamari. I haven't eaten since I arrived."

I'd never seen Tony order so much food before. This was going to take forever to prepare and film; simply ordering had consumed nearly a quarter of our entire allotted time—and we'd only just got the order in!

"Okay, Tony, why don't you go have a cigarette while we set up the table," I said, hoping to keep him separate from Omar before the scene.

"May I join you?" Omar asked.

Fuck! I knew from experience Tony would blow all the good content before we were rolling. It was like clockwork. If I appeared too worried—over directing as Tony called it—that could be just as bad.

"Umm, please try not to talk about things we might want to discuss on camera," I said.

"Relax," Tony said. "If we say anything good, I'll bring it up again when we're filming."

Fat chance, I thought. But if we were going to stay on schedule, I didn't have time to babysit.

"Reda, tell the restaurant we need to scale down the order," I said, entering the kitchen, where I promptly stepped in a pile of fish guts.

"Okay, what should they eat?" Reda asked.

"Whatever. Nothing that takes too long," I said, and went to check on the DP's progress setting up the table.

"What's the problem?" I asked, seeing that Zach and Todd were arguing over the seating arrangement.

"Even if we put all the drivers in the background, it's going to be tough to make the place look full," Zach said.

"It's postwar Libya, it doesn't matter if the restaurant looks empty," I said. "Todd, as soon as you can, please go to the kitchen and try to make something out of the food prep. We're not going to be able to come back or do it afterward."

I looked up and saw Damien was staring at me from the doorway. He shook his head, tapped his watch, and said, "Tick tock, tick tock." I checked the time; we'd already been here for twenty-five minutes! Ack! We hadn't even started yet! I needed an update on the food prep and to make sure Josh was working on the releases but decided to check on Tony and Omar first.

"Gaddafi regime took all the restaurants and moved them here," Omar said. "Even the restaurants were oppressed by Gaddafi."

"Arlp!" I squeaked. "Let's wait to talk about the restaurant until we're filming!"

"Oh yeah, I'm so sorry!" Omar said.

Finally, I got word that the food was almost done and the cameras were set up. I put on my trusty IFB, a device that allowed me to dial into Tony's microphone. We hit the table with only twenty minutes left, if Damien stuck to his guns. When the food arrived, I relaxed slightly.

"Oh, that's delicious," Tony said, taking a bite of calamari stuffed with rice. "So how quickly did your life change when the war started?"

"Wow, it drastically changed. When the war comes and goes . . . you will value life more. Even the dishes that I'm tasting right now, they will taste better," Omar said.

As Omar relayed his experience fighting in the revolution, Zach was telling me to move the straw that was blocking his view of the food. And Todd said he missed Tony asking the question, three questions ago; we'd need to get that again. I could also see Damien, who saw I could see him and tapped at his watch again. My attention snapped back to the table. Oh my god, was Tony asking me a question?

"Ummm . . . yes," I said, having no idea what I was agreeing to.

"It's like two years, I think," Omar said.

"Okay . . . so about two years, only two years later," Tony said. "This is a country where for forty years you had all power emanating from one guy. Once he's gone, you'd think it would be complete chaos. But the airport is working, they're stamping passports. The traffic lights work, okay, the traffic's not so great, but it's okay. There are a lot of problems . . . especially in the last week, and a while back in Benghazi, but generally speaking, this seems to be a functioning society. When you've been fucked over so badly by a leader so monstrous as Gaddafi, for so long, I gotta say I'm a little surprised things are going, so far, so well. Am I crazy?"

"There's a system right now. Kind of," Omar said. "It's done by the people. Nobody done it. Not the government. Nobody. People they want something for their children. Want something for themselves in the future."

"And you think in the next five years it'll come together?" Tony asked.

"I think it's going to be awesome," Omar said, grinning proudly. "Everyone is free to do their own thing."

"Man, this is good food, you brought me to a good place," Tony said. Then, looking up at me: "You want to reconfigure for wide shots?"

"Uh . . . yes," I said, surprised at how well the scene had gone.

"We have significantly overshot our budgeted time," came Damien's voice over the walkie.

"Copy that, we just finished the meal," I replied. "Zach, can you go outside and get an exterior shot? Todd, finish up any outstanding food inserts. Josh and Reda, double check releases. Let's get on our way to the next location in five minutes." I lit a cigarette and relaxed, just a little bit, for the first time in what felt like forever.

"How was the food?" I asked.

"It was fantastic," Tony said.

"CNN, CNN!" OUR DRIVER SHOUTED as we arrived back at the hotel that evening. Damien had remained silent the entire drive back, and now I could see his left eyelid was twitching.

"This afternoon has made it abundantly clear just how outmanned and boxed in we were," he said, once we were back inside.

We'd just come from filming at the Bab al-Aziziya, Gaddafi's ultra-luxe palace and former seat of power, turned unrecognizable pile of rubble. Midway through the scene, militia in several white pickup trucks had surrounded us. They claimed we didn't have the right paperwork to be there, and the situation escalated to the point we had to flee before they destroyed our footage. It had gotten a little dramatic. The slight twitch in Damien's left eyelid was not encouraging. "If we'd needed a quick exfiltration, our vans didn't stand a chance. Our current vehicles are not fit for that purpose, and the drivers are incompetent. The situation could easily have escalated further, and we would've been completely helpless. We need to upgrade, or it will be necessary to abandon filming."

"What are you suggesting?" I asked.

"One of your sidekicks, Hamid, from the Misrata militia," Damien said. "Bowler met him on the recce and couldn't help but notice his rather impressive array of toys. The possibility of assistance was discussed should the situation escalate and support be deemed necessary. We've checked in with them today, and Hamid has reiterated his desire to lend a helping hand."

As Josh and I learned, the Misrata militia could in fact provide us with security. And vehicles, brand-new Toyota Land Cruisers no less. Our new friends would be armed to the teeth for our protection. They could be here in the morning. There was just one little detail to work out. It was going to cost somewhere in the neighborhood of $30,000, give or take. Considering all the potential unknowns, Damien suggested to be safe we needed at least $50,000 *cash* on hand to keep the lights on.

Everything about the Libya episode had been spiraling out of control, including the budget. Due to visa delays, we'd been forced to reschedule the shoot. That had meant new plane tickets, additional security and vehicle costs, and losing nonrefundable hotel deposits, among countless other kill fees. We'd had to cancel a satellite trip to Benghazi. Including Reda, we had a total of four fixers working on the show. Before arriving, we'd been required to double the number of security consultants. But it would be pretty awkward, and ultimately a much larger financial loss, if we had to leave the country without a show. Sure, this was going to be a lot more money than we'd ever spent on an episode. But, then again, we were in a much more dangerous place than we had ever been before. Josh called Sandy, our executive producer, back at Zero Point Zero, to tell her the good news. While Josh and Damien spoke to Sandy, I went to update Reda and let him know Hamid's militia might be joining the shoot.

"Oh my god," Reda said. "Your security guys are too paranoid! It wasn't such a big deal what happened today. We were never in any danger, this is just how people in Libya talk."

"If it's going to make Damien relax, the militia will be worth its weight in gold," I said. "That way we can all get back to focusing on actually making the show."

"I don't trust these guys," Reda said. "They won't be good for the representation of Libya. I got for you Omar and Johar to be in the show. Both of them are already revolutionaries. Why do we need Hamid?"

"Reda, we've been talking about freedom this whole trip," I said. "Revolutionaries who don't want to put down their guns like Hamid and his militia represent another side of Libya's struggle for freedom. Also, I don't have a choice."

"WELL...THE COST FOR THE MILITIA has been approved," Josh said at breakfast. "You won't believe this part: the office wanted to know if the Libyan militia had a US federal tax ID number!"

In addition to not having a federal tax ID, the militia didn't accept credit cards or travelers' checks. And Libya being Libya, a standard wire transfer in the amount of $50,000 was not an option either. So later that morning a man with a perspiring forehead, British accent, and pressed blue suit arrived at Josh's hotel room carrying a duffel bag full of Libyan dinars. We were officially back in business.

When I found Tony, he was outside smoking. Before I could fill him in on the details, I was interrupted by a voice from behind us.

"You should cook for us . . . I heard you are the best French cooker or something . . . I'm Hamid, your new head of security."

So, this was the famous Hamid I'd heard so much about. And "head of security," eh? Damien was not going to like that, I thought with a chuckle. Hamid was young, probably in his mid-twenties, and spoke with a Libyan-Canadian monotone. His shaved head and the rings under his glazed eyes made him vaguely reminiscent of fat Brando from *Apocalypse Now*. Hamid had come back when the fighting broke out and had chosen to remain in Libya rather than return to his family in Montreal. He wore spotless olive-green fatigues with matching cap and a color-coordinated avocado scarf. He pulled out a grenade and used it to light his cigarette.

"Have you tried Libyan alcohol?" Hamid asked.

"No," Tony said with a slightly uncomfortable laugh. "I hear it's brutal."

"Yeah, it's gonna destroy you," Hamid said.

"We haven't had a chance to meet yet. I'm Tom," I said. "Thank you so much for all your help, I really appreciate it."

"No problem," Hamid said.

"Yeah, we're excited about Misrata," Tony said.

"WHERE'S TODD?" I ASKED. "WE need to wait for him before we start."

"Well, *we did our best*," Tony said, checking his Rolex. "We gotta get going."

"Let's begin then and catch him up when he arrives," Damien said, addressing the crew. "Big company move today, the roads here are known for being treacherous, and we'll be encountering many checkpoints. Hopefully most of them will be legitimate. If we come up against anything unpleasant, we're going to drive straight through. If for any reason the vehicle has to be stopped, get out of the car and get away from it if it's being shot at. Okay?"

"Uh, and preferably on the side—" Tony began.

"Correct, not on the side that's being shot at," Damien said. "Like I taught you in Virginistan, endeavor to stay out of *the Killing Zone*."

This was a reference to one of Damien's memorable training exercises. On the second day of the course we ran into a roadblock, and our car started to take fire. While we all ran for cover, Damien, who'd been playing the role of our local fixer, took a bullet to the chest, and dropped to the ground, spurts of arterial blood erupting from his chest. Amid a very realistic soundtrack of screaming and machine gun fire, it became clear the exercise had morphed to a moral quandary about what to do if a member of the team is injured. Risk more injury by helping, or flee and protect yourself?

"We have to go, we have to go now!" Zach had yelled.

"Please! Please don't leave me!" Damien cried.

"No man left behind!" I shouted.

"Leave the fucking fixer!" Tony cut in. "What's he gonna do, recommend a good restaurant?"

"*STOP!*" Damien shouted. And just like that, the simulation was over. "You're all dead," he said. "While arguing about what to do, you all got shot up like Swiss cheese . . . I can tell you the wrong decision was made today . . . You should have found cover sooner. I can't tell you the right decision to make in the future. Every situation is different. What I can tell you is that leaving a friend or colleague behind is something you live with forever. If you choose to do so—for your own peace of mind—you'll want to be able to tell his or her family you did your best."

It was a sobering moment that put in perspective the path we'd elected to take. And *"We did our best"* became an instant recurring crew joke from that day forward.

"Also, we have a slight issue in Misrata. We've just got word a council member was assassinated today," Damien said, snapping me back to the present. "But apparently we're told by the guys from there that it's not going to result in a big blood feud in the city. We'll be keeping our eyes on the situation."

"Wait, what?" Zach said.

"Is this where I get all Geraldo and shit?" Tony said. "I better go back inside and put on the khakis."

"Did I miss anything?" Todd asked when he arrived.

"We've got some much better mitigating measures than khakis," Damien said. "Our colleagues from Misrata have come up to look after us. They're going to escort us around for the rest of the show, which is really good news. And they brought some tools to do the job."

In addition to our three production vans, we now had four shiny new Land Cruisers full of semi-automatic weapons and some badass security. I needed to introduce all these elements narratively and decided a transport beat would be perfect. So I assigned Todd to shoot POV and b-roll and Zach to film Tony. It was a chaotic scene as everyone climbed into random vehicles. I'd be riding in one of the Land Cruisers with Damien, who, in his infinite wisdom, had decided it would be best for Tony to travel with Bowler in the "gun truck." But once I got in our Land Cruiser, I realized "gun truck" was something of a misnomer. All the SUVs were full of guns.

The highway between Misrata and Tripoli ran along the coast. Turquoise waters of the Mediterranean out one window, yellow sand of the desert out the other. Once we broke free from Tripoli's gravitational pull, our convoy accelerated.

"You're aware there's a rifle behind you, right?" Damien said.

"Yeah, it's right here," I said, tapping the gun next to my leg.

"There's another one behind you as well," Damien said.

Despite the move to CNN and the more "high-risk" locations, at the end of the day this was still supposedly a food and travel show. It was pretty surreal, I thought. I'd be filming in Copenhagen at the world's best restaurant in a couple of months, but at the moment I was surrounded by a bunch of AK-47s.

"Umm . . . those can't go off if we hit a big bump or something?" I asked.

"That depends on the position of the safety," Damien said. "However, I'd consider the case of grenades and road traffic collisions to be of greater concern."

Driving was dangerous everywhere, but our security briefing material listed Libya as number one in the world when it came to traffic deaths per capita. It cited "obstruction caused by camels on the road, other vehicles, and heavy traffic," as principal causes of accidents. Seeing the lawless auto brawl on the highway, the concern didn't seem unfounded. It wasn't reassuring that we'd left late and were speeding to make up for lost time; driving at night in Libya was considered highly inadvisable.

"Is that Aerosmith?" I asked, hearing a familiar song come on the radio. "Turn it up." Damien obliged, and sure enough "Sweet Emotion" was playing on the local station.

"I'm not usually a big Aerosmith fan," I said, looking out the window at the desert flying by. "But right now it's perfect."

"It's natural, at a time like this, to desperately cling to any reminders of home," Damien said.

A flatbed truck overloaded with camels tore past us at what must have been 100 miles an hour. "Todd! Camel truck coming up in the fast lane!" I called over the walkie. "Get that shot!"

It was dark by the time we finally arrived in Misrata. The city had been the scene of some of the heaviest fighting during the revolution, and it looked the part. We drove past piles of rubble, melted and twisted metal, what had once been vehicles. Everywhere there were bombed out and abandoned buildings, honeycombed with holes from bullets and mortars. A few new brightly lit furniture stores and a functioning restaurant called Stalingrad were an odd juxtaposition to the smell of burn and oil.

"Attention," Damien called over the walkie. "When we arrive at the hotel, get out of the car and move quickly inside, then stay inside."

THE NEXT MORNING DAMIEN WATCHED us loading up the vehicles, hands nonchalantly clasped behind his back in what Tony called the "I'm just an innocent bystander" pose.

"Hamid has informed us there's a large-scale protest being planned for this afternoon," Damien said. "Unsurprisingly, the local population is rather bent out of shape about yesterday's assassination. We'll have to be clear of the War Museum and downtown area before it begins. That will give us roughly an hour to film."

Fuck. I'd been counting on Misrata being a more relaxed environment so we could catch our breath. There were two important scenes scheduled for today, and I didn't want to rush through them. I traveled to location in the truck with Hamid.

"So, what do you guys do when not helping out film crews?" I asked, making small talk.

"We hunt down former Gaddafi supporters," Hamid said. "Torture and kill the fuckers."

"Ohh . . . okay . . . cool," I said. Note to self: stay on Hamid's good side.

Misrata's War Museum was set up to honor the revolution and those lost fighting for freedom. Out front were a collection of tanks, mortars, RPGs, makeshift slingshots, a beached yacht, as well as Gaddafi's famous sculpture of a golden fist crushing an American fighter jet. Inside was one large room, photos of the martyrs plastered floor to ceiling, on every wall. They looked like everyday people of all ages, including children. Below each face was a name and their date of death. Several families with children wandered, looking at the exhibits and taking pictures. Hamid walked Tony around the room telling him stories of the fallen. He'd known at least a dozen of them personally. In addition to the martyrs were improvised weapons used to fight Gaddafi, like a periscope constructed from PVC tubing and a makeup compact as well as a jury-rigged rocket launcher.

"This one is a homemade rifle," Hamid said, pointing to a hand-gun with a two-by-four handle on one end and a pipe mounted to the other.

"Unbelievable," Tony said, genuinely impressed. "You gotta have a lot of courage to go out with that as a weapon."

"We had no other solution," Hamid said.

Among the war trophies was a collection of personal items once belonging to Gaddafi, many taken from the Bab al-Aziziya compound in Tripoli. There was Gaddafi's silver-and-gold-plated AK-47, gold-fringed china, a golden saber, and even what looked like chairs from the *Golden Girls* set.

"It seems whenever they kill a despot, turns out their things are always tacky," Tony said. "Like a pimp."

"This was Gaddafi's shaving kit," Hamid said, kicking what remained of a medium-sized Louis Vuitton suitcase. "He wore hair dye and beauty masks." Among the items was a set of gold-plated combs and brushes, various hair and grooming products, and sure enough, a Deep Cleansing Pure Clay Formula Mudd Mask.

In one corner of the museum a TV was showing unedited cell phone footage of Gaddafi, bloodied, surrounded by a wild mob of revolutionaries. The graphic video played silently on a loop.

"Gaddafi's lucky day," Hamid said with a chuckle.

"This is when he gets the good news," Tony said.

"Tick, tock. Tick, tock," Damien called over the walkie.

On our way out, Tony stopped to sign the guest book. *It's nice once in a lifetime to see the good guys win. Respect. Anthony Bourdain,*" he wrote.

"Thank you, Hamid," I said. "That was a powerful scene. I hate to rush, but we have to be out of here before the protest."

"What protest?" Hamid asked.

"I thought there was a big protest here this afternoon?" I said.

"You mean the funeral?" Hamid asked.

OUR CONVOY BOUNCED DOWN A dirt road kicking up a cloud of dust before finally stopping at a cinder-block structure. It was a beautiful spot perched on a small promontory overlooking the Mediterranean. "Most meals in Libya are eaten at home, but it's not uncommon to get together with friends for a beachside barbeque on the weekend." Or so I'd written in the treatment.

"I told you that goat was not worth two hundred dollars," Reda said. "And it's not even a goat, it's a sheep."

Reda was right, a sheep was bleating away, tied up in the back of a pickup truck. Frankly, I didn't care what kind of animal we'd procured or what it cost, as long as it wasn't an endangered species. I was impressed at Reda's willingness to stand up to a well-armed militia to ensure that we weren't taken advantage of in his country. While the crew unloaded gear from the van, I took a look around to check out the location. On the leeward side of the shack I came across Hamid and a couple of his militia buddies. He didn't look happy.

"Is everything okay?" I asked.

"This is shit," Hamid said, slapping down a newspaper on the table. On the cover I could see a group photo of the GNC, Libya's first democratically elected government in over forty years. "All of them were in London, they only came here after *we* fought the revolution!" Hamid said. "These are not real Libyans . . . "

"Umm . . . While we have a minute can we go over the plan for the barbeque?" I asked, wanting to change the subject as quickly as possible.

"Yeah, just catch this first," Hamid said, and threw a grenade at me. I recoiled from the explosive, which hit the ground with a thump. Over the ringing in my ears, I could hear laughter. Hamid and his friends were doubled over. "You should see the look on your face!" Hamid gasped. "Relax, man, it's just a lighter!"

I tried to smile, but I don't know how successful I was.

"No hard feelings, have a drink." Hamid opened a recycled plastic cola bottle and filled a cup halfway. "This is our famous Libyan boha," he said, handing me the drink. "It's like homemade vodka."

With alcohol strictly prohibited in Libya, it had been days since any of us had hit the booze, and I greedily swallowed the boha in one gulp. A warm, comforting sensation instantly radiated throughout my body. "Oh, wow, that feels good," I said.

"That's because you're an alcoholic," Damien said.

Todd and Zach started filming b-roll, the landscape glowing in the mellow late afternoon sun. A steady breeze blew off the sea, kicking up the surf along an empty beach stretching to infinity. Tony and the militia guys were drinking non-alcoholic beer when the cameras were around—and boha when they weren't—everyone was having fun. An eight-year-old valet parked cars for late arriving guests. I made sure we got that shot. All in all, the scene was turning out quite well, considering.

Everyone gathered around to pray, which meant it was time to get the obligatory slaughter shot. I hid behind Zach so I wouldn't have to watch as one of the militia members held down the struggling sheep and slit its throat.

"Halal style," Damien said matter-of-factly. "That's exactly how al-Qaeda does it."

"That's not funny," I said, my voice a bit shaky.

When we'd finished filming for the day, a joint was passed around, but I declined. I watched Tony laughing with Hamid. He was really in love with the militia. He'd even nicknamed them "the Misrata Boys."

"Okay, everyone," I said over the walkie. "We have to get back to the hotel before sundown."

"DID YOU HEAR ABOUT WHAT'S happening in Mali?" said a very worried looking Zach. "Damien told me jihadists could be moving this way, and they're saying the first to burn will be Westerners!"

I looked past Zach into the hotel lobby where Damien and Josh were watching a local news channel broadcasting footage of French troops landing in Timbuktu. Josh put his head in his hands.

"Mali is thousands of miles from here," I said, returning my attention to Zach. "Do you really think that a van of jihadists is going to make it all the way through countless checkpoints just to target us? That's not rational. Pull your shit together!"

Zach was frightened, and I should have had more sympathy. He wasn't crazy; it was scary being here, and "Why are we even here in the first place?" was a totally legitimate question to be asking. On top of that, Damien had been filling our heads with images of jihadists beheading journalists and suicide bombings for days now. If the threats were as grave as he was telling everyone, why hadn't he pulled the plug? He had the power to terminate the shoot with the snap of his fingers. But if he pulled the plug and we all went home, and it turned out there was no real threat . . . well, that would be *very* bad for Damien. Instead, if I was the one that threw in the towel—either because I was frightened or I had to bow to pressure from the crew—then no skin off Damien's nose. It was the only logical explanation. Or was it? At this point I had no perspective. Was Damien capable of playing such intense head games? Could Damien be right? Damien's job wasn't to scare us. He'd never done that before. What was different this time?

Lights, Camera, Action!
Jaffna, Sri Lanka, 2017.

Tony and I on Ipanema
Beach. Rio, Brazil, 2012.

Todd Liebler

Tony fulfilling his
cowboy fantasy.
Ghost Ranch,
New Mexico, 2013.

Panavision cameras
used on the "Heel of the Boot"
episode. Fasano, Italy, 2017.

"Parking lot time" before the scene. Jaffna, Sri Lanka, 2017.

Crew meal. Bahia, Brazil, 2014.

Tony and director Darren Aronofsky doing some souvenir shopping. Punakha, Bhutan, 2017.

Tony getting a tattoo for the episode. Chiang Mai, Thailand, 2014.

Between takes. Fasano, Italy, 2017.
Jeff Allen

(Bottom left) Me in Halong Bay near the start of my travels. Vietnam, 2006. *Rob Tate*
(Bottom right) Me in Halong Bay ten years later. Vietnam, 2016. *Do Hung Phi*

Tony getting "mimed." Paris, France, 2012.

Tony waiting by the Colosseum while filming *The Layover*. Rome, Italy, 2011.

Layover wrap party
at the Tonga Room.
San Francisco, 2011.

The "unblinking electric eye."
Seattle, 2012.

Getting a ticket for
filming without a permit.
Rome, Italy, 2011.

Nari Kye

Market scene. Seoul,
South Korea, 2014.

Goat head soup.
Tehran, Iran, 2014.

My birthday / wrap
party. Colombo,
Sri Lanka, 2017.

Jeff Allen

Ferran Adrià's El Bulli kitchen. Roses, Spain, 2011.

Molecular gastronomy peanut snack at El Bulli. Roses, Spain, 2011.

Crew meal behind El Bulli. Roses, Spain, 2011.

Tony getting photobombed after winning his first Emmy.
Los Angeles, 2013.

View from the stage while Tony accepts an Emmy. Los Angeles, 2015.

Getting ready for the Emmys.
Los Angeles, 2017. *Jeff Allen*

My dad, Chris, Lydia, and I at the Emmys.
Los Angeles, 2014.
Todd Liebler

Proudly grasping my Emmy. Los Angeles, 2013.
Joe Caterini

Tony in the therapy session filmed for the episode. Buenos Aires, Argentina, 2016.

(Left) Suitcase full of production cash (and a flask). The money changer asked Jeff if we were purchasing land. Antananarivo, Madagascar, 2014.

(Right) Dried squid and M&Ms, a popular karaoke drinking snack. Seoul, Korea, 2014.

Asia Argento with Tony at the Chateau Marmont. Los Angeles, 2017.

Tony managing his empire while waiting for our boat to arrive. Asunción, Paraguay, 2014.

Josh being Josh. Istanbul, Turkey, 2015.

Tony offering me a glass of amaro at the end of the shoot. Amalfi Coast, Italy, 2011.
Frank Vitale

Tony and Darren Aronofsky eating before an archery tournament. Phurjoen Village, Bhutan, 2017.

Crew meal. Chiang Mai, Thailand, 2014.

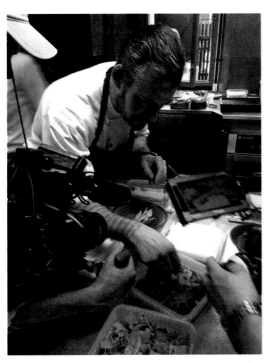

Cameras film the meticulous preparation of a dessert course in the Noma kitchen. Copenhagen, Denmark, 2013.

Gammel Dansk (Danish bitter) flavored ice cream made from dehydrated milk and soy, garnished with sorrel leaves. Noma. Copenhagen, Denmark, 2013.

Excess baggage.
Kuching, Malaysia, 2015.
Jeff Allen

Testing an experimental camera rig before filming with Tony. Seoul, South Korea, 2014.
Helen Cho

Jeff and local crew. Dochu La Pass, Bhutan, 2017.

Tony and I on the Cajun Mardi Gras shoot. Lafayette, Louisiana, 2018.
Todd Liebler

Village meal scene.
Luang Prabang, Laos, 2016.

Tripas lunch scene.
Porto, Portugal, 2017.

Scene with director
Francis Ford Coppola.
Bernalda, Italy, 2017.

Lost at sea. Naxos, Greece, 2015.
Jeff Allen

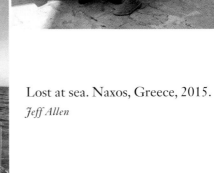

Tony and I take a break while filming the funeral scene.
This is the last picture I took of him. Bali, Indonesia, 2018.

"GUYS, REALLY... WHAT ARE WE DOING here?" Zach said, pacing back and forth. "This isn't what we do. This is *Vice* territory."

"Look, I get it, I get it, Libya is scary," Tony said. "Frankly, I'm scared too. But we're telling a story that's really, really special. And we're being well looked after by the Misrata Boys."

"Damien's talking about a lot of scary shit, but it's nothing different than what was going on before we arrived. I think he's mind-fucking us," I said. Having found myself in the truly terrifying situation of not trusting the people hired to protect us, I'd convened a private meeting in Tony's hotel room, no security guys. I was worried about our safety, but I had to keep a level head, and according to everyone but our security team, the situation was stable.

"I'm not buying it either," Todd said. "Something's up. I've heard what Damien says and then how he changes his tone depending on who's around." Oh, thank God! Another voice of reason. Somewhere on the spectrum between strong-willed and stubborn, Todd was not highly susceptible to manipulation.

"Bottom line, what uncertainty exists is more than made up for by the certainty that we are getting really good footage," Tony said. "Nobody's seen this side of Libya before. Let's finish what we started. Who's with me?"

"I am," I said.

"Me too," Todd said.

"It's only another couple days," Josh said.

"*Arrgh. Fuck it*," Zach said.

"Tom, hang out for a minute," Tony said. He waited for everyone else to leave then closed the door. "Good work holding it together," he said, clapping me on the back. "Your dedication has not gone unnoticed."

"Thank you," I said, genuinely flattered by the rare compliment. "You know, if two—"

"Need be we can get rid of Damien too," Tony said. "Now that we have our own militia. I mean, it's not like we're in a fucking war zone with bullets flying over our heads or people throwing grenades at us."

THE NEXT MORNING AT BREAKFAST, Damien informed us that the UK Foreign Office was issuing another statement, something regarding an imminent threat against the embassy in Tripoli, which happened to be where we were headed. Midway through loading the vans, Reda appeared.

"Can we talk?" Reda asked. "It's important."

"Yes, of course," I said, happy to see him. "What's up?"

"It's about the mili—" Reda was cut off by my phone ringing.

"Fuck, it's Tony," I said. "Can we talk once we get on the way?"

The trip ended up being filled with last-minute logistical details, though, so we arrived in Tripoli without having had the chance to talk.

Once there, I sent Todd to get some time-lapse images from the hotel roof. Meanwhile Zach and I went down to the corniche to film a walking beat with Tony. The late afternoon sun reflected off the Mediterranean. We set up outside an amusement park in the shadow of large buildings that had been frozen mid-construction since the civil war broke out. The call to prayer competed with "Do You Think I'm Sexy" coming from loudspeakers in the park, and seagull calls mixed with the sound of kids laughing and screaming on the rides. I was caught off guard as, unprompted, Tony began talking to the camera.

"It's the perfect moment, you know . . . smiling, happy kids, the mosque . . . Rod Stewart playing in the background . . . and a pickup truck with militia off camera. Looking at us. Smiling, but talking on their cell phones," Tony said. "Who are the good guys? Are we the good guys? It's a very complicated issue here, by the way. Who the good guys are . . . Cotton candy, anyone?"

Finally, some good luck. This was just supposed to be a walking beat, but Tony was paying out triple sevens on content. He walked over to the water's edge and continued talking.

"Look, what do I know? I've been here a week. There's a lot going on. A lot of it good, a lot of it bad . . . But, in spite of the fact this has been a really hard shoot, for me this is a happy show. Whatever you think about Libya—and whatever happens here—I very much feel like the good guys won. I'm not an optimistic guy, but I generally feel—and this experience reaffirms it—the world is mostly filled with pretty nice people, doing the best they can . . . " Tony smiled and looked off at the setting sun. "All right, back to the ranch?"

"WE NEED TO TALK," DAMIEN said as I arrived back at the hotel.

"Okay," I said, preparing myself for whatever mental torture he was cooking up. "What's going on?"

"We have a little problem on our hands," he said. I knew it. Damien was probably about to tell me that the latest intel suggested Tripoli was sitting on an active volcano. He took a sip of tea, his yellow eyes trained on me, unblinking. "Hamid has informed me Adnan, one of the production assistants, accused Reda of raping him."

"I'm sorry?" I said.

"I took the liberty of sending Adnan home," Damien said.

"Wait, wait, wait. What the fuck happened?"

"While you were out filming, I interviewed Adnan independently. His story seems credible. Hamid, along with the rest of the militia, are extremely upset. They wanted to arrest Reda immediately. I was able to convince them to wait twenty-four hours until we can all be on a flight out of the country."

I slumped down into the couch, head spinning. Was this what Reda had wanted to talk to me about? I didn't want to believe Reda had done what he was being accused of. I also didn't want to discount Adnan's accusation out of hand, but certain words kept repeating in my head. Like "militia extremely upset" and "arrest Reda." I knew what that meant. Homosexuality was a criminal offense in Libya but, in this case anyway, I was worried it would be dealt with by vigilante justice. "Oh, my fucking god." I stammered, "We-we have to warn Reda!"

"I understand you're upset, but our objective is to protect you all who have hired us to do so," Damien said.

I searched Damien's face, desperate to discover that this was just some awful and inappropriate joke. Other than the twitch in his left eyelid, he seemed as calm as ever. "I'm sorry, but this is Reda's country, and as much as our more *delicate Western sensibilities* may be offended by such practices, this is how justice is delivered in Libya."

"But they might kill him!" I said, trying to control my voice.

"They very well might, they also might not," Damien said. "Militias *are* the authority here; police, judge, and jury. It's far from our place to interfere with how they do their business. We have no choice but to let nature take its course. Ultimately, this is not our concern."

"This is insane!" I said, losing control of myself. Since this was Libya, clearly I wasn't going to make a public protest, but I sure as shit wasn't going to stand by and let an injustice like this occur. "Even if Reda is guilty, he doesn't deserve to be tortured or killed. And on top of that, if we weren't here, he never would've met the militia, and none of this would be happening. So, I do think it's our fucking concern!"

"I believe you're failing to grasp the gravity of the situation," Damien said. He was right. I was having trouble grasping what was happening. It sounded like we were talking about a *National Geographic* lion-hunts-the-zebra scenario. I'd held it together so far, but I'd reached my breaking point. The shoot was definitely over.

"We at least have to have a meeting," I insisted. "Like we've been doing, let the rest of the crew weigh in. I know they would agree with me, we have to give Reda a heads-up!"

"You need to do what's best, not what's right," Damien said. "Getting involved in any way would present an *extreme* danger to yourself, as well as the rest of the crew. Even telling them about the situation will put everyone in a state of jeopardy. You must say nothing. Go pack."

It sounded like a tea kettle was boiling next to my ears, and I was getting that funny metallic taste in my mouth. Something didn't add up. But at the same time, things in this world rarely did. And the risk of a misstep, given the circumstances, could be catastrophic. Maybe I wasn't thinking clearly, maybe Damien was right. I went to my room to call Sandy, and explained the whole situation as far as I understood it.

"I think you're absolutely right," she said. "It doesn't matter if Reda did what he's being accused of or not. The punishment is so far outsized compared to the crime. And we *are* involved. I know Damien has everyone's best interest in mind, but I think having a meeting and letting everyone decide for themselves is the right thing to do."

"I'm so glad to hear you say that," I said, starting to regain my composure. If nothing else, I'd always seen Sandy as having a sober hand on the tiller, so her reassurance meant a lot. I was the only gay crew member, and everyone knew, but it almost never came up. I'd never taken a stand, but it was time. I called a meeting, and thirty minutes later, everyone but Todd and Damien were impatiently waiting to hear what I had to say.

"How much longer are we gonna wait?" Tony asked. "Let's just get this over with. Josh can share the minutes with everyone who isn't here."

"I'm sure they'll be here soon," I said.

Not long after, there was a knock at the door. Through the peephole I could see Damien and Todd, and they seemed to be chuckling about something, which I took as a good sign. On his way in, Todd greeted me with a jovial, "Good evening, Tommy."

Damien paused and said, "Mind if we have a brief word in the john?" He closed the bathroom door after me and stated more than asked, "I presume you've taken what I've said to heart and we will not be discussing anything related to Reda."

I took a deep breath. "I'm sorry, but I have to. I talked to San—"

Before I even knew what was happening, Damien had cleared the four feet between us and forcibly shoved me down onto the toilet seat. As I looked up at his towering frame, the veins on his forehead and neck bulged red, and his eyes cut into me. Gone was the wry and jovial, cool-under-pressure Damien I'd known for years. In his place was a Damien that reminded me he hadn't been just any old soldier, but one of those specially trained killy soldiers.

"You little fucking faggot!" Damien was somehow screaming and whispering at the same time. "You have no fucking idea what you're doing. We're talking about the safety of your entire crew! You have no right to let your actions put them in danger!" Everything about him was getting redder and redder as he hissed, "If you say *anything*,

ANYTHING about Reda, I promise you, I will make sure you regret it . . . Am I making myself perfectly clear?" I think Damien's nose was starting to bleed. I'd never been more terrified in my life. I was unable to speak or even nod. "Good," he said.

Straightening his posture, Damien opened the door and grabbed a tissue on his way out of the bathroom. I emerged a moment later trying to conceal my shaking hands. It felt like I was dreaming. The hotel room and everyone in it looked so normal, and yet what was going on was *so* not normal. This was one of those pivotal moments that would probably define my character; whatever I was about to say would have long-lasting implications, perhaps as Damien had said, for the rest of my life. "I wanted to let you all know . . . " I said, clearing my throat, "we're going home. We have enough material to complete the episode."

"Halle-fucking-lujah," Zach said.

"At least we're done with these damn meetings," Tony said, getting up to leave.

"Is there anything else?" Damien asked, daring me to defy him. I said nothing. "Right then . . . Wheels up out front tomorrow morning at 0900 hours. Our friends from Misrata will be escorting us through the check-in process to make sure we don't encounter any issues. If all goes according to plan, we shall be in Istanbul in time for cocktails."

I couldn't believe I'd chickened out. Over the years we'd filmed with people who were overtly homophobic. Not knowing I was gay, they'd make jokes and say "fag" every fourth word. I'd wanted to say something, but I never did. This time was so much worse.

"I have an idea," Sandy said after I'd updated her on the situation. "I'll wait until you are on the airplane, then I'll call Reda and explain what's happening. He should still be able to get a head start."

"Tom, Tom, are you in there?" A persistent knocking came from the other side of the door.

"Oh my god, he's outside," I said, my voice dropping to a whisper.

"Tom! It's Reda," he said. "I need to talk to you. Are you in there?"

"I have to go," I said to Sandy and let the receiver slide into its cradle.

Knock, knock, knock, knock, knock. "Tom, what's going on?!?! You're not answering my phone calls or SMS messages, I think you are in there!"

I wiped the tears out of my eyes and barely felt myself walking over to the door and opening it.

"I have something important to tell you," Reda said. "I found out what you were paying Hamid. In Libya, it's the law that if a journalist asks for protection, the militias have to provide it. Not for a cost. Hamid was stealing from you. I confronted him and he—"

"Reda, I need you to listen to me very carefully," I said, my racing heart in stark contrast to the slow and careful enunciation of every syllable. "I can't explain why, but I need you to go home, get some things, and leave Tripoli for a little while, and don't speak to anyone or tell them where you're going. I know this sounds crazy, but please, you have to do what I say."

I didn't know if Reda was here trying to save me $30,000 or prove he was innocent or if he even knew he'd been accused. There wasn't any time to lose, and none of it mattered. I think it was more the bughouse expression on my face than what I said that caused Reda to take several steps backward, his eyes widening.

"Okay," he said in a quiet voice. "These are for you and Josh." He bent over slightly, dropping a plastic bag to the floor, then he turned around and left. I waited for the sound of the elevator doors to close before picking up the bag and locking my door. Inside the bag were a few trinket souvenirs, as well as a decorative metal dish engraved with a traditional scene and delicate cursive that read, "Tom Loves Libya."

A large storm was kicking up off the Mediterranean. Repeated gusts of wind slammed into the sliding glass doors of my balcony, the percussive rattle making a sound reminiscent of mortars or artillery shells. I couldn't wait to get the fuck home.

Chapter Eight

SHINY OBJECTS

THREE MONTHS AFTER TONY'S DEATH, MY SUITCASE REMAINED UN-
touched. I dreamed about Tony a lot, and often had the eerie sensation of catching a glimpse of him out of the corner of my eye. Simple
tasks like paying bills and laundry were getting more difficult. Even
when I ran out of clean underwear, I didn't dare open that suitcase.
Truth be told, I'd intended to never unpack. I'd fallen victim to a
maudlin superstition that if I even touched the zipper, I might have
to admit to myself he was really gone. But I hadn't managed to get
it together to buy a new one, and I had a ticket on a flight to Los
Angeles leaving in the morning. I didn't have much need for a new
suitcase now anyway.

Somewhere over the Midwest, the cabin started shuddering.
Nervous flyer that I am, my mind raced with images of wind shear
snapping off the wing or the horizon inverting as the plane entered
a death spiral, the result of a jammed rudder. The shaking increased
while engines throttled up and down. My heart rate caught up with
my imagination as the "fasten seat belt" sign illuminated, and the
pilot's voice came over the intercom.

157

"We're encountering a bit of rough air, it won't last long. In the mean-time we ask you to please stay seated with your seat belts fastened."

Hearing from the flight deck was a good sign, I reminded myself. In an emergency, they're far too busy to bother talking to the cattle. Tony enjoyed severe turbulence; he said it broke up the monotony of a flight. If he looked over and saw the panic on my face, he might smile and say something like, "Relax, Tom. You're not going to die in anything as glamorous as a plane crash. It'll be a slip in the bath-tub that gets you." I always felt a hell of a lot better, at least until I had to take a shower. But his words didn't sound nearly as comfort-ing in my own voice. As the wings distorted over air pockets, I tried to imagine Tony in an empty seat across the aisle.

For the eighth year in a row, I'd be spending a couple of days in mid-September at the legendary Chateau Marmont. I checked in to 55, my regular room. I smoked a cigarette on the terrace overlook-ing Sunset Boulevard and watched the smog of downtown LA light up with the day's end. Everything appeared the same, but of course it wasn't. I didn't know who, if anyone, was next door in 54, but it wasn't Tony. Even though it felt like he was here in a tingly phantom limb sort of way, the 2018 Emmys would be my first without him. I'd debated whether or not to stay at the Chateau, or if I should even come out for the awards ceremony. There were so many good memories turned painful wrapped up in the ritual, but ultimately I'd given in to the force of habit.

"WHAT ARE YOU GONNA SPEND your money on anyway? You can't take it with you, Tom," Tony said, sipping a Negroni on the hotel's colon-naded garden terrace. His drink glittered ruby red in the late afternoon California sunshine. "You'd look good in a Tom Ford tux. And actually you *can* take a tux with you." He pantomimed a crossed-arm coffin pose. "Everyone will say, 'He looks so handsome in there, slim, rosy-cheeked, and smart. I wish I'd known him when he was alive.'"

"I'm not spending ten thousand dollars on a tuxedo," I said. For someone who'd lived the majority of his years paycheck to paycheck, Tony seemed to have no concept of money.

"So, anyone else staying on campus, or is the rest of the herd at the ghetto hotel?" Tony asked. "Campus," of course, referred to the Chateau. It was Tony's favorite hotel on earth and for good reason.

"You can get *anything* you want," Tony said, eyes wide with Christmas morning juvenescence. "Call down to the front desk at three a.m. you can order cocaine, some Hell's Angels, and a donkey. They'll even help you dispose of a dead rodeo clown should the need arise. As long as you're discreet and don't disturb the other guests."

Even though I couldn't afford it, staying here with Tony was worth every penny of the frightening bill. Over the years and across the continents, we'd resided in a wealth of fine hotels, but you couldn't stay anywhere else like the Chateau. For nearly a century it had been a haven for Hollywood's elite, as famous for its eccentric elegance as for the staff's discretion when it came to scandalous behavior. The sordid history was part of the aura, and French gothic architecture definitely added to the charm. But there was more to it than that . . . something paradoxically exquisite.

The hotel was gloriously out of step with time and possessed a haunting boutique-*Shining*-meets-Hollywood-royalty ambience. Opening in 1929 as an apartment building, it immediately went belly-up with the stock market crash. Every room was a suite and retained vintage kitchen equipment, as well as at least ten ashtrays. Despite September being peak season, it always felt like you had the place to yourself. The public spaces were eternally dim, making it easy to trip over antique deep-pile Persian rugs, especially after a few Negronis. Medieval revival cast-iron wall sconces and titanic chandeliers did little to illuminate Spanish tiles and the delicately stenciled coffered ceiling of the sunken lounge. Mismatched and slightly worn oversize sofas and tasseled Moroccan lampshades surrounded a grand piano that had been played by everyone from Jimi Hendrix to Judy Garland. After a few more Negronis you almost expected to bump into James Dean on the staircase or F. Scott Fitzgerald at the kidney-shaped pool.

The scent of gardenias and a supernatural hint of vanilla mixed with cigarette smoke hung in the air. There was no such thing as a non-smoking room, or hallway, or even elevator. Not all the light

switches worked, and a mathematically perfect number of my bathroom tiles were mismatched. The hotel was *just* the right touch
shambolic and gave the impression both damage and repair were
the consequence of cosmic design rather than bacchanalian excess.
It was an eccentric attention to detail that continued throughout
the property.

"Cinematography is a shoe-in," Tony said. "But we'll never win
series."

It was 2013, the Burma and Libya episodes had received Emmy
nominations across five categories, and the first season of *Parts
Unknown* had surprised everyone including the network by exceed-
ing ratings expectations. The show was a hit. Even reviews had been
universally positive, although one pithy comment had questioned
the wisdom of shooting despotic regimes like a Pfizer commercial.
Zach did not find that funny. But he, Todd, and Mo were nominated
for the episode, so they were over the moon.

"It has a Faraday cage," Tony proudly explained as he handed
me a shiny new Rolex. "The Milgauss was originally designed for
scientists who worked in nuclear power plants, and then got adopted
by the TV industry back when they were surrounded by all that
electromagnetic broadcasting shit."

As a thank-you, Tony had bought himself, Zach, Todd, Mo, and
me matching watches with "Parts Unknown O.G." engraved on the
back. Tony was a bit of a watch nut. Perhaps his most prized posses-
sion was a vintage 1960s Rolex he'd inherited from his father, whom
he missed dearly. He often wore his dad's watch on shoots; maybe
it was Tony's way of bringing him along on the trip. To me, anyway,
Tony's gift held special significance well beyond the watch itself. I'd
never been given something this expensive before. I half-heartedly
tried to refuse it, but Tony just laughed.

My new watch was so beautiful and had a cool lightning-shaped
seconds hand, but something didn't feel right. I'd always had trouble believing the "A-Team" thing, and even though this was pretty
irrefutable proof, I still had trouble believing it. Add in the Emmy
nomination, and I was sick to my stomach. How had the most difficult, traumatizing shoot we'd ever done led to all of this?

Parts Unknown had begun with a bang. I'd filmed Burma, Libya, and Congo in rapid succession over the span of three months. Our itinerary had given me real pause—pretty much for the first time— about blindly following Tony on the increasing number of trips to "high-risk environments." It was becoming ever clearer that in the world of high-stakes travel TV, it was easy enough to stumble into ethical quagmires and danger without even trying. Did I really want to be in the business of actively courting the kind of dangers—to myself and others—that we'd encountered with those shoots?

Unlike the old days, when the worst outcome might be fallout from some off-color Dracula jokes, it was clear we had the power to ruin lives. Almost nine months later, Reda still hadn't been able to go home because of the show, and I felt like we didn't deserve the Emmy nomination.

When I had raised the issue with Tony and expressed my frustration over not telling the full story in Libya, it was clear he wasn't experiencing the same ambivalence.

"This show was not about us feeling scared," he said. "That sort of shit might have worked for Travel Channel, but this is CNN, and plenty of their journalists are in much more perilous situations all the time. What were our options? Realistically? It was a catch-twenty-two. If we told the truth, that's just throwing more fuel on the fire. We don't go for low-hanging fruit. The bigger picture is the message." I could see his point: we had made some compromises and saved our own skins and had gotten a great show as a result.

"Barbeque may not be the answer to world peace, but it's a start," Tony said in the episode. The show had been powerful and uplifting, even if it was far from reflecting the reality of our experience. Tony was also right about plenty of CNN journalists often being in much more perilous situations. The difference was, they were foreign correspondents, and we were supposed to be making some version of a food show. Technically I'd succeeded, at least insofar as I'd held it together and we got home with a show that brought us to the Emmys tonight. But at what cost? Which was the greater disservice, to gloss over those edges, or to perpetuate the image viewers already had?

Later that night when they called our names, Tony bounded toward the podium. I followed on autopilot like a deer in the headlights. We'd won our first Emmy. I don't remember much more than the bright lights when we were standing up on stage or what Tony said. It was all a blur. Backstage, they let us smoke cigarettes before posing for group photos. Afterward Tony talked to a reporter.

"It feels pretty good," he said with a hint of mania. "Uhh, I mean, I screwed up my life in every possible way a human being can screw up their life, I made every awful decision that a person could make. I was standing there dunking french fries at age forty-four with no future . . . and it seems to have worked out . . . Failing upwards, I'm a big believer in that."

I couldn't have imagined what it felt like to hold that impossibly heavy, cold, glorious electroplated gold statuette in my hand. The moral dilemma with which I'd been wrestling seemed to have evaporated. They say everyone has a price, and I guess this was mine. I'd sold my soul for two incredibly shiny pieces of metal.

Chapter Nine

FAME

TONY ALWAYS SAID HE DIDN'T WANT A FUNERAL, AND IN ACCORDANCE
with his wishes no such event was held. But funerals aren't for the
dead, they're for those left behind. Tony's brother, Chris, arranged a
memorial service at a vast Cantonese dim sum parlor located on an
upper floor of a Chinatown office building.

The banquet room housed a bar, a small stage, and about twenty
tables decorated in red and gold. Along one wall stood a buffet of
steamed pork buns, spring rolls, dumplings, gluey lo mein as well as
a host of other offerings including Popeye's chicken, one of Tony's
guilty pleasures. Many of the letters that had been left at Les Halles
were displayed around the room. Affixed to the podium was a four-
foot-tall poster-board enlargement of Tony wearing a somewhat
goofy half smile. Music from a raucous wedding party one floor
above spilled down the elevator shaft and mixed with the small talk.

Guests included a good number of people who had appeared on
the shows throughout the years and was a who's-who of Tony's culinary, cinema, and travel Criterion Collection. Tony watched over the
gathering from his poster, looking perhaps bemused to see everyone
together. The whole evening was bathed in the fluorescent glow of

163

unreality, and I had to repeatedly shake my head as if resetting a magic eight ball each time the thoughts piled up and threatened to overwhelm. Seeing all of these people brought so many memories and conversations I'd had with Tony to the surface.

On a trip to the Netherlands, I had been prodding Tony for some content and, per usual, he was resistant.

"Why do I have to say anything?" he said, taking a sip of coffee. "You didn't tell me this was a talking scene."

"Aww, c'mon, what could be better? We're here in Amsterdam on a beautiful sunny morning sitting by a canal," I said. "How does it feel being here?"

"Okay, you really want to know how I'm feeling?" Tony said, straightening in his chair. "I'm a fifty-six-year-old smoker. Realistically, how many years do I have left? I travel all the time and the only thing I want right now is to be home with my daughter but instead I'm stuck here being prodded to deliver some inane content by people who get paid to be my friends."

"Go wide," I called over the walkie.

Tony always knew what to say to get whatever it was he wanted. With one comment he'd succeeded in getting out of having to talk to the camera and making me feel both complicit and cheap in the process.

Chris delivered a powerful eulogy at the memorial that managed to be alternatingly heartbreaking and funny. Tony brought so much joy as well as so much pain. Though I don't think he did it on purpose, Tony's demons ensured he was a difficult and, at times, fearsome person to be around. Anthony Bourdain was a great man, even though he could, at times, be a less successful human being.

About fifteen people spoke, and each time someone finished, the audience applauded. Even Tony's memorial service was some form of entertainment. One of the last people to take the microphone was the indefatigable chef José Andrés, with whom I'd traveled on a few shows.

"I asked Tony a lot of questions all the time," José said. "One day he responded, 'Who do you think I am, the Wizard of Oz?' But Tony gave all of us the heart to bring people from far away to feel closer together, realize that people who are different aren't our enemies, and gave us the courage to do the things we wanted to do. And though Tony didn't answer my question, he gave me the power to come up with my own answer. I guess at the end of the day Tony really was my Wizard of Oz."

Looking around at Tony's famous friends, it occurred to me they probably hadn't spent much time with him unless there was a camera involved. The same went for nearly everyone else in the room. I was startled to realize there were fewer than a handful of people here who weren't associated either with fame or television. After another moment or two, it hit me kind of hard when I recognized that less than charitable incrimination included myself.

Rather than bringing any kind of closure, the memorial instead served to make the impossibility of Tony's death that much more impossible. How was it that the most brilliant and amazing person I'd ever known, someone whose words could touch millions of fans, had done so poorly when it came to his personal life? It just wasn't right. Tony was capable of better. No matter how hard I tried, I wasn't able to shake away the image of paid mourners.

FROM RURAL MINNESOTA TO URBAN Manchuria, Tony got recognized and approached everywhere. Through the years we got to meet so many fans while filming, at dinner off camera, during cigarette breaks, or Tony's favorite: mid-dash for the airport bathroom between flights.

"I am so sorry," the maître d' apologized, chagrined that Tony's meal and my cameras had been interrupted for the fourth time. "I don't know what's going on. Michael Jordan was here last night, and nobody bothered his table!"

Something clicked when she said that. I'd seen it endless times all over the world. Tony could strike up a conversation with someone he'd never met, and twenty minutes later they'd be talking like old friends. He possessed a charisma that made him distinctly accessible, familiar even. His magic radiated out through the television to people he never met. Complete strangers greeted Tony with a sense of intimacy, like they'd either already shared a beer together or, if they offered one now, Tony would just sit down and the two of them would casually pick up the conversation where they left off. It was one of Tony's super powers, and befitting a man of his complexity and contradictions, it was both a blessing and a curse.

Tony's ability to connect with anyone from all over the world was strangely at odds with the shy and often insecure man I knew. Tony openly admitted he couldn't complain, nobody was going to sympathize with the burden of being popular. He saw it this way: if you're going to enjoy the perks of being famous, you have to be obliging to the people who make it possible. Tony bent over backward to be gracious to anyone who wanted a book signed or to pose with him for a picture, unable to stand the look of disappointment on someone's face if he refused. It was an existential trap for a self-conscious man who lived much of his life on TV.

Often, when one person asked for a picture, all of a sudden, a line would form. Tony called it the "Kissing Booth," and it could ruin not only Tony's mood but an entire day's worth of filming. So that presented quite an incentive to gently protect Tony from his public. But if I went overboard, seemed "uncool," or was ever harsher than necessary when rebuffing a selfie hound, Tony would turn incandescent. One memorable instance, I went too far.

We were filming a walking beat with Tony at the end of a long day shooting in Hong Kong. Everyone was jet-lagged, dehydrated, and running on fumes when I spotted the look: a not so subtle bulging of the eyes mixed with disbelief, mixed with adrenaline.

"OMG, is that Anthony Bourdain?" I heard the man say.

I was praying he at least waited until the cameras went down, but of course he beelined it right to Tony, ruining the shot.

"Wow! I'm your number one fan! What are you doing in Hong Kong? Can I get a picture with you?"

Tony obliged the photograph, but instead of moving on, his number one fan kept talking despite the fact that we were obviously in the middle of filming. I could tell by the look on Tony's face he was losing patience and might decide to return to the hotel at any moment.

"Excuse me," I said in a practiced tone, intended to be polite yet firm. "We're filming right now—"

"Umm, do *you* mind?" the man said, glaring at me, clearly upset I'd interrupted his conversation with Anthony Bourdain. That's when the jet lag and the stress and lack of food caught up with me.

"Do I mind? Do *I* mind? *YES*, I fucking mind!" I said, my voice getting louder. "This is my *GOD DAMN FUCKING TV* show and *RIGHT NOW* you're ruining it!"

"Woah. Chill out, dude," he said, and walked away.

"Good work, Tom. That's how it starts," Tony said, shaking his head. "Piss off one fan, the word spreads, and next thing you know, I'm public enemy number one, jerking off motorists on the West Side Highway."

AS A PART OF OUR 2016 Buenos Aires episode, I pitched a therapy scene, and surprisingly, Tony agreed. Even more surprisingly, he showed up prepared with notes. Reclining on a daybed across from a local therapist who'd agreed to the shoot, Tony opened up.

"I suspect that by being on television and by writing books that I am already borderline personality," he said. "It's crushingly lonely. I travel over two hundred days a year . . . I feel like, uh, Quasimodo, you know? If Quasimodo stayed in nice hotel suites with high-thread-count sheets, that would be me."

I was surprised by Tony's on-camera honesty, though he did often talk about the subject. Tony's awkward relationship with the camera was in some way related to his morbid fear of clowns. Perhaps a phobia of *being* a clown. He compared TV to a nightmarish carnival in which he was the side-show freak.

"It's unnatural," Tony said to the therapist. "The camera hanging there waiting for you to do something entertaining. Shove the chicken leg in your mouth, say something funny, fall down and stand up . . . They used to hire like desperately poor people who were in terrible circumstances who they would dress up as the 'wild man of Borneo' and they would bite the heads off chickens, eat disgusting stuff for the entertainment of the carnival goers and—and the patrons. I feel like that sometimes."

Though he came off as extremely adventurous, in reality Tony was—increasingly, in later years—even becoming agoraphobic. Though he knew it was never going to happen, he said, "In a perfect world this show wouldn't have me in it. You would see what I see and I would write everything. . . . I like making television; I just don't want to be on television."

Oddly, in addition to clowns, nurse shoes, and alpine vistas, Tony had developed a phobia of ordering room service, and would often go hungry rather than place an order. When I'd connected the dots, I offered to call the hotel from wherever I was and have them send up an order of spaghetti bolognese, which he gladly accepted. Presumably either embarrassed or fearful of bothering me, Tony never actively requested I order him food, but he was always extremely grateful when I did.

Adding to the complication of someone like Tony wrestling with self doubt, he had a talent for attracting people from the most extreme fringes of the fan world. In Paraguay a group of crazed individuals camped out for days in our hotel lobby waiting for Tony like he was John Lennon or a new iPhone release. We once worked with an American expat named Jasper who was normal enough until he finally got to meet Tony. He whipped out a dog-eared copy of *Kitchen Confidential* from his trench coat like Hinckley pulling a gun on Reagan and gushed, "I'm so, so, so sorry for panting like a schoolgirl, but when I was recovering from surgery your book was what kept me going. You're so so brilliant, and now getting to meet you, this is like *seriously* the highlight of my life! I feel like Inigo Montoya from the end of the *Princess Bride*, I mean, what am I going to do next after reaching the mountaintop?!"

Tony handled the awkward and slightly creepy compliment gracefully, saying, "Yes, we get a lot of mail from hospitals and prisons, apparently I'm very popular with that demographic."

My personal favorite was Karen of catsworking.wordpress.com. She devoted herself—fully—to blogging about politics, cats, and Tony. Karen's investigative skills would put the FBI to shame. Her in-depth and insightful blog posts about Tony were often chillingly accurate. Tony spoke of her often, and spent a fair amount of time devising ways to ensure he remained on Karen's good side.

Usually it was the road crew who interacted with Tony's fans, but Pam, our office production coordinator, who never worked in the field and never met Tony, still managed to get a taste for herself. Pam was a devotedly punctual redhead who wore too much makeup, but her most defining characteristic was a chronic sour disposition. Then one day everything changed. Out of nowhere Pam became bright-eyed, bushy-tailed, and delightfully helpful. It was quite the mystery, but we didn't have to wait long to find out what was going on.

Pam's new friend came by the office to visit her the next afternoon. He was a handsome chef several years her senior, and had brought an enormous tray of delicious cupcakes he'd baked for the office. Day after day Pam radiated happiness, and we were graced by the occasional visit from the chef, now her boyfriend, always with some kind of pastry in hand. Soon Pam was positively glowing, relaying how Chef Husband Material was taking her on a cruise over the holiday.

"It's getting serious," she said, while opening boxes of resort casual clothing and accessories ordered for the trip.

Three days before the cruise, Pam showed up to work late, wiping tears from her mascara-streaked face.

"Shithead dumped me," Pam cried.

Eventually it emerged that the shithead chef had only been dating Pam in the hope of running into his idol, Anthony Bourdain. But after two weeks and no sighting at the office, creepy stalker chef had realized Pam wasn't the way to Tony's heart.

The *ultimate* award for *super, superfan* goes to a meth addict who binge-mailed Tony letters when not in prison. Let's call her Tammy. Sometimes she loved Tony and wrote him poetry, other times she was irate and threatened his life. Often these letters were scrawled in lipstick or crayon on the blank side of a Denny's placemat or a grease-stained paper bag from Arby's. Tammy seemed to believe she was Tony's illegitimate daughter and on multiple occasions threatened to go public unless he gave her the "Bourdain Jewels," to which she was the rightful heir. Tony actually appreciated Tammy's letters, especially the menacing ones. If she made a few more threats, the NYPD would approve his concealed carry permit.

AS TONY'S NOTORIETY INCREASED OVER the years, famous people started appearing on the program. In general this was, for me, a giant pain in the ass. I'd like to be able to say it was because the true stars of the show were the local everyday people who made it what it was. And celebrities have rigid schedules, demanding special attention. And celebrity doesn't impress me. And though all those things are sort of true, the bigger reason was that I was already socially anxious around everyone we filmed, all strangers, really, let alone famous people. Similarly, Tony often seemed a bit off his game, habitually mystified as to why celebrity guest stars had agreed to participate. It's not like they got paid. Suffering from what he called "fan-boy-itus," I'd notice Tony saying some "non-Tony" things, his voice a little high-pitched and squeaky.

One of the first household names was Christopher Walken, who could only be reached by fax. Billy Joel canceled at the last minute, and because Iggy Pop didn't think Tony was "too much of a dick," he agreed to come on the show. In Haiti we filmed with Sean Penn. He was the real deal, genuinely giving his all to help victims of the 2010 earthquake, no helicoptering in for a photo opp.

When we were delayed before filming a scene for our Southern Italy episode with *Apocalypse Now* and *Godfather* director Francis Ford Coppola—a legend among men and one of Tony's heroes—the only thing that calmed Tony's nerves was my telling him the delay was the result of Francis being nervous about appearing on camera as well. Which happened to be true.

With an inside understanding of how film and TV was made, directors were, for me, the most intimidating type of celebrity guest. I was terrified they'd discover just how disorganized we were, or even worse, judge us as inept. But Darren Aronofsky came along for the entire Madagascar shoot, and he turned out to be an awesome guy. At the end of a long day spent filming on a train, I sat with Darren on the nose of the engine as it twisted through mountainous countryside toward the coast. After five days together, I finally worked up the nerve to ask him why he wanted to be on the show.

"I wanted an adventure, and Tony's amazing," Darren said, taking a swig of his beer. "I didn't really know him, but my girlfriend was a big fan. She showed me the Iran episode, and I thought it was one of the smartest pieces of TV I'd ever seen. Tony has this way of speaking to everyone, both sides of the aisle. That's really rare."

Wait, had a director I'd looked up to since school just said something I did was one of the smartest pieces of TV he'd ever seen?! Though one hell of a compliment, it had made me even more nervous about the Madagascar episode living up to expectations. I needn't have worried. Darren enjoyed himself so much, he came along with us for a second shoot in Bhutan.

I was profoundly grateful and thankful for all of these experiences, at least in retrospect. But the unfortunate reality was that I was so stressed in the moment that I rarely ever enjoyed the trips enough to be thankful for them while they were happening. A big part of it was that at every moment, I felt like a fraud. Even sixteen years, 100 episodes, and five Emmys later, that feeling never went away. As the outside praise and recognition grew, the self-deprecatory voice inside my head only got louder.

I think to some degree Tony suffered from the same sense of imposter syndrome that I found so paralyzing. Whenever a personal hero, let alone someone as powerful and respected as President Obama, requested to appear on the show, it confused Tony. His increasing social anxiety and agoraphobia was, I think, connected to this pervasive fear of being exposed as a fraud.

Tony was more at ease when there wasn't a camera in his face, and that's probably why most of my favorite memories happened between scenes. One of the more unforgettable experiences of my life wasn't that we got to film with Bill Murray for the Hudson Valley episode, it was what happened after the cameras cut. Bill was late for an appointment in New York City, and Tony—thinking quickly—offered him a ride while I grabbed the keys to the Tahoe. By the time I stopped at the second yellow light in a row, Bill was visibly fidgeting.

"All right, that's it," he said, jumping out of the back seat and opening my door. "Get out, I'm driving."

More than a little surprised, I glanced at Tony, who shot back a "just go with it" look. As soon as the light turned green, Bill floored it, swerving onto the parkway.

"This is a rental, right?" he asked. "Let me show you how to drive one of these things." Already at highway speed, Bill down-shifted into second gear and jammed the accelerator. Engine redlining and making a strange high-pitched whining roar, the SUV lurched forward like some massive four-wheel-drive sports car. "In order to get optimal performance, you need to keep the RPMs up there."

Perfectly at ease manual shifting on the Henry Hudson at what must have been near eighty-five miles an hour, Bill nonchalantly alternated between telling Tony about Charleston—"You'd love it there, the people are really down to earth, good food too"—and giving me driving advice—"Don't signal, New York drivers never let you in"—cutting off a taxi to demonstrate. When Bill jerked the wheel, the SUV didn't just move from one lane to another, it vaulted. Tony looked like a schoolboy on Christmas, and I was terrified, convinced we were going to die. Really, though, when you think about it, there are worse ways to go.

"No E-ZPass . . . ?" Bill said as we approached the toll booth at Spuyten Duyvil. "Amateur move."

He came to an abrupt stop behind a white van that appeared to be asking for directions. Bill sighed audibly, and after about fifteen seconds of waiting he leaned on the horn. Finally, the van drove off, and we pulled up to the tollbooth attendant, who was clearly about to yell at the jerk who'd been blowing his horn. That is until she saw it was Bill Murray, at which point she froze with her mouth open. Bill dropped the money in her hand, politely saying, "Thank you," before peeling out.

After continuing down the West Side Highway at breakneck speed, the SUV veered off at 96th Street going so fast I don't know how we didn't flip over. "A couple years back I invested in a minor league baseball team, the Charleston Riverdogs. They're pretty good," Bill said, running a red light at Riverside.

"Aren't you worried you'll get a ticket?" I asked.

"Tom. Let me tell you something about police in New York. They really appreciate people who keep traffic moving," Bill said.

I'm pretty sure this is only true if you're Bill Murray, who I'm guessing doesn't get tickets. Accelerating onto 86th, we cut across the park before screeching to a halt behind a big line of slow-moving cars. After about three seconds of patiently waiting, Bill sounded the horn. That is until he was distracted by an older woman Rollerblading past us, a bundle of plastic bags slung over a tattered pink winter coat.

"Look at that woman, she's amazing," Bill said, completely fixated.

The traffic started moving, and we caught up to the woman in pink, at which point Bill slowed down to Rollerblade speed and lowered his window.

"What's in all those bags?" he asked.

"My food," she said with a thick accent.

"Is it good?" Bill asked. "Can I try some?"

"No, it's my food!" The woman said before the recognition flashed across her face. "Wait . . . You're a movie star! You're a movie star!"

"Who? Me? Nooo," Bill said in mock surprise.

Punching the accelerator, we launched across Fifth Avenue, just making the light. He yanked the wheel, pulling off a ninety-degree turn onto Park Avenue at what felt like forty miles an hour, and screeched to a halt.

"Thanks for the ride!" Bill said, stepping out of the car.

We sat there, not moving, in stunned silence, for a minute or two listening to the engine chug and wheeze. Tony finally turned around to face me and broke the silence saying, "Okay, we can die now."

Chapter Ten

JAMAICA ME CRAZY

OUT THE WINDOW THERE WAS NOTHING BUT GRAY. THE STEELY WINTER sky reflected in the sober expanse of the Hudson River. But inside was a kite from Bali, an antique map of the Sarawak, a commedia dell'arte mask from Rome, a Russian fur hat, an alligator-skin flask, a delicate Vietnamese paper lantern, and a totally bizarre Holstein cow briefcase from Medellín, to name a very few. After years of traveling, I'd curated quite a collection of memorabilia, each item a physical manifestation of a memory, and my house had become a museum of these souvenirs from an alternate universe.

A decade before, when I had traded my apartment in Chinatown for a rambling old clapboard house upriver, I had something to get away from. I loved the tall ceilings, warrens, unexplained noises, and steeply pitched gables draped beneath a cobweb of gingerbread. In the right light, the house looked mysterious, and proud. Other times its weathered façade looked like what it was, run-down.

On a half broken mantel sat a carved wood dog with a broken foot named Mr. Papers. He stared at me with an "I told you so" expression, a reminder that June 2014 had been one of the most bizarre months of my life. It began with my thirty-fourth birthday in Iran and ended with Tony's fifty-eighth in Jamaica. A *lot* happened in the time in between.

AFTER A WEEK IN IRAN, I was feeling emotional and a little confused. While we were filming festivities honoring Ayatollah Khomeini—founder of the Islamic Republic of Iran—a group of women clad in full-length black chadors smiled and waved. They'd been sitting in the shade until prompted, when they stood up for the cameras and began chanting, "Down with America! Down with Israel! Nuclear energy is our inalienable right!" In between, one of them said, "Do you speak English?" Another called, "I love you!" Iran was just that sort of place. The Persians themselves—at least the ones we met—had been pretty fucking cool, shockingly friendly, and welcoming to us as Americans, and also open about their likes and dislikes and even feelings regarding their government. We'd all been surprised about what a good time we were having on this trip.

Iran was also a paranoid and closed-off country that had proven a *somewhat* challenging location to make a TV show. It might best be described as a constant balancing act, walking a treacherous political tightrope, never more than one misstep away from catastrophe. Highlights included repeated threats by the government of confiscating our footage, losing a valuable production day while half the crew was held hostage by the Bisaj (Iran's ultra-right religious youth), not to mention that getting to Iran in the first place had required several years of trying, a mountain of paperwork, as well as an act of Congress to approve the trip. These were all actually indications it was going to be a good show. After many years spent traveling with Tony, inconveniences of this sort amounted to "just another day at the office." In fact, to refer to the Iran shoot as "pretty good" is something of a grotesque understatement.

Tony, however, was furious. The production company, in a misguided attempt to turn a profit, had released a fox into the henhouse and hired a new line producer who'd been cutting back everywhere she could, including the quality of accommodation. Tony essentially lived in hotels, and after a long string of sheets of questionable thread count and infinite varieties of bad plumbing, Tony had finally reached his breaking point. A self-proclaimed "hotel whore," he described our Tehran home-away-from-home as "only slightly less soul-destroying than the Soviet equivalent of a midrange Hilton." And it wasn't even much worse than the last several.

Tony knew the accountant was the problem, but he couldn't understand why we didn't just push back harder. Problem was, Greta was really good at her job. She was a vaguely European line producer who spoke with an accent that landed somewhere between "German war criminal" and "Stalinist henchman." After a glorious decade of laissez-faire accounting, Greta began making outrageous demands, like we needed to file production insurance and it was now required to turn in receipts for petty cash. She had a penchant for fractions, and could sense the smallest discrepancy in currency conversion on an expense report before it was even submitted. I could go on, but suffice to say, above all, she was a formidable adversary.

Fortunately, Greta blundered the first battle of the Budget Wars. Speaking French, she went along on the shoot to Lyon to "keep an eye on the expenses" and do the accounting on the ground. On the first day of shooting—after a crew meal with Tony present— Greta got the bill, did a quick calculation, and asked everyone to contribute a percentage. Tony's face went white.

"This is bullshit. You guys are winning all these awards. You deserve more, not less," Tony said. He paid the bill, and Greta was banned from *ever* going on the road again.

But that barely slowed her down. Overnight Greta completely rewrote the rulebook. Previously we'd enjoyed a gloriously free-wheeling approach to logistics and accounting that was ideally suited to the run-and-gun, chaotic nature of making a show in ever-changing locations with an ever-changing set of rules. So much of the way we'd made the show had been about good will, trust, and making friends. You'd be surprised how much having to ask someone to sign a receipt on the back of a leaf really killed the vibe.

Greta instituted a crippling policy of curtailing expenditures greater than $200 without prior authorization. *Two hundred fucking dollars*. Filming a single meal cost at least that much. It didn't matter that we were always in sudden death lightning round with no time to explain; forget years of loyalty and success, if we wanted to spend $201, it was going through Greta. To her credit, despite the twelve-hour time difference Greta always answered her phone, even in the middle of the night. She also almost always denied the funding request. It was just so frustrating how the conversation had shifted from creativity to the bottom line, and these days it felt like we all spent half our time tripping over dollars to pick up pennies.

I'd never been purposely reckless with the budget, even if it might not always have been the *first* thing I'd thought about when making any given decision. But that was a big part of what made the show great. It was an ethic that came from the top. And, yes, true, I'd become accustomed to having large amounts of cash on hand to buy my way out of problems. But time is money, and the way I looked at it when it came to Tony, time was very valuable.

"I have run zee numbers unt discovered it vould be cheaper to canzel zee show," Tony would joke, imitating Greta's accent.

To be fair, Greta had expertly navigated the byzantine process of securing our Iran visas. I wasn't kidding when I said it took an act of Congress. Due to the trade sanctions, we needed special permission to import items like our computers, phones, and of course the film equipment. Greta managed it, the State Department approved it, the IRS made an exemption, Congress voted, and under the Iran sanctions, we were exempted from prohibitions 31 C.F.R. §560.210(d).

Most Iranians we met were excited to talk about how much they loved the USA. But the old hardline establishment still existed. The sinister sounding Ministry of Culture and Islamic Guidance controlled our access, permits, visas, as well as monitored our trip and what we filmed. We were warned that our hotel rooms and vehicles would likely be bugged, our phone calls recorded. Tehran was also a modern, cosmopolitan city of over 8 million that reminded me a lot of Los Angeles, as well as being perhaps the friendliest place I'd ever visited.

IF IRAN HAD DEFIED EXPECTATIONS, GoldenEye lived up to them perfectly. It was about as close to paradise as I'd ever seen. Sequestered on Jamaica's wild, less touristy, northeast coast, this was a part of the island where old banana plantations mixed with dense jungle and spilled right down to waves breaking against coral cliffs. The historic seaside estate turned ultra-luxury hotel was once home and writing retreat of Sir Ian Fleming, author of the James Bond series. The entire complex was situated behind a phalanx of tall trees, gated, guarded, and absolutely private. The villa had gleaming white walls and an elegant hipped roofline, and sat between a large teal blue swimming pool and sunken garden framed by almond trees. But the location was the real selling point. Perched on the edge of a cliff overlooking the Atlantic Ocean, a winding staircase led down sixty feet to a private beach that included a grotto. Our personal butler, Nicholas, provided a never-ending flow of delightful rum punches. Looking around, it made total sense that James Bond would be conceived at a place like this. But Tony's adoration of Fleming and Bond wasn't the reason we were staying there. As we had departed Iran, Tony made it extremely clear that the top priority for our next location—and last shoot of the season—was "some low-impact beach time" and accommodation of "unspeakable luxury."

So, with only a week before the Jamaica shoot was to begin, Josh and I headed to Jamaica to scout out Tony's "creative vision" for this trip. Out the window went the gritty and non-touristy capital city Kingston, along with our two months of research, careful pre-production, and planning. When we touched down on the Caribbean island synonymous with Rastafarians, white sand beaches, and mass-market tourism, we had our work cut out for us.

By the end of the season I was also a bit worse for wear. In the last six months I'd been to the Punjab, Himalayas, Bahia, Brazil, Thailand, Paraguay, Iran, and now Jamaica. There was the ever-present pressure to keep raising the bar creatively, and now, thanks to my new nemesis Greta the budget czar, there was the added complication of trying to economize at the same time.

Tony was right, it was time to take a stand, fight fire with fire. If Tony really wanted a five-star luxury episode, well, we all needed a little luxury more than we'd ever needed it before. The more I thought about it, the more I realized billing Greta for an all-expense-paid five-star shoot in Jamaica was the perfect act of budgetary disobedience. Every shoot I'd ever done to this point, all sixty or so of them, nearly every moment on the ground had been spent beating the show out of however many dead horses I could get my hands on. But not this time. I bought a carved wooden souvenir dog, named him Mr. Papers, and immediately put him in charge. He spoke with a cockney accent and took over when it came to the decision-making process, leaving me blissfully free to relax. I'd never really relaxed before. So this Jamaica scout was a completely alien experience, and my goodness, Josh and I were having so much fun.

Josh reconciled mutually exclusive mandates of finding "unspeakably luxurious" accommodations while staying within Greta's restrictive hotel budget thanks to an extremely helpful Fifth Avenue public relations firm representing GoldenEye. From what I understood, Fleming's original villa was sort of like the presidential suite of the larger hotel complex and rented for about $12,000 a night. In exchange for filming on the property, we'd been given an extremely generous media rate. It was arguably the most exclusive place to stay on the entire island of Jamaica, and Tony loved James Bond. It was perfect. Apparently GoldenEye's owner, Chris Blackwell, had taken a special interest in us and was even flying down to Jamaica just for the shoot. In addition to being a hotelier, Blackwell was one of the most successful record producers of all time. He was responsible for bringing reggae music to the world outside Jamaica by discovering Bob Marley, among others, and had founded Island Records. Blackwell had instructed the hotel staff to do anything we wished in order to facilitate the logistics. We'd gratefully obliged, and much of what we planned on filming in the surrounding area was being arranged through our butler, Nicholas, who had turned out to be a treasure trove of good ideas. Nothing left to do but get stoned and pretend to scout for the show.

"What the fuck is that?" Josh said.

"It's probably just a seed. I think I missed a few when I was rolling the joint," I said.

"No, I mean we just drove past a sign with an arrow that read Dr. Hoe's; what's Dr. Hoe's?" Josh asked.

"Let's find out," Carleene, our fixer, said as she wheeled the jeep around.

Turned out Dr. Hoe's was a charming beachside rum bar where fishermen get a drink after returning from work. We ordered a steel bottom, rum and beer. Everyone was getting stoned. Obviously we had to film here. I mean not only was the place called Dr. Hoe's but it was located on James Bond Beach. Strangely, Dr. Hoe's and James Bond Beach hadn't been suggested to us, even though it was literally adjacent to the GoldenEye property.

"Another steel bottom?" the bartender asked. We were recklessly racking up a pretty big bar tab, and the shoot hadn't even begun yet.

"Greta said no alcohol, but she didn't say anything about expensing weed," I said. "I mean, it's practically legal here. Clearly pot is going to factor into the shoot. We're just scouting."

"Technically true," Josh agreed.

We worked long days, and it had always been an unwritten rule that, since we got no health insurance or overtime pay, we did get some perks, like a few drinks at the end of a long day. But now Greta had closed the bar, and the days weren't getting any shorter. Tony found the new alcohol guidelines just as upsetting as the hotel situation, and he'd donated his per diem, about $1,000 per shoot, for crew drinks in what became known as the "Alligator Fund." He also offered some accounting advice.

"It was fucking brilliant," Tony said. "Nixon instructed Kissinger to nervously let slip that he was acting irrationally, completely obsessed with eradicating communism, crazy enough to launch a nuclear attack. Kissinger would 'confidentially' tell the Russian ambassador, 'I'm worried about the president's mental state. He's got his finger on the button and I just don't know what he's capable of . . .'" Not responding to the uncomfortably confused look on my face—or perhaps feeding off it—Tony counseled me to call up the office and demand all sorts of crazy things. "Just say, 'I don't know what Tony's going to do next. I'm the only one that can control him, so you better listen to me and approve the purchase of that gold-plated duck press Tony's been raving on and on about.'"

I wasn't comfortable with either the Nixon Madman Strategy or Tony's alternate suggestion to plant flesh-eating bacteria on Greta's computer keyboard. Between Tony, whatever surprises presented themselves in the field, and now the office, well, I didn't think I could handle a three-front war. But like it or not, in the midst of a war is exactly where I found myself. As well as a cruise ship port of call.

As the "scout" continued, our jeep arrived at Ocho Rios, ground zero for the mass market commercial tourism "all-inclusive" set who swilled tropical drinks while stuffing themselves on nachos grandes. Walking around, I spotted a Margaritaville. I'd never been to one; all I knew was that the vacation-themed bar and restaurant chain was owned by Jimmy Buffett, who Tony had practically made a career of publicly trashing. Mr. Papers whispered that we should go there for lunch. Josh cheerfully agreed, though Carleene seemed a little less convinced. But believe it or not, Margaritaville was like the most fun place ever! I ate nachos and burgers; there was a waterslide, a giant shark where you could take selfies in its jaws, a jukebox playing all the classics, and there was even a beach.

"Let's get another round of margaritas!" I said, having the time of my life.

"Uggh. Greta just texted again," Josh said. "She's demanding an updated petty cash funding request. *Again.*"

"What? We've only been here a few days, and we're starting almost from scratch!" I said, *extremely* pissed Greta was managing to cast rain clouds over my Margaritaville date with Josh and Carleene. Tony's Nixon Madman was tempting, but it was just too insane. Then again, I was wearing a tie-dye T-shirt reading "BUMBO KLAAT" along with oversize novelty sunglasses, not to mention I was following orders from a carved wood dog who spoke with a cockney accent.

"You know what . . . Let's really end the season with a bang," I said. "Send Greta something so crazy she won't know how to respond."

Josh smiled, got out his laptop, and opened an email. "What did you have in mind?" he said.

"Let's submit a PC funding request based on the most half-baked ideas we've been thinking about. Something that makes no sense whatsoever. I don't know . . . like Tony has us pursuing a Jamaican cinema à la *Harder They Come* meets *James Bond* hybrid theme for the episode," I said, getting inspired. "Let's tell Greta Tony wants us to film a swinging Bond party requiring performers. So we'll need a troupe of dancers for musical numbers that can be on call through-out the shoot. We'll use them for a classic underwater Bond title sequence as well as a bus beat to reference 1970s-era Jamaican cinema. So we'll also need to arrange a city bus as a picture car for the duration of the shoot."

"Let's tell Greta Tony is demanding a pirate ship so he can talk about the history of Errol Flynn and old Hollywood in Jamaica while on the water, because he says it wouldn't be appropriate to have that discussion on shore . . . " Josh said. "If she denies the request, we'll say we *might* be able to convince him to settle for a less expensive luxury yacht or catamaran."

"Perfect! And wait . . . what's that, Mr. Papers? . . . YES!!!" I said, looking around. "Mr. Papers says we should send Greta on a wild goose chase, giving her the impossible task of securing permission to film . . . here . . . at Margaritaville! Let Greta know Tony feels it's *absolutely, absolutely* necessary for the creative to film at Margaritaville. Tell her we know how hard it can be to secure permissions from major corporate chains, and we only have a few days left, so she should start on it ASAP. Make sure to emphasize, Tony says Margaritaville is *really* important. That should keep her busy for a day or two."

"Are you sure we should be doing this?" Josh asked. Actually, I was not. Mr. Papers was a terrible influence. Or maybe it was the frozen margaritas and the pot. But this was no time to admit weakness of resolve.

"Do it," I said.

"You guys are mental." Carleene laughed. "But if that's what you want, we can make it happen; it's your show." And I believed

Carleene *could* make anything happen. Even though I had only just met her, it was obvious she was one of those people with a gift to move mountains. Carleene was Jamaica's top music-video producer, and part of her magic was that you never saw it coming. She was creative, gorgeous, had a good sense of humor and a tough-as-nails attitude. Pity the waiter or cook who didn't send our order out fast enough. Carleene would get up from the table, go back to the kitchen, and personally resolve the holdup. She was a force to be reckoned with, and everyone respected her. These were all ideal traits in a fixer. Best of all, Carleene was fun to hang out with. And she seemed to like Josh and me more than she liked Greta!

"I can negotiate a good rate for the extras by hiring local exotic dancers rather than the more 'traditional' type from a conservatory in Kingston," Carleene said. "And we can talk to the Trident Castle about the Bond party. You'll probably need flashing colored lights, strobe and smoke machines. It's a tall order, but we can get a city bus as well."

"There's no way Greta will approve a funding request that cuckoo," I said. "We just need her off our backs." While I tried out the waterslide, Carleene and Josh crunched some numbers.

"Ooohhh, nice shell necklace," Josh said when I returned from the gift shop. "So, this is what we came up with."

JAMAICA SCENE COSTS:

Piggy's (Jerk Chicken)—$200

Tony at GoldenEye—$500

Baby Lex Bar and Car Wash Scene—$600

Blackwell Drinks—$200

Dr. Hoe (local fishermen rum bar near GoldenEye)—$300

Meal at Chris's (local's restaurant near GoldenEye)—$300

Bus (need to rent a bus for driving beat throughout show)—$900

Beach Scene—$400

Home-Cooked Meal—$500

Boating Scene—$1,000

Trident Castle Meal and Bond Party—$3,500

Rio Grande River/Wild West Meal and Raft—$700

Crabbing Scene (Crab Hunt & Meal)—$300

B-Roll/Vendors—$800

Extras for Dance Sequences—$1,000

TOTAL: $11,200

"Perfect!" I said. "Just make sure to let Greta know the figures are estimates and subject to upward revision."

"Sending!" Josh said, and clicked his trackpad with a flourish. We laughed and toasted our drinks. Almost instantly, Josh's phone started ringing. Of course, it was Greta.

"Don't pick up, we have to let this sit," I said. "Let's get another round!"

We successfully evaded Greta's repeated emails, texts, and phone calls for about two hours until Lisa, Josh's friend from the office, called.

"Please hold for Sandy and Greta," Lisa said.

"Fuck," Josh said, his phone in one hand, a rum punch–filled coconut with cocktail umbrella in the other. "They tricked me!"

"Put it on speaker," I said, taking off my novelty sunglasses and putting out the joint.

"Josh, zis iz Sandy unt Greta," Greta said sternly at the other end of the line.

"Hi, Josh," Sandy, our executive producer, said. "Are you guys having a good time?"

"Ve have been trying to reach you az I vould like to interrogate you regarding zee budget request. For instance, vhat iz zis six hundred dollars for zee Baby Lex Bar unt Carvash scene?"

"Well, due to the schedule, we can only film at Baby Lex's in the morning," Josh said. "We need to buy drinks for people in the background to make the bar look full."

"Vhy don't you put zee drivers in zee background?" Greta asked.

"Oh, that's a great idea, Greta, let's give the drivers alcohol," Josh said.

"Vhy not, zee drivers can drink juice," Greta instructed.

"Greta . . . no, Greta, no . . . " Josh said. "Ain't nobody drinks juice at Baby Lex's Bar and Carwash." There was a prolonged silence at the other end of the line. I could only imagine what they were thinking, and I had to hold my nose to keep from bursting out laughing.

"Unt explain yourself regardizing zee three thousand five hundred dollars for a James Bond party?" Greta demanded.

"Well, the dance troupe and voodoo priest might be more expensive than we'd originally hoped," Josh said. "But on the bright side, we can get a great deal on a fire eater."

"Hi, this is Sandy," Sandy said. "I appreciate how much of this is coming from Tony and that you're pulling the shoot together quickly, but the current creative costs are about double what we're budgeted for."

"Hi, Greta, this is Tom," I said. "Any progress on securing permission to film at Margaritaville?"

"It iz a large organization unt zo far I have been having trouble reaching zee right department," she said. "But ze procezz has been started."

"Okay, well, it's extremely important to Tony, and he knows you're working on it." There was no way in hell Tony would have wanted to film at Margaritaville, but Greta didn't know that. And even better, I'd recently discovered that "Tony knows you're working on it" was a magic set of words that sent the office into a terror.

With Greta preoccupied chasing her tail and Tony and the camera guys arriving soon, we still had to figure out what the show was about . . . so Josh and I went to the beach to get stoned.

"Hear me out," Josh said. "What makes a Bond film? What's the formula? You need a hero . . . "

"Bourdain, Anthony Bourdain," I said, sparking another blunt.

"Yes! And an ultra-luxurious tropical location . . . " Josh said.

"Some place so perfect it's practically evil?" I said, gesturing to our private beach.

"Plus, a villain with an evil master plan and some over-the-top HQ with henchmen," Josh said, taking a hit.

"Well, Greta is bent on nuking anything fun in the Western hemisphere," I said.

"No, Greta is just a henchman trying to distract from the true villain. Isn't there someone else you can think of?" Josh said, passing back the blunt. He began humming the lyrics to the song "Margaritaville": "There's booze in the blender . . ."

"Wait . . . so, the villain is Jimmy Buffett?" I asked. Josh had a point. Buffett could have made for an archetypal Bondian villain, and the Margaritaville Organization was the perfect cover to steal all the beaches from the Jamaicans. The more of the island we'd seen, the more difficult it was to ignore the harsh contrast between resorts and the communities that serviced them. All the waterfront real estate had been snapped up by hotels, restaurants, and private vacation homes, and there was basically a tall concrete wall all along the coast. Shockingly, it appeared Jamaicans didn't really have much access to their own beaches, unless they worked in the resorts.

"Shit, man," Josh said. "If we expose Jimmy Buffett, it'll make the next rock star think twice before starting an evil restaurant chain to buy up all the beaches."

"It's too bad there's no chance Greta will come through with permissions," I said. "Bond is just a historical and visual nod with the party."

WHHHRRRRRFFFLLLLUUUUSSSSCCH. Tony exited his bathroom wearing a huge smile. "Did you hear that flush?" he asked. "Like the sound of a 747 taking off."

Everything was coming up roses. Tony was happy with the hotel. And shockingly, the Nixon Madman seemed to have worked. Maybe too well . . . somehow—*unbelievably*—most of our cost requests had been approved. I was as flabbergasted as Mr. Papers. Now all of a sudden we had a new problem: figure out how to fit together all the disparate elements Greta was willing to pay for.

"You should have a rum punch," Tony said. "They're excellent."

"I can't, Greta is really cracking down on our drink bills," I said, throwing a little gasoline on the fire.

Tony looked at me from over his iPad. "I'd like sixteen rum punches, please," he said to Nicholas when he came to check on us. "You can have one of mine."

Rum punches in hand, Josh, Tony, and I went to our private beach to smoke a joint. I decided this was as good a time as any to come out to Tony about our experiment with Nixon Madman and how it had gotten a little out of control. To my surprise, Tony thought it was hilarious.

"Just as long as I don't have to be any part of that shit, shoot your heart out," he said.

"We have Greta on a wild goose chase to secure permission at Margaritaville," I added cautiously. "We went there on the scout, but it wasn't any fun."

"You went to Margaritaville?! Where's my robot piranha? Summon the robot piranha!" Tony said, slipping into evil villain affectation while pacing the beach. "Fucking fat herpetic with a novelty drink. Someone should put a stop to his reign of fuckin' terror right now, and every other bald fuck with a ponytail. Things to do tomorrow: Destroy Margaritaville. Start worldwide revolution ... Find paracetamol with codeine, 'cause I could really use some right now ... Actually ... this being a former British island, you could probably get codeine in the pharmacy. *Where's the fixer?*"

When we got back to the villa, Carl was in the lounge waiting for us. "Respect is true," he said. "We are the two percent. We the two percent have to inform, keep adjusting. We are the newsmakers."

Upon hearing we wanted to visit James Bond Beach, our host, Blackwell, had insisted his friend Carl accompany us. We'd tried to demur gracefully, but Blackwell had refused to take no for an answer. In his seventies, I guessed, Carl was rail-thin, flamboyant, bald, with dreadlocks, a thick beard, and pale blue eyes. He told us about the history of the island, his acting credentials, and a few details relating to the shoot at James Bond Beach in the morning before showing himself out.

"Fuck," Josh said. "We're out of papers."

"I know how to make a bowl out of an apple and a pen," I said. "It's too late to bother Nicholas, but I bet we can get an apple at the concierge desk."

We stumbled through the night jungle to the hotel office. While Josh asked for an apple, I took in the room. Nouveau Caribbean minimalist pastel chic. I noticed a large architect's model beneath Plexiglas. Looking closer, I could see GoldenEye, and even the building we were in. There was the village of Oracabessa just on the other side of the perimeter wall. My eyes followed the coastline down to James Bond Beach. But instead of a rum shack and fishing boats, there was what looked like an extension of the hotel complex . . .

"Josh! Come over here!!!" I whispered.

We waited until we got back down to our beach, which we were pretty sure would be hard to bug, and packed the apple before talking. Though we were employing paranoid stoner logic, Josh and I started to put the pieces together.

"Shit . . . " Josh said. "The neck bone's connected to the hip bone! No wonder the hotel didn't recommend we film at James Bond Beach!"

"And is that why Blackwell is insisting on sending Carl along?" I asked.

"Blackwell purchased GoldenEye from the Fleming estate in 1976. Since then, he's expanded the original property into a fifty-two-acre world class resort positioned as the flagship of his ultra-exclusive Island Outpost Hotel consortium," Josh said, reading from the hotel's promotional literature. "We'd better tell Tony!"

It was looking like the villain might not be Jimmy Buffett after all.

"So I think the ghost of Ian Fleming might be inhabiting this wooden dog I have and . . . well, anyway, that part is complicated," I said, taking a hit of the joint before passing it to Tony.

"What Tom means to say, the important thing is that in the process of fucking with Greta we may have . . . " Josh paused to gather his thoughts.

"Accidentally uncovered a plot to steal the last public beach in Oracabessa," I interjected. "And we sorta . . . "

"Might have stumbled into a Bond film!" Josh said.

"It sounds more like a tired *Scooby-Doo* mystery than a Bond plot," Tony said, unimpressed.

THE NEXT MORNING WE ARRIVED early at James Bond Beach to find Carl already there. Everyone else at Dr. Hoe's were local fisherman. But Carl looked like he'd come right from the salon, and he obviously wouldn't have been here if we weren't filming. He was dressed in—I don't know what sort of style you'd call it—maybe like Studio 54 meets *Tales from the Crypt*. The Mona Lisa was emblazoned on his bright orange silk shirt, half her face dissolving into twisting snakes, a hundred eyes bedazzled with rhinestones.

"Jamaica is fortunate to have Mr. Bourdain and CNN in our presence," Carl said.

"It's just a normal conversation," I said. This was supposed to be a nice, natural scene. Local fishermen went out each morning to haul in the catch. After the day's work was done, they gathered at Dr. Hoe's for a typical Jamaican fisherman's rum breakfast. Tony would sit with them and talk, but Carl had placed himself in the middle of it all, interfering with the atmosphere and standing out like a sore thumb. I actually wasn't sure why he was here. In the sobering light of the morning, our paranoid Bond delusions seemed a little far-fetched.

"Hello, gentlemen," Tony said. "So is business better these days or worse these days?"

"Worse," Carl said. "Overfishing is a problem. So right here has actually become a fishing sanctuary where we're trying to now revive the fish stock around the island."

Carl proceeded to cut everyone off and answer for them almost every time Tony's questions related to fish. Which of course were most of Tony's questions, given that we were talking to fishermen at a fishermen's bar. This scene was going to be worse than my hangover.

"So, if this becomes a protected sanctuary, what are you going to do for a living?" Tony asked anyone but Carl.

"Yeah, so you have to go—" one of the fishermen began.

"Further out to sea for deep-sea fishing," Carl interrupted.

"I guess what I'm asking," Tony said, "is there a future for the traditional—old school, subsistence, fishing industry in Jamaica? Or do you think, like every place else in the Caribbean, is it going to end up an entirely tourist economy?"

"This is going to belong to the tourists," said a fisherman wearing a checkered yellow shirt. "You got a point, and I'd like to clear up a point with you now all right. There's a lot of things going on here, right? I read a piece of paper a couple months ago, what's going on down here. Right? The native here, don't have no beach in a few months' time. They're gonna have an ID to come inside here."

"I don't care about truth, man, we kill people for truth, man!" Carl said, suddenly losing his temper.

"Umm . . . did Carl just make a death threat on camera?" I asked Josh. But before he could answer, a fairly sensational commotion had erupted among the local fishermen, and the group began turning on Carl. There were shouts that the local school kids wouldn't be able to use the beach road to get to classes anymore. It was only the second time in all my shows that such an unexpected fracas had erupted seemingly out of nowhere. The previous time it was to get out of paying the check at a Roman trattoria. This time it seemed a lot more serious. I could see in Tony's eyes that his bully alarm had been triggered. Mr. Papers got knocked over in the chaos, breaking his foot. Carl pulled the fisherman in the checkered shirt behind the rum shack, making the classic mistake of forgetting his microphone was still recording.

"In order for the program to work, assuming, you just kick back and be cool," Carl said menacingly. "You can't expose yourself. 'Stand me?"

"What did he mean when he said 'for the program to work'?" Josh asked.

Carl and the fisherman came back to the group, which is when it got even stranger . . .

"It's a joyous day! Let us find the spirit in man and travel to the unknown," Carl said in a booming voice that immediately quieted the other fishermen. "We are what you call astral travelers, so traveling dimension to dimension. If one man die, all men dead, and if one man live, all man live . . . " I couldn't believe what I was seeing: on a dime everyone had gone from yelling to quietly nodding in agreement, seemingly hypnotized by Carl's words. "Everything is relative," Carl preached. "The cure, the money, everything is connected to the universe. One person does not realize how vulnerable we are within the changes of time. Earth will not disappear my brethren. *As eye and eye.*"

"SEE WHAT THIS SHOW'S ABOUT, right? It's all coming together for me, who owns—who gets to live in paradise, right?" Tony said to the camera in the afternoon light on GoldenEye's private beach. It was a beautiful spit of sand surrounded by a clamshell of cliffs and dense foliage. Small black-and-yellow bumblebee fish scooted through the coral pools that broke the Atlantic surf and ensured gentle bright turquoise waves. With every conceivable luxury only a call to Nicholas away, Tony mused on the strange plot unfurling around James Bond Beach just down the coast. "Let's accept, as a basic premise, this is about as close to paradise as it gets, right? It's Jamaica. Jamaicans live here. I mean . . . this place I'm staying was built by a guy who planned to live here, and lived here two months out of the year. You know, who gets to live like this? Well, me, clearly. Look, here I am, fully aware of the irony of the situation. The whole preservation thing: preserved for who? Save the reef, for who? Save the beach, for whom? Not you, motherfucker. Probably."

While Tony talked to the camera, Josh and I were reading. After Carl's impromptu performance, I'd texted Greta that we needed to know everything possible about GoldenEye and James Bond Beach and Tony knew she was working on it. By the time we got back to the villa *The GoldenEye Environmental Impact Assessment Study* was waiting in my inbox. It made clear the government had in fact licensed James Bond Beach to the hotel for its expansion project, and James Bond 007 was no longer to be designated a fishing beach.

"Restricted use of the lagoon is *an essential component of the GoldenEye experience,*" I said, reading from the document. "*There are several advantages to this, including the protection of a marine sanctuary and enhancement of security and safety for guests.*"

"Ouch," Josh said. "It says here several permits have been issued in order to '*Incorporate the fishermen into the ambience and essence of the development.*'"

"Wait, so this *actually* explains what happened today, right?" I asked.

"Where's my cocktail? Where is my cocktail?" Tony interrupted.

"Umm . . . it's coming right now," I said.

"If this were a Bond film, you'd be being torn apart by piranha now," Tony said. "Piranhas would be swimming in ten different directions with your genitals." Fortunately, Nicholas arrived shortly with a rum punch. "Thank you, sir. Life is beautiful," Tony said. "I'd like twelve more of these, please."

Despite really only wanting to get high, have a vacation of sorts, we'd somehow basically stumbled backward into our own real-life Bond film. Josh and Mr. Papers had been right. And we were getting it all on film.

"How do you do this and be a good person?" Tony said to the camera, sipping his rum punch. "If you wanted to spend three months out of the year in a hammock, looking out at the Caribbean, on a secluded beach like this. Could you do that and also be a good person? No, you—you have to do bad things to do this, right? James Bond's a hustler, he gets this for a couple of days before he moves on to the next location. The guy who lives here is the Bond villain. That's what I've been missing. Ian Fleming was much closer to Blofeld or Hugo Drax. Those guys had lots of leisure time, sitting in hammocks, trying to figure out how to take over the fuckin' world. Lot of downtime in world domination. Bond was a working-class motherfucker." Tony looked out over the ocean and sighed.

"BAD NEWS," JOSH SAID WITH a worried look on his face. "I just heard from Greta. She says the PR agency representing Margaritaville is ready to move forward with the shoot. They love the show and have agreed to our release."

"No fucking way," I said in utter disbelief. "Are you kidding me?"

Damn, damn, damn. I glared at Mr. Papers. This was a double-double backfire. Not only had I inadvertently given Greta the opportunity to shine by pulling off the impossible, more worrisome, now we actually had to film at Margaritaville, even though we'd realized Margaritaville was just a red herring. Most of all, I was concerned Tony wasn't going to take it well.

"I'm sorry, but it seems like the permission for Margaritaville somehow came through," I said, bowing my head in shame. "But we have a plan. Josh will play oversize tourist number one. He'll represent the worst-case outcome—the all-inclusive resort douche tourist threatening to take the beach from the Jamaicans."

"Blofeld actually said yes?" Tony muttered. He thought for a long moment looking out at the ocean, hands folded behind his back. "Well, *excellent*. Wasting away in Margaritaville? Too slow for my tastes. Let me help you with that. Bleeding away in Margaritaville is more like it. *I don't expect you to talk, Mr. Buffett, I expect you to die!*"

Tony stayed at GoldenEye while the rest of the crew headed behind enemy lines, prepared to attach limpet mines to the hull of the SS *Margaritaville*.

"You ready?" I asked through the door.

"Oh, boy, ready as I'll ever be," Josh said, emerging from the men's room, his six-foot-five king-size frame squeezed into a teensy-weensy "Jamaica Me Crazy" T-shirt with cut-off sleeves, sunglasses, and floppy straw hat.

"You look amazing!" I said. "Okay, let's do this!"

I added enough money to the jukebox to keep the "Margaritaville" song playing on repeat for twelve hours. We filmed Josh in slow motion emerging from the ocean, double fisting margaritas, eating a massive plate of nachos, line dancing with the friendly and totally accommodating staff, as well as enjoying the waterslide— basically, just having one hell of an awesome mini vacation, all of it in extreme slow motion. Josh nailed it, the most fun takedown imaginable. When we finished filming, we all sat down for a crew meal. This bunch of ultra-highly experienced, battle hardened, jaded, off-the-beaten-track travel pros all had a fantastic time at Margaritaville. Not that we could ever tell Tony.

"HOW HAS NICHOLAS BEEN TAKING care of you?" our mysterious host asked when we finally met. "Everything to your liking, I presume?" Blackwell was dressed in all black and spoke in a refined British meter while continuously twirling the skewer in his rum punch, crooked pinky finger slightly raised. The only thing Blackwell lacked was a long-haired white cat to stroke. He maintained a home at GoldenEye and had invited Tony to his private bar tucked away in a secluded grotto in the cliffs. Carl was there wearing gold silk pajamas. He sat cross-legged and mute, blowing clouds of smoke from a pipe. Everything was right out of evil villain central casting. Or maybe I was just so stoned it looked that way. But I don't think so.

"Welcome," Blackwell said when Tony arrived.

"Long overdue," Tony said. "I've been living in your house."

"So have you been getting any good material while you've been here?"

"Oh yeah. Eating well. Beautiful scenery. Nice people."

"Rum punch?" Blackwell offered.

"Yes, I'll have one of those," Tony said. "You grew up in paradise. You had a successful career signing some of the coolest bands like ever. Life has been pretty good. What thrills you?"

"I'm trying to break a little resort town here," Blackwell said. "Something that filters into the town, filters into the parish, filters into the country."

"Is it an inevitability that basically all of the Caribbean is essentially going to end up as a service economy?" Tony asked.

"Well, yes, I think, yes, I think mainly so . . . service and agriculture," Blackwell said. "Bring people here and give them fresh food, Jamaican food, that's my mantra."

Chirping of tree frogs mixed with the sound of waves crashing against the coral. There was a shake of ice cubes as Blackwell's butler prepared another round of rum punches. Carl exhaled a cloud of smoke, and Blackwell twirled the skewer in his nearly empty drink.

"If life were a Bond film, who would you be?" Tony asked.

"Well, there's only one hero in a Bond film," Blackwell said with a hint of a smile.

"You wouldn't be the . . . " Tony stammered, a bit surprised by Blackwell's answer. "You wouldn't put yourself in any other role? You'd be the hero?"

"CAN YOU BELIEVE BLACKWELL ACTUALLY said he'd be James Bond?" Tony asked in disbelief when we retreated to the Fleming villa.

"We better be careful on the roads or we might get forced off a cliff by a Blackwell Industries truck," Zach said. Then, switching to his evil villain voice, *"What a pity . . . we warned them the roads were dangerous."*

Leaving GoldenEye, we headed further east along the rugged coastline toward Port Antonio. Once a getaway for the wealthy and Hollywood elite, the area had been nearly forgotten when the airport was built on the other side of the island. Known affectionately as Porto, it was as stunningly beautiful as it was undeveloped. While there, we filmed a Bond Party that Tony didn't go to, but we did make good use of the fire eaters, voodoo priest, and dance troupe. We even filmed that underwater Bond opening credit sequence. Generally, a great time was had spending Greta's money. But with several days left to fill, the show was missing something.

"I think I know what Mr. Papers is looking for," Carleene said. "Winnifred is the only public beach left in Portland. A woman, Cynthia, has a cook shop there, and she's fighting in court to keep the beach from being turned into a resort."

"If the food's good, I'm sold," I said.

We arranged a saltfish and ackee scene with Cynthia and her friends Joy and Marjorie—fellow beachside food purveyors and compatriots in the fight to save Winnifred Beach. Arriving at the beach was like a mirage: an unspoiled, untouched swath of coast-line. White sand, clear water, locals relaxing and having fun, and plenty of beachside food options. And like a mirage, Winnifred Beach was also in danger of disappearing.

"Winnifred Beach is a public beach. It has been one of the best beaches in Jamaica," Cynthia said. Not only did she run her restaurant every day, but she'd taken on the entire Jamaican government in a legal battle that was stretching into seven years. "The government want to make like a resort here. And when they make a resort, you know that it is not public for everyone to come in because they want to build hotel and villas around. So, it won't be open like a lot of people could come and enjoy it like now."

"I mean that would be sort of ridiculous if Jamaicans can't go to the beach in Jamaica," Tony said.

"Fight on, fight on," Cynthia said. "Here is where we relax. When we have our problems, we come down here and—"

"Take a swim," Joy said. "And you lay back."

"And things are better," Marjorie said.

"Well, it's a beautiful beach," Tony said. "I gotta come back here. Better yet, in my bathing suit tomorrow." Tony genuinely seemed to be having a good time, and if he was serious about returning, then we'd have our missing last scene of the show. "Well, good luck in your struggle," Tony said. "Because I would like to say, what kind of monstrous human being or organization would displace the people from their own beach?"

"If they take this away from us, we would live like we're in prison," Joy said, getting emotional. "'Cause when the time is hot, we would have nowhere to come and swim."

"I would like to be your minister of propaganda," Tony said. "I would like to direct the public relations campaign against this."

And Tony was true to his word. We returned to film an even bigger feast on Winnifred Beach. He really liked those ladies and their beach and genuinely hoped to bring attention to their cause.

The last day of the Jamaica shoot happened to be Tony's fifty-eighth birthday. Tony's father had died at fifty-seven—as had a string of male relatives before him—so we were all relieved that

Tony had outlived the Bourdain Curse. Josh, Mr. Papers, and I figured the best gift for the man who had everything was to cancel the
day's shoot and go to the beach for some prime ray time. It's strange
how often Tony gave the impression of being on a permanent vacation, because in reality he never stopped working. He only got to lie
in a hammock or do all those amazing looking vacation-y things if
there was a camera in his face. But there was nothing relaxing to him
about a camera. Even Bond got to enjoy the moments for himself.

TWENTY-THREE DAYS EARLIER, TONY HAD been looking histrionically
bored as the cameras followed him on a tour of the Milad Tower,
Iran's equivalent of the Seattle Space Needle and a symbol of national pride.

"Upon completion, the Milad Tower was considered the fourth
tallest freestanding telecommunications tower in the world," our
government-approved tour guide droned in clear but stilted English.
"As you see, it offers breathtaking view of Tehran set against the
Albroz Mountains."

Tony rolled his eyes and audibly sighed, then huffed. If anyone
got to make a fuss, it was me, I thought. It was the latest installment
of what was nearing a decade of my birthdays spent on the road.
Unlike previous years, I put my birthday on the schedule in ***BOLD
ITALIC CAPS*** to make sure Tony didn't forget.

"Good morning!" I had said enthusiastically at breakfast. Any
second now the attention was sure to start rolling my way.

"So, how old are you, Tom?" Tony asked, looking up from his
coffee.

"Thirty-four today." A smile of anticipation broke across my
face.

"You know, that's the same age Jesus was when he died and look
at all he accomplished," Tony said, not missing a beat. "So, why the
hell are we filming an 'observation deck scene'?"

As much as I hadn't appreciated the joke, it was pretty damn
funny. However, I managed not to laugh. After the observation

deck tour we stuck around getting b-roll shots of tourists and the view. The sky was a strange color; lightning flashed in the distance. Putting out my cigarette, I noticed everyone was pointing, taking pictures, and filming with their phones. I looked and saw some sort of sepia-tinged cloud stretching clear across the horizon. There was a low wail, the breeze began to pick up, and whatever it was, it seemed to be getting closer, and fast.

"There's a sandstorm coming!" Zach called from behind his camera.

I ran over to grab Tony from inside. By the time we got back out, a massive sand spout was nearly upon us, and conditions had intensified to a whirlwind. The cameras kept rolling as security guards started pushing people inside for cover.

"Here it comes!" Tony said.

We made it inside just in time. As the doors closed behind us, a wall of pressure hit the building with a thud and my ears popped. The sky darkened as the sun disappeared and the floor started moving beneath my feet. Coin-operated binoculars on the observation deck violently rattled in the wind. Lights flickered. What a great scene this was turning out to be!

"Is this normal?" I asked.

"This is the first time that we have experienced such a thing!" our guide said in what looked like shock, grabbing at her hijab. Then the realization of what was happening hit me. *This has never happened before* was not the sort of thing you wanted to hear from a nervous flight attendant, or in this case your panicked tour guide when you're in the middle of a fucking tornado atop a 1,000-foot-tall curio. The cameras kept rolling as the floor swayed ever more dramatically, buffeted by winds from all sides. When the lights cut out, they momentarily revealed a sickening murky green sky before jittering back on. Pieces of the building started to sheer off, catching in the swirl. Benches and larger panel cladding dislodged and crashed along the observation deck, threatening to ricochet into floor-to-ceiling windows.

"Stand away from the glass!" Tony shouted.

"Leave now! Leave now!" a security guard yelled over the howling. "It's dangerous!"

A sense of fear and dread deeper than I'd ever experienced before reached up and clenched around my neck as we were ushered into a stairwell. I could now officially add skyscrapers to my list of phobias. Everyone was running down the steps carrying film gear as the structure groaned and lights continued to flicker on and off.

"Please stop filming!" our guide cried, distress in her voice. My mind raced with images of shady contractors, substandard steel girders, and how it was common practice to mix sand into the concrete in so many countries, then when an earthquake hits, collapse! I'm not proud to admit it, but at one point I whimpered something like, "The building is going over! The building is going over!"

Hanging green emergency exit signs pendulated, caught as we were in the middle of the tempest. I thought of lighting a cigarette. What did it matter? I was sure I was going to die on my birthday.

Like all storms, eventually this one passed, and though it took some damage, needless to say, the Milad Tower did not fall.

That night we all went out for an off-camera meal to a banquet hall. On discovering we were from America, the restaurant owner came over to welcome us personally.

"He says he usually likes to put the flags of foreign guests at the table," our fixer Afshin translated. "He apologizes, he is all out of American."

Moose and Afshin must have informed the owner it was my birthday, because at the end of the meal a cake made its way to our table and all 200 people in the restaurant—led by the house band—began joyously singing the familiar "Happy Birthday" song in a mix of English and Farsi. I'd have to say it had been perhaps the most memorable birthday of my life. As I got ready to make a wish and blow, Tony leaned over and whispered in my ear, "Nice to see they went for candles over burning mini toothpick American flags."

BACK IN JAMAICA, TONY WAS lying in a hammock tanning with no camera to bother him, no content to deliver. He generally hated his birthday, but today he looked genuinely happy. We ordered bad pizza and had a cooler full of Heineken and Red Stripe. As the sun set, we presented Tony with a rum cake covered in powdered sugar, slices of starfruit, and cocktail umbrellas. Written in chocolate, it read "Rum Lives Forever." Tony smiled as he blew out his candles. It didn't get much better than this, the sort of day you wished would never end.

The next morning Josh and I sat mostly silent—painfully hungover and exhausted—through three hours of nausea-inducing mountainous twists and turns across the island to the international airport in Kingston. With each curve we listened to a dozen or so mostly empty rum bottles and leaking forties clink and clank as they rolled from one side of the gear van to the other. Mr. Papers sat there looking at me with one of those superior "I told you so" expressions. What a bizarre month it had been, I thought. The emotional, confusing, and life-changing shoot in Iran, then off to Jamaica, where somehow every boneheaded stoner blunder seemed to have worked in our favor. I don't think we could have got there sober. Even Greta's penny pinching had been a part of the magic recipe. And, damn, we'd had a good time.

I didn't know it yet, but the Jamaica episode would inspire a "Who gets to live in paradise? You do!" hotel promotion. More important, a judge ruled in Cynthia's favor, and Winnifred Beach was saved from development. I don't know if international attention from our Bond film helped, but it couldn't have hurt.

What I *did* know for sure at that moment, as I tried to keep from being sick, was that we'd never be able to go back to Golden-Eye; and Mr. Papers *might* owe Greta an explanation when we sobered up.

Chapter Eleven
SHOOTING NIGHTMARES

TONY OFTEN SPOKE OF HOW THE CAMERA WAS A LIAR; SIMILARLY, THE edit was inherently manipulative. And he was right. As time went by, what we chose to show or not show in the finished episodes had a funny way of recasting what had really happened in my mind. The constructed retelling somehow became more real to me than the actual experience had been. I found myself forgetting what had really happened, and what I did remember became edited, as if it were the show.

In the wake of Tony's death, I continued to be flooded with memories, both good and bad. Some that pushed their way in contradicted the versions of the trips I'd chosen to remember, ones I had previously blocked out. I wanted nothing to do with them, but they persisted.

I AWOKE FROM A NIGHTMARE—IT was about work, of course, something about missing the shot of our train running off the rails into a rice paddy. Jet lag and antimalarials make for cheap thrills. Cold comfort in the sweltering heat. My eyes blinked as I struggled to remember where I was. Bright light streamed in through the window. A fan was on, laboring to move the heavy tropical air. I saw my hastily half-packed suitcase. Last night slowly came into focus. Flashes of drunken revelry.

"Pretty crazy party, are you doing okay?" Jeff asked, forcing a smile.

"I want to go home," I said, rubbing my neck.

"Yeah, man, do you remember trying to swim back to Kuala Lumpur last night?"

I did remember, and despite my best efforts I hadn't made it very far.

"Hopefully Emong helped you get all the leeches off," Jeff said. He averted his eyes. "Ummm . . . so Tony wants to see you."

Hoping against hope this was somehow all a dream, I closed my eyes tightly . . . and opened them. Unfortunately, I was still in Borneo. We were here in the remote Iban village of Entalau retracing Tony's steps from ten years ago. It was a special trip, one that I'd thought would be like living a dream. Instead, it had turned into a waking nightmare. Getting out of bed, I checked again for leeches before starting the 1,000-foot walk of shame toward Tony's hammock "office."

Tony's first visit to Borneo in 2005 was a trip that had marked a turning point in his life and career, as well as mine. Back then *No Reservations* had just been commissioned by the Travel Channel and I'd been hired by the newly incorporated ZPZ to post-produce the first season. I'd be screening footage, writing voice-over, and working with the editors to craft each episode. That meant I'd spend all my time in the New York office, and the closest I'd get to traveling would be through the raw footage playing out on the edit room screen.

That trip to Borneo during the first season of *No Reservations* had been an emotional one for Tony. His marriage of twenty years was breaking up, and he'd fallen in love again and was feeling unusually poetic around the camera. Brand-new to the job, I'd sat in the edit room watching as the PD150 focused and Tony, on the banks of the Skrang River, had said,

Travel isn't always pretty. It isn't always comfortable. Sometimes it hurts, it even breaks your heart. But that's okay. The journey changes you; it should change you. It leaves marks on your memory, on your consciousness, on your heart, and on your body. You take something with you. Hopefully, you leave something good behind.

Unfortunately, the footage was unusable because of an unrelenting dog barking in the background, but I transcribed what Tony said, repurposing it as a line of voice-over for the end of the episode, and it became my favorite quote about travel.

Tony's words as well as the episode's theme had been inspired by the Bejalai, an Iban philosophy about taking a journey of self-discovery. An indigenous group native to the vast jungles of Borneo, the Iban considered the Bejalai central to their culture. The general idea is you go on an adventure, and learn something about the world. When all is said and done, hopefully you're better for what you've seen, and you share the knowledge you've acquired with your home village. The Iban then commemorate the experience with a hand-tapped tattoo, à la "travel leaves marks." It was literally a perfect theme for an episode of TV about travel.

Back in New York the edit—my first—was going well and developing a distinctly cinematic arc. In addition to being practitioners of the Bejalai, the Iban had once been fearsome headhunters. Tony's guide, Itam, was in his eighties, the tattoos on his fingers an indication he was one of the last surviving Iban to have engaged in the delicate art of taking heads. So of course Tony fell in love with him immediately. At the end of the trip, Tony and Itam sat beneath a bouquet of human skulls knocking back shots of rice whiskey. Before Tony left, Itam invited him to return for Gawai, a three-day-long raucous Iban drinking festival sort of like Thanksgiving, Christmas, and New Year's combined. Tony thanked Itam warmly and promised to return.

Watching that raw footage, something clicked. I remember Tony and the crew hiking through sweltering jungle, blundering and wheezing up and down over steep, slippery, thorny, leech-infested bush. I didn't really like damp jungle or leeches, but I realized I needed to be there. I'd never be happy in the comfort of an air-conditioned edit room. So I set about figuring out a plan to transition to the road crew. The rest, as they say, is history.

FOUR DAYS BEFORE MY WALK of shame to Tony's hammock office, I'd been standing on the banks of the Skrang River watching the crew load up our fleet of colorfully painted longboats. This was Tony's second trip to the jungles of Borneo; he was back to fulfill his promise to return for Gawai. I'd edited that first episode a decade ago, but this time I was going to live it.

"Okay, everyone, we're fighting daylight," Jeff called. He was producing the episode, and over the last year had proven himself to be a valuable creative collaborator on our trips to Madagascar, Beirut, and Greece. Jeff was gifted with homecoming king confidence, the laser focus of an ER resident, and according to Tony, "eyes like an Alsatian." Best of all, Jeff had turned out to be a good friend. "Let's carpe diem this shit and head out!" he said with a smile.

Resembling motorized canoes powered by 15-horsepower outboard engines, our longboats sailed over opaque jade-colored water that was turned a frothy greenish-white swirl at intervals by small cataracts. Short of a helicopter, the Skrang River was the only way to reach the many Iban villages located deep in the jungle, and we roared past other colorful longboats laden with cargo and revelers returning for the holiday.

We filmed boat to boat, pass-bys, action shots, and footage of fording the rapids. Tony drank Tiger beer while watching the late afternoon sun filter through the dense canopy. As the river snaked its way deeper into the jungle toward the longhouse, I thought about how I'd somehow been given a magic opportunity to step through the TV screen into the episode that in a lot of ways, for me, had started it all. On that long-ago trip, Tony had talked whimsically about how travel leaves marks. He'd delivered that wisdom at what had been the relative beginning of his traveling career. I was determined to outdo the original episode and coax an even more brilliant realization from Tony this time. Now, with another decade of experiences under his belt, he'd surely have something far more profound to share. He must have learned something in all those miles.

As dusk began to settle, the sky turned gray-pink, and we got shots of a magnificent rainbow stretching above the river. And much like the episode a decade ago, our boats arrived at Entalau just after dark.

THE NEXT MORNING WE AWOKE to find much had changed in the decade since Tony's last visit. The old longhouse where the whole Iban village lived together under one roof in apartments off a communal hallway had been torn down and replaced by a newer one. The tribe had converted to Christianity and been convinced to bury their bouquet of skulls. Much of the jungle had been clear cut by loggers, and Itam was dead.

But here we were anyway, the crew and the whole Iban village preparing to celebrate Gawai. Fred, our newest DP, and Todd set about filming b-roll after a quick stop to play ball with the Iban kids. Tony was situated in his hammock checking emails, thanks to Jeff having found the only bar of cell signal in the province. Meanwhile I was continuing to deal with a number of pressing concerns. We had decided to devote half the shoot to Gawai, but nothing was happening aside from repetitive drinking. At Gawai, everyone drinks. Kids, adults, the village elders, and *especially* honored guests like us. Every five feet, you're obliged to accept another shot of lankau, a homemade rice whiskey only marginally lower octane than jet fuel and known to induce mildly hallucinogenic effects. It's considered an insult to refuse, which is probably why our travel doctor here in case of emergency was lying passed out drunk on the floor.

In addition to that, I'd discovered that the translator-sidekick I'd brought along to the drinking festival was a recovering alcoholic and didn't drink. Which didn't really matter because, as it turned out, he also didn't speak Iban. And none of the Iban spoke English. As if that weren't enough, I didn't have much to visually connect this visit to Itam—the narrative backbone of the episode. Worst of all, Tony had decided he didn't want to go through with the Bejalai tattoo scene. I was counting on that damn tattoo!

I wanted to believe we'd been on a Bejalai, but deep down I was terrified the last decade had just been aimless wandering while making a TV show. On some level I'd convinced myself the tattoo would be proof there was meaning in the chaos.

I couldn't say that to Tony so instead I pointed out how we'd structured the entire episode around the tattoo. But Tony didn't seem to care because that's what he called a "Tom problem," and "don't worry, we'll fix it in post," which meant I'd have to fix it in post and give up the next two months of weekends in the process. But I was really freaking out because travel was supposed to leave marks, not a feeling of emptiness!

Also, it was my birthday and everyone but Jeff forgot. Again. Suffice to say I was not reveling in the experience of being here and fulfilling a personal dream.

Festivals were one of the most challenging things we filmed, and this one had so much riding on it. One of my jobs was to be the eyes of the shoot, directing the cameras toward narrative elements needed for the edit. It was now the last night of Gawai, and with little to show for our efforts, I was unsuccessfully navigating a minefield of Iban hospitality, but still sober enough to spot the hitherto elusive widow of Itam. Ninety-five years old, she was knocking back shots from a handle of Johnnie Walker Blue with her preschool-age great-grandson. Now, that might have been a useful shot to bring back to New York, but, of course, there were no cameras to be found. Getting no response over the walkie, I rushed around desperately looking for the crew, going from apartment to apartment. Finally, I found everyone seated with Tony around a table relaxing, laughing, and enjoying something to eat.

Now, I worked *very* hard to arrange the schedule so that there was a proper one-hour-long break every six hours (maximum) and that days weren't longer than twelve hours. If the *Titanic* hit an iceberg outside of the shooting window, I would think twice before asking anyone to get the shot if it happened outside of the allotted time. In return I expected the cameras to be on during our scheduled filming blocks, especially when I was struggling to eke out a story. Which, admittedly, was all the time. But anyway, this was not a crew break, and I was beyond stressed, and also now feeling left out.

"What the fuck are you guys doing?! I found Itam's widow, get the fuck up, we need that shot!" I shouted.

Without question, I shouldn't have had so much to drink, and I was totally out of line to speak that way to the crew. But my biggest mistake was doing it in front of Tony. I'd been pushing him for content all day, which always got under his skin. But drunken behavior and being "uncool" was even worse. Quite drunk himself, Tony got to his feet and yelled, "That is fucking it! You're done, demoted. Jeff, you're in charge. Tom, if I see you one more fucking time tonight, you're off the show! For good! Now get upstairs to your fucking room and sleep it off."

Tail between my legs, I was escorted to my prison cell. Cursing the heat and the mosquitos and the snakes and the leeches and the jungle and my "best fucking job in the world," I tried to fall asleep. Worst birthday ever. I lasted roughly fifteen minutes hearing the increasingly rowdy festivities below, fretting over the cameras missing shots, before I caved and slinked downstairs to check. From the presumed safety of a darkened room, I squinted out at the party through the slats of a vented window.

Of course, having hawk vision, Tony zeroed in on my position immediately. Next thing I knew, he was barreling toward the room. I scrambled back against the wall as Tony charged through the doorway. In the dark, he stumbled over a couch, then lunged and tackled me, his hands closing around my neck. It all happened very fast. As I hit the floor, Tony squeezed as tight as he could. I didn't fight back. I don't know if I tried to scream or if I even could. I just looked up at his reddened face, veins inflamed, bloodshot eyes popping out of their sockets, his pupils darting back and forth like my dad's used to when as a kid I'd done something really, *really* bad. The next thing I knew, the light switched on, and Jeff and Fred were pulling Tony off me, sputtering, his limbs flailing.

I don't remember exactly what happened next, but the general impression was that it was my fault. I was led back upstairs, Tony still screaming. This time, a member of the local crew was assigned to stay with me, but I escaped again, slipping down to the river. I knew there was no way I could really make it all the way to Kuala Lumpur, but I had to get the hell out of there.

The next morning, as I walked to Tony's hammock office, I was hungover, cloudy headed, chagrined. I felt like a line had been crossed. If he didn't fire me, I had resolved to quit. Even if Tony apologized, there was almost nothing he could say that would make me change my mind.

Arriving at Tony's hammock, I found he was engrossed in his iPad, responding to emails.

"We need to talk about what happened last night . . . " Tony said, flicking the ash from the end of his cigarette.

"Yeah, we do!" I said with uncharacteristic intention.

"We will never speak another word about it again," he said without looking up. "Is that clear . . . ?"

I stood in stunned silence, caught altogether off guard. This I was not expecting, and I was completely tongue-tied.

Tony peered up at me over his reading glasses for the first time, waiting for an answer.

"Okay then, good," he said, taking my silence for acquiescence. "What time is that tattoo scene you want me to do?"

As instructed, we never spoke another word about it again.

AS THE MONTHS PASSED BY after Tony's death, I was in the midst of a deep depression that only seemed to be getting worse. Maybe my brain had been protecting itself, shutting out emotions like the pop of an overloaded circuit breaker. What happened in Borneo was only one of many inconvenient realities that had been surfacing since Tony's death, dramatically contradicted the made-for-TV version of how things were supposed to be.

I hated thinking about it, I hated that Tony had killed himself, I hated lying in bed doing nothing with my life, I hated the conflicting memories that kept flooding back no matter how much I tried to drown them with alcohol.

One night at the end of March, halfway into a handle of Johnnie Walker, I just couldn't shake the horrifying image of Tony's hotel room in France. I saw it whenever I closed my eyes, and I couldn't make it go away. Feeling like I had no options left, I decided that, like on TV, I needed to reenact the crime scene. I went upstairs to the bathroom, removed the belt from my bathrobe, tied it around the doorknob, sat down and leaned back. I wasn't attempting suicide; even in my inebriated state I knew not to tie the other end of the belt around my neck. I just needed answers. Lying on the floor, I stared up at the ceiling. Through tears, I checked the watch Tony had given me. The time since having the idea to where I was now had taken less than five minutes. My experiment brought me a moment of peace. It made it easier to imagine what happened was some kind of an accident. Not like jumping off a bridge or putting a gun in your mouth. It wasn't violent, it was so quick, so easy. And incredibly terrifying that it even seemed like a good idea to try to find out.

I needed to get the fuck out of the house. I called United Airlines and used some of my frequent flyer miles to book a one-way ticket leaving for Rome in a few hours. There was a guy I'd been seeing in Italy before Tony died, and a half-baked plan was formulating in my mind. If there were answers, or any kind of absolution anywhere, I would find it in Rome.

Chapter Twelve

ROMAN HOLIDAY

I LANDED IN ROME ON APRIL FOOL'S DAY, INTERESTINGLY ENOUGH. I found a room in a cheap hotel, and drank and smoked lying in the bed, staring up at black mold stains on the ceiling. Fuck. I'd gone all the way to Italy just to do the exact same thing I did at home. This must be what rock bottom looks like.

My phone buzzed with a text. It was Asia. "Tom, yes, it would be great to see you. Really. So happy to hear from you." It all seemed clear to my addled brain now. I lit another cigarette and exhaled, watching the curls of smoke lose shape.

As the show got bigger, everything else in Tony's life got bigger too. His fame, the stakes, the problems, the phobias, all grew at an exponential pace. In hindsight it's clear how Tony had become more and more isolated and lonely, and more dependent on his relationship with Asia Argento. They'd been on-again, off-again for the two years before his death. She wasn't only beautiful, fascinating, and exhilarating. Being famous, Asia understood Tony's lifestyle, but the relationship was far from a honeymoon. I'd seen how intensely Tony seemed to love her, and how heartbroken he was each time she dumped him. As time went on, Tony's moods oscillated along with the ups and downs of their relationship, an ever-amplifying cosine wave. When Tony was filming in France, they broke up and, according to the crew who were there with him, he became despondent. A couple days later Tony was dead. I wanted somebody to blame. If I was ever going to get on with my own life, I needed answers.

We met at an upscale restaurant in the northern suburbs of Rome. The dining room was a late Monday afternoon of still white tablecloths, that dead zone between lunch and dinner. Asia was already there waiting for me behind a pair of dark, oversize sunglasses. She was ghostly pale, a stark contrast to jet black hair. She looked thinner than I remembered—rail thin and somehow smaller too.

"Tom, it's so good to see you," she said, her deep, gravelly voice bigger than her frame.

When the waiter arrived, I declined food and asked for a bottle of Talisker. I was here to get Asia to confess she'd killed Tony, and I had a plan. I poured myself a drink. Asia circled for a moment, then took the bait.

"Nobody will talk to me, I'm completely cut off from everyone in Anthony's life," she said, emptying her glass. "I have no idea what's going on. I read in the newspapers about his will, where's the rest of the money?"

"Rest of the money?" I repeated, pouring us another. "I don't think there is more money. Tony always spent more than he saved."

"Well, what about the book he was working on?" She held out her glass.

"I don't know anything about what he was writing," I said, downing another drink.

"He was always complaining, especially at the end, about his writer's block," Asia said. "It started when we were in Hong Kong. It mortified him, he felt he had to write this book, but he couldn't finish it. He said he was haunted by 'the great blank white page staring him in the face.'"

"SHE'S AN AMAZINGLY TALENTED ACTOR, brilliant director, and smoking hot," Tony said, finishing his cigarette. "She's like the Angelina Jolie

of Italy ... Her father is Dario Argento." He waited for a flicker
of recognition on my face. "The famous Italian horror director?"
I stood there with a stunned goldfish expression. The words coming rapid-fire out of Tony's mouth had no meaning to me. "Never
mind." He rolled his eyes and continued. "Asia has agreed to help
with the Rome show; it's going to be fantastic. She's a treasure trove
of inspiration and ideas and is going to set up the entire shoot."

Okay, that was great. But at the moment, we were filming in
Argentina, and I had a lot to worry about before I could start thinking about Rome. We'd been in production for fourteen years, and
the job was getting harder. Dealing with ever escalating logistics,
variables in the field, and unhelpful bullshit from the office was
taking a serious toll. In addition to Argentina, I was behind schedule on the Manila edit, and two weeks after Rome, we had a super
top-secret—tell nobody, or it will not happen—shoot in Vietnam
with President Obama.

"Wow, that sounds really exciting," I said, too wound up to
appear genuinely enthuasistic. "How did you and Asia meet?"

"We haven't met," Tony said. "We started direct messaging
through Twitter."

Hadn't met yet? Well, that was a red flag. I shuddered at the
realization that the next several months of my life would be hinging
on the strength and reliability of a Twitter relationship.

"How do you know you're not getting catfished?" I asked.

"I want you to keep me copied on all correspondence," Tony
said, ignoring my question. "Everything, I mean everything."

Copy Tony on every email? It kept getting better. Micromanaging
pre-production to this extent wasn't just unusual, it was insane.
Anytime Tony paid special attention to a location or scene it spelled
trouble. Putting the show together required a million little details,
and it had pretty much become my survival strategy to keep Tony
Bourdain as far away from the nuts, bolts, and gnashing gears of the
machine as telegenically possible. The big picture was where Tony
did best. Choosing episode themes and outlining his critical artistic
direction, his intense involvement in the edit that ultimately defined
the show, all that was what made each episode an intensely personal

expression. Tony's knowledge of literature and film was encyclope-
dic, and we often riffed on a cinematic reference for each episode.
But as the bar rose, these references placed increasingly outrageous
and logistically challenging demands on the crew, resulting in
extreme stress, though pretty much without exception a relentlessly
improved TV show.

"So, I'm thinking Bertolucci's *The Conformist* as the style of
cinematography for Rome," Tony said. Gears started turning in
my head. A film shot in the 1970s, set in the 1930s with a powerful anti-Mussolini, anti-fascist message mirrored by the use of
super-wide-screen anamorphic cinematography and a cold, brutalist, dehumanizing architectural landscape. Seemed like a perfectly
straightforward reference for a food show being shot in 2016. Really,
though, I knew I wasn't being fair. To Tony, the more important the
episode, the more important the style, and for this one he definitely
had a plan. There would be no Colosseum or picturesque cobblestone piazzas this time.

"Start gathering archival footage of Mussolini and fascist-era
Rome that specifically evokes the current Trump campaign and
political mood at home," Tony said. Trump wasn't even the official
Republican nominee at the time, but Tony was already concerned by
the comparisons. "It's fascinating and so timely. I've been reading up
on fascism and it's coming back, big time. I think there's even a clip
where Mussolini says, 'Make Italy great again.'"

Speaking faster than I could write, Tony instructed me to begin
assembling a list of possible brutalist filming locations on the
outskirts of Rome, "with an emphasis on examples of fascist architecture, remnants of monuments, bland suburbs subtly drawing a
mostly unspoken line to present-day Trumpism."

By this point I'd been to Italy many times. It's a lovely place to
visit, has, in my opinion, some of the best food in the world, and
is without question one of the most difficult places to make this
show. And now with Tony's focus on details and his obvious desire
to impress Asia, this was going to be a whole new level.

Perhaps the biggest challenge of all was that we would
be shooting anamorphic. We'd be using Arri Alexa cameras and

anamorphic lenses to get an authentic, extreme widescreen aspect ratio that would recreate Tony's Bertolucci-inspired vision for the episode. But it meant spending roughly an additional $38,000 in equipment rentals (which would eventually spiral to a $90,000 cost overrun) and lugging massive studio-size cameras all over Rome while trying to make the episode look like a scripted film, even though we had no script or shot list. It wasn't just the mammoth cameras we had to contend with. Filming anamorphic required additional equipment, lighting, a dolly and track, and a massive local Italian film crew to haul and operate it all. It would look cool, if we could pull it off.

Tony's ethic of relentlessly pushing the envelope—the very drive responsible for getting us where we were—had reached such a fever pitch, it felt like the pace was becoming unsustainable. Flexibility and margin for error were shrinking by the episode.

If it hadn't been for Jeff, I think I would have lost my mind long before we ever touched down in Rome. He negotiated equipment, and managed fixers, logistics, and the local crew with seeming ease. These were logistical and diplomatic challenges that would have killed a lesser producer.

We didn't have an assistant director to run the production—someone to make sure we were on schedule, that everyone was where they were supposed to be, and they all got fed on time—which was normally a necessity when dealing with a crew this size. The qualified locals we'd hired were all used to studio-style, union-approved conditions, including regular coffee breaks. When they realized they needed to work between the hours of one p.m. and three p.m., the local team essentially went on a food strike and flat out refused to allow lunch to be rescheduled.

"We make a show about lunch," Jeff patiently explained. "We're all going to have to work through lunch." Eventually everyone came to an understanding that involved a food break every three hours. The enormous equipment box truck immediately blocked the hotel freight entrance. Our film permit didn't include "traffic obstruction," and I could tell we were going to have an issue on whatever narrow Roman street we were supposed to film.

With the giant camera setup for Rome, success hinged on the good action wandering into a rigid and narrow field of view. Which was pretty much the opposite of how the real world worked.

Setting up inside the restaurant—for our first scene, our equipment footprint was so large it took over a third of the dining room—there was no chance of fitting into the background as usual. I was terrified at what Tony would say when he arrived, but not only did he not mind, he seemed impressed.

"Nice lenses, are those rentals or do we own those?" Tony asked, sitting down for a solo meal to camera. "Apparently we blew out our equipment budget for the entire year." He smiled at the camera proudly. "Wow, look at the size of that fuckin' tripod. Are we blocking the bathrooms? We're terrible people. No one in this restaurant can pee without going through us."

The restaurant owner brought out some raviolis, which Tony declared delicious. "I wanna die here already, and I might yet," he said, enjoying himself very much.

Total Murphy's law. Whenever I was at my wit's end, Tony would show up chipper as a Girl Scout selling cookies.

FOURTH DAY OF FILMING IN Rome was a big one, our first scene with Asia. Tony came to location early and was looking nervous. Asia arrived exactly on time and gracefully exited from the rear of a chauffeured Mercedes in what looked like a slow-motion shot. There was something about Asia that made her feel larger than life. Dressed in all black with a bob of black hair and bright red lipstick, she was stunning, vaguely reminiscent of Greta Garbo.

"Hello, Asia, I'm Tom," I said. "Thank you so much for doing this."

"My pleasure. How goes the shoot?" Asia asked, her voice surprisingly deep and raspy.

"It's been somewhere between a little and a lot hectic," I said. "But Rome is always a good time."

"When everything under the heavens is in chaos, the situation is perfect." Asia smiled.

For the scene she'd chosen a simple Roman family-run restaurant from her childhood located in the ancient part of the city, the sort of place where the customers wear pearls or mustaches and the house nonna prepares fresh fettuccine by hand. We'd been sure to set up early so we were ready to start filming right away. The scene was mostly unremarkable at first, starting off a little rocky, but by the end of the meal Tony and Asia were practically finishing each other's sentences.

"You guys can go wide," Tony said, signaling the meal was over.

"Okay, thank you very much," I said. "After wides you guys are done for the day." Clearly, even I wasn't stupid enough to prod Tony for content today. Turned out the restaurant was too small, and the cameras were too big to fit a lens that could get a wide shot. Fortunately, Tony and Asia continued talking and didn't seem to notice.

"I have reasonable expectations for happiness, I think," Tony said. "Three minutes here or there . . . I mean, I'm sitting there and I think, God, everything is really beautiful, this is a great moment, I'm really going to enjoy it, because it's going to be two or three minutes."

"How about serene?" Asia asked.

"Never," Tony answered. "Happy is one thing, but serene . . . "

"Happy and sad are the same thing," Asia said.

"You know, this really fucking sucks, but when I'm thinking, 'That's a good shot,' I'm happiest when life is kind of like a film . . . "

"You're happy with the illusion, because film is an illusion," Asia said.

"Yeah, I am," Tony said.

"I know, me too, I understand," Asia said. "But then I thought, this is really wrong. This is no way to live, when you're a grown-up. With this illusion. Does that make me bad? What is bad? What is good? Are you a bad person?"

"I don't know," Tony said, thinking. "A bad person is a person who hurts other people, either deliberately, or just because they don't really think about other people, and yeah, that was me for a long time."

"Me too," Asia said.

"I mean, there was a lot of collateral damage," Tony said. "To be my friend was not necessarily going to work out for you."

"Everybody wants to fuck people over," Asia said. "They do, they really do."

"You know, I'm coming around on that," Tony said. "I think, actually, that it's not that. It's the people who act in their perceived self-interest, and I think most people do the best they can, and a lot of times that means they're going to fuck you over. And you know, it's on me if I have unreasonable expectations of people, which I do."

"I do too," Asia said. "From everyone."

After a few more glasses of wine, Tony and Asia walked off together, continuing their conversation. I watched while Zach's camera captured them disappearing into the late afternoon sunlight reflecting off the cobblestones.

I WATCHED ASIA KNOCK BACK another Talisker. We'd put a sizable dent in the bottle by this point, and we were both feeling the effects.

"After we filmed that first scene at my fettuccine place, he brought me to the English cemetery. We sat on the bench by Keats's grave and drank wine and we spoke about our families," Asia said.

Fitting, I thought, that Tony's relationship with Asia both began and ended with death.

"You broke up with him repeatedly," I said. "It crushed him each time that happened . . . I knew him for sixteen years. He felt like he'd finally met someone worthy of him, and it made him cuckoo. It made him crazy."

"Like why? How?" Asia asked.

"Like happy and nice," I said. "He was supposed to be mean. That was his job. But after he met you, he got fucking nice. In retrospect, I should have realized that was a big-ass fucking warning sign that something was really wrong."

"Even before we met, Anthony told me so much about you," Asia said. "He told me you live alone, out of the city in that strange house with all the cats. He wrote this lengthy thing, his admiration and love for you. He told me how you were lonely too and he wanted you to move into his building. He told me things about your craft and your art that maybe he never told you."

"There's no place to say goodbye to him," I said, overcome with emotion and a wave of booze. "If I can't say goodbye, then how am I going to move on?" I asked through tears.

"We're never going to move on or get on with it," Asia said. "There will never be a goodbye to him. I have to live with it. Thirty times a day, everything I see reminds me of him, everything I do relates to him. We will always be like this."

ON THE LAST DAY OF the Rome shoot, we started off with a solo scene. Tony sat at an outdoor café in the Mussolini-built Garbatella neighborhood, constructed in the 1930s in what was then the suburbs of Rome. Originally intended as a fascist design for model living, the ochre middle-class housing flats built around communal gardens were still inhabited by working-class families, many of whom may well have lived there since the neighborhood's inception. There was a sole remaining Roman ruin in the center of the square, where the unassuming café was located: a stump of a pillar with a carving of Romulus and Remus. A mixture of historic Italian and Art Deco architecture, everything seemed both timeless and faded. The locals seemed unaffected by the presence of our cameras. The unassuming location was a perfect fit with our aim to film a scene on the outskirts of the city that reflected the darker side of twentieth-century Roman history.

Tony was quite happy with how the shoot had gone. Even more, it was clear from the beginning that he was in love with Asia.

"All right. A traditional Roman breakfast. There's no dignified way to eat this," Tony said, playfully taking a bite of his bomba, essentially an Italian jelly donut. "Oh, that's going straight to my hips. Oh fuck, that's good. I'm gonna eat the fuck out of this thing . . . I gotta get a real job."

"We're going to the Angry Cousin restaurant after this for crew meal; it's nearby," I said when we wrapped the scene.

"Oh, really? I could use a couple bowls of pasta, maybe some carbonara, a nice bottle of wine," Tony said.

Ever since we filmed at the hole-in-the-wall trattoria years before—when the whole dining room erupted into a fight—the Angry Cousin was my favorite restaurant in the world. Our legacy fixer Sara had introduced us to Mama, Papa, and Margareta (the "angry cousin"), who were all like family. I'd gone back every time I'd been to Rome since we first filmed there for *No Reservations*.

Located in a basement, the restaurant occupied what was once an auto garage in a grand, if faded, Art Deco building. Mama was perpetually perched by the cash register; Papa was frequently napping at his lounge recliner that looked like it belonged in a private residence. The walls were covered with pictures of famous actors and their prize-winning Scottish terrier. The familiar and comforting aroma of tomato ragù accosted the senses as soon as you walked in. Tattered and outdated, the refrigeration unit had fake walnut seventies-era laminate, and the kitchen was the size of a postage stamp. It was utterly lacking in pretense. It felt like stepping into someone's well lived-in home, and I loved it.

The food was good, but it wasn't that. It was the memories. On one of our many previous trips to Rome, Tony, seeing how exhausting the shoots had been, how the travel was starting to grate rather than feel like an opportunity, perhaps sensing I needed a pep talk, took me to the Angry Cousin.

"Tom, you have your whole life ahead of you," he'd said, thunder and lightning crashing outside the window. "Just think, one day—many years from now—you'll come back here as an old man, with so many travels under your belt, and you can tell the story of what happened here and the stories of your life."

Entering the restaurant, massive Roman film crew in tow, the expression on Mama and Papa's faces were of utter surprise to see us again. Mama kissed her rosary and professed, "A cardinal from New York City came to eat here because he saw the show."

All sixteen of us sat down at a large table in the center of the dining room and ordered the usual, carbonara and amatriciana.

"Why are you looking so stressed?" Tony asked. "Don't worry, man, everything's going great. It's gonna be a beautiful show."

Tony was right. Despite the cameras, or perhaps because of them, Rome ended up being an amazing shoot, miraculous, in fact. The episode became a poignant anti-fascist warning against Trump.

"There is the undeniable and obvious fact that this is a love story," Tony would write during the edit. "Given the grim, melancholic, ominous message, this show gives a sense of what could be lost, what is at risk, what and who is threatened by fascism. Faces on the bus, in the park, the patches of grass and flowers SHOULD look magical, enchanted as if from a fable. LOVE IN THE TIME OF FASCISM. It begins and ends that way."

Tony's style was not to offer effusive praise, but when he did, it somehow made the stress and demands of the job feel worthwhile.

"You have painted your masterpiece," Tony said to me when the edit was complete. "It made me cry. Just from how beautiful and awesome it is. Breathtaking. Never been prouder of a show. Thank you for all the work and an incredible job. Really."

I FIGURED BY NOW ASIA and I were both liquored up enough, it was time to go in for the kill. "Everyone thinks he killed himself because of you," I said. "You broke up with Tony. You sent him the pictures of you and that guy from the tabloids two days before he killed himself."

After the internet furor that had exploded against her in the days after Tony's death, she seemed resigned to the accusation. "I saw this guy, he came to Rome. I saw the paparazzi, they took a picture of me hugging him."

"I've seen the pictures. You were doing more than hugging," I said.

"It's true. But this guy was nothing to me. I told Anthony before."

"Nothing you did tarnished the way he thought about you," I said. "These are some of the things I look back on that are signs that I should have seen . . . I think that so many things in his life were like a drug. You were like a drug to him. If somebody overdoses on a drug, do you blame the drug or do you blame the junkie?"

"Both," Asia said, taking another drink. "I didn't break up with him . . . I just got a job on this big TV show, I was so excited . . . I have to live with this . . . but I told him I felt trapped and I didn't like it. Because he was like angry about my job. He asked me to man up and tell him what I wanted. So, I told him, 'My kids come first. My job, second. You are third.' I never said, 'I'm leaving you, I don't want to be with you.' Fuck. I was so happy to start this job. Finally, it was a job for me, it was gonna be really good. But he was really scared that this would somehow take me away from him."

I don't know. What Asia was telling me didn't fully line up with what I knew about Tony's last days from the people who were there. That said, I believed her life had been ruined just like mine. It seemed to me Asia was desperately seeking to absolve herself of guilt—the kind of sorrow, pain, and guilt that eats away at you like a cancer. I knew the feeling. I'd come to Rome for answers, but they weren't the answers I was looking for.

"I want a reason," I said, my fingernails digging deeply into my palm below the tablecloth. "I want you to tell me, you broke up with him, I think you broke up with him."

"There's no fucking reason," Asia said. "I'm sorry."

PART THREE

PART THREE

Chapter Thirteen

THE QUIET AMERICAN

LANDING IN HANOI, I KNEW SHOCKINGLY LITTLE ABOUT WHAT TO EXPECT. At least the surroundings were familiar. Heading into town from the airport, my car was adrift in the usual sea of motorbikes, some carrying well-dressed commuters in suits or high heels, others laden with an impossible cargo, like a mattress or a family of eight, toddler perched on the handlebars.

Ever since Tony's extremely formative first trip to this part of the world back in 2000, Vietnam, more than any other country, had staked a claim on his heart. Ten years later I got to return with him and experienced firsthand how Southeast Asia can ruin you for your old life. Over the years I'd had so many wonderful experiences here: riding on the back of Tony's motorbike, hanging on for dear life as he sped along rural highways in Hoi An, slurping pho at sunrise after a night of Saigon partying, getting lost in the Central Highlands, kayaking in Halong Bay during a torrential downpour. Gin and tonics with Tony on the roof of the Majestic Hotel, feeling like I'd just won the lottery, when Tony asked me, "You're gonna stick around until this train gets to the end of the tracks, right?"

I'd almost forgotten how easy it was to fall in love with this country. From the start, not only had I been captivated by the beauty, but even more I was humbled by how welcomed I felt as an American, given our nations' troubled histories.

Out the window passed larger buildings and an ever-increasing number of new retail shops and neon lights, but also just as many restaurants with those low plastic stools as there'd always been. Since my first trip to Vietnam a decade ago, I'd learned it was one of those rare places with the ability to change as much as it stayed the same. But as far as our shoot was concerned, there was going to be one rather significant difference this time.

It was May 2016, and President Obama was traveling through Asia, solidifying support for the Trans-Pacific Partnership trade deal and, for some reason, taking time out of his busy schedule to have a meal with Tony on camera. I couldn't wrap my head around how or why it was happening or that we'd even passed the background checks. But this was no time to ask questions. Despite all the bewildering shit we'd done over the years, this promised to be the most impressive, insane, wonderful, and terrifying experience yet. That is, if I didn't fuck it up.

The Secret Service had warned that in the interest of security we were to tell absolutely *nobody* about the shoot. Not significant others, not parents, not Vietnamese members of the crew, not even the camera guys. If word leaked, the shoot wouldn't happen. This presented a slight problem, as Vietnam was one of those countries where government minders are supposed to track your every move, and there was a lot that still needed to be figured out and arranged over the next week before the shoot began. Namely, where would we be filming the scene with Tony and President Obama?

The locations I'd proposed had been vetoed by the Secret Service, who offered a counter list of venues, all of which had to be scouted. There were meetings and logistics to work out with the White House media team, and all of it had to be done in secret. Fortunately, Jared, the producer, and I had a believable cover. In addition to the scene with "Eagle 1" (the not-so-discreet code name Tony assigned the president), we still had the rest of the show to figure out.

The first couple days went by without incident. We did all the usual planning, organizing, and scouting. It helped that we were working with our old and trusted friends and fixers Ha and Phi, who had worked with us since my first trip to Vietnam in 2006 as well as every one of the many trips since. It seemed like our government minders, Mr. Lihn and Mr. Tuan, didn't suspect anything. Jared and I had even managed to surreptitiously visit the locations suggested by the Secret Service. Predictably, all of them sucked. When it came to restaurants, local atmosphere and authenticity rarely went hand-in-hand with sprinkler systems, ease of exfiltration, and proximity to a helipad, all required for this particular special guest.

"You don't negotiate with the Secret Service," I said. "We're lucky it's even happening."

"Trust me," Jared said. "When we meet with the White House people today, we need to push back."

Jared and I used to go everywhere together, but he'd stopped traveling on the show years ago after being promoted to an executive office job within the company. I was beyond thankful he'd dusted off his producing hat for this particularly high-profile and complex shoot. We'd both been in our mid-twenties when we started together on *No Reservations* and had shared some pretty transformative experiences along the way. As a result, our relationship was sort of fraternal, and Jared always looked out for me, especially when I was coming apart at the seams. Now that we were in Vietnam, the reality of filming with President Obama was sinking in. I knew it was the pressure getting to me; but I was so deep in the weeds I felt powerless to stop it from clouding my judgment.

"We only got one chance at this," Jared said as we were driving to meet with the White House team. "Think about it. The president, or at least somebody powerful on his team, wants to film a scene with us, because of what we do. So let's do what we do! I know you liked the Bun Cha place as much as I did."

Jared was referring to a local noodle shop we'd scouted the other day. Located in the old part of Hanoi, it was so much more visual and in line with the ethos of the show than the safe and sterile locations where the Secret Service wanted us to film. But who were we to interfere with their judgment? Enough people had been put in harm's way over the years as we pushed boundaries with the show, and I wasn't eager to add the leader of the free world to that list. In fact, it was keeping me up at night. At the same time, I was also terrified of under-delivering with the stakes so high.

"Yes, the Bun Cha restaurant was amazing, but I don't know. The place has gotta be a firetrap. If one of those woks bursts into flame, we'd all be fucked!"

"Pull yourself together," Jared said, shooting me one of his trademark withering stares. "For starters, let's *not* talk about shit that we don't know—like whether or not the restaurant will blow up," Jared said. "Let's talk about what we do know, *like food.*"

"You're right, you're right," I said, trying to calm myself. "But what if the president gets food poisoning because of us?"

"Woah! Pump the brakes!" Jared ordered as we pulled up to the JW Marriott. The high-end hotel was nearly completed but hadn't officially opened yet. Situated atop a hill lording over a neighborhood that had only recently risen from rice paddies, the structure seemed to have been designed with a futuristic "Evil *Star Wars*" theme. The American delegation would be taking over the entirety of the gargantuan property when they arrived the following week, but at the moment it was ghostly desolate.

Even though we'd just stepped out of the car, I was already sweating, but not from the tropical heat and humidity. I put out my cigarette and took a deep breath in an attempt to appear sane to our White House liaisons. It wasn't hard to spot them, as they were the only other people in the cavernous lobby. Nicole and Rachel worked in the Executive Office of the President where—as best I understood—they helped to communicate Obama's message.

It wasn't just that we were filming with the president. Thanks to the years of accumulated stress and overstimulation, my confidence, perspective, and nerves were generally shot. I'd developed some repetitive ticks, and worst of all, I'd started to catch myself talking to myself. Out loud. In public. I really needed a vacation from my vacation.

"We're all really excited about the opportunity to work with you guys," Nicole said as we sat down on a bank of sofas.

"Everyone on our end too!" I said. No sooner had the words come out of my mouth, I realized I'd managed to gaff in the first two seconds of talking. "I don't mean everyone, I-I just mean everyone who's allowed to know about the shoot. I mean *filming*, filming, not shoot . . . I didn't mean to say shoot, and no random extraneous people know about our plans."

A silence descended on the conversation. Despite the lobby being kept at refrigerator temperature, I felt the sweat break out on my forehead. After a pause that felt like it lasted forever, Nicole asked, "Sooo . . . what did you think of the locations the Secret Service suggested?"

"Well . . . frankly, we didn't love them," Jared said, turning to me. I knew this was my cue to mention the Bun Cha restaurant, but I couldn't quite find the words to speak up. So Jared continued, "The Secret Service suggestions didn't exactly have the local vibe we go for."

"Yeah, those spots were a little stuffy," Rachel said. "It's tough. I know one of the big sticking points is the guys prefer a restaurant with a private dining area instead of general seating."

"The big sticking point is a private dining room?" I asked, sensing an opportunity.

"There's this great locals-only bun cha pork noodle soup shop." I took a deep breath and did my best to channel Jared-style confidence. "The restaurant has a separate upstairs overflow room we could take over for the scene."

"That sounds interesting," Nicole said.

"We could fill the other tables with trusted people," I said. As always, Jared's instincts were spot on. There was only one opportunity to get this right, and we owed it to ourselves to film at the best possible location. "So it would be totally safe as long as windows aren't an issue. Is line of sight a problem?"

Both Nicole and Rachel's faces went stone cold. By the way they were staring at me, I could tell I'd said something very, very wrong.

"Line of sight?" Nicole repeated.

"It's just that we don't wanna—" I shut up, seeing Jared flash me his "I didn't come all the way to Vietnam for you to fuck this up now" look.

"What Tom means is that we just want to make sure we don't get in the way of anything you guys do," Jared said, saving me from self-immolation. "The restaurant Tom mentioned is one of the best places for bun cha in Hanoi. We can have lunch there if you like."

After a taxi ride across town through bustling traffic, we arrived at Bún Chả Hương Liên.

Rows of stainless-steel tables jam-packed with hungry locals lined the narrow, tiled dining room. A never-ending procession of trays loaded with bun cha came from the kitchen, along with the savory aroma of grilling pork. The atmosphere was punctuated by an occasional flash-bang, the result of a pyrotechnic wok-related explosion. We ordered a bun cha for each of us and went up the staircase to the overflow rooms.

"Oh, wow," Rachel said, tasting the rice noodle and pork meatball soup. "This is delicious."

"I see what you mean," Nicole said. "The energy here is so much better than the other locations we've been considering."

"According to Ha, who's been fixing our Vietnam episodes for a decade, bun cha is *the* quintessential Hanoi dish," I said. "Eating it on camera is definitely the sort of thing that 'makes the home team proud.'"

"Maybe we should bring the security detail here for lunch?" Rachel suggested to Nicole. "It might be a good way to try to sell it to them."

Nicole and Rachel were sold; now it was up to them to convince the Secret Service. Jared and I were anxious to get back before our government minders realized we were missing, so we agreed to keep each other updated on plans as they fell into place, and we parted ways.

"It was a meeting about noodles," Jared said, once we were safely on the way back to our hotel. "'Shoot,' 'windows,' and 'line of sight' was too much sniper terminology for meeting with White House people. You don't need to be worried about stuff like that. There are plenty of real things for you to worry about."

I was so thankful Jared was here. I decided not to mention it, but I was starting to think I was either on the verge of, or already having, a mental breakdown, and Jared was probably the only thing keeping me from going over the edge. Ugh. This shoot with the president was the absolute most inconvenient time to be going insane.

"You're single-handedly managing to depress everyone at the bar," Jared said later that evening. "I'll buy you another scotch if it'll cheer you up."

"What kind of scotch?" I asked. "And in case I haven't said it, thanks again for coming along. I know how busy you are."

"Are you kidding?" Jared said. "I love being on the road again. This job is too good to be true."

"It's a fucking widow-maker," I said, on the verge of whiskey tears.

"Aww, c'mon! What's happened to you? Where's the Tom who used to take pleasure in regularly outwitting government tourism boards? You *love* your job! How could you not, it's the best job in the world! We've stayed in palaces, hotels built for royalty. We've eaten food made by grandmothers in the favelas in Colombia. And now, somehow we've ended up in Hanoi about to shake the hand of our president . . . ? As long as you don't scare him off . . . "

"Too late, probably," I said, and we both laughed.

Jared was—again—correct. Having him here had brought into focus just how much I'd changed in the last couple years. And not for the better. I needed to reconnect with my old lighthearted self. For the last several years I hadn't been stopping to smell the roses like I used to. Jared was right: it really was the best job in the world.

SEVERAL DAYS LATER NICOLE, RACHEL, and a very serious-looking Secret Service agent named Mitchell came to our hotel for a clandestine poolside meeting. Mitchell was wearing dark aviator sunglasses and a Hawaiian shirt. The whole thing reminded me of some sort of B-movie spy thriller. I was about to say as much when I thought better of it and decided to keep my mouth shut.

"Mitchell is head of the president's detail the day we're filming," Nicole said. "Great news, he's agreed to the bun cha restaurant!"

"Oh my god, that's fantastic!" I practically shouted. "Thank you, thank you!"

"There are some logistics I want to go over," Mitchell said. "You'll have forty-five minutes with the president beginning at seven-thirty p.m. Local Vietnamese authorities will be performing security checks throughout the day and then begin shutting down the area surrounding the restaurant in the early afternoon. So anybody and anything you want there needs to arrive by one p.m."

"Everyone?" I asked.

"Yes," Mitchell said. "Is that a problem?"

"No, no, of course not," I said, swallowing hard. I usually had Tony arrive about ten minutes before we started rolling. I couldn't imagine what it would be like having him there six hours early.

"We do have one very important request," Nicole said. "The upstairs air-conditioning unit is broken; can you have it fixed? We don't want the president sweating on camera."

"Absolutely, of course, no problem," I said. "It's the least we can do."

I was overjoyed. Thank God Jared had pushed to shoot for the stars. That afternoon the crew and Sandy arrived from New York. As executive producer, Sandy didn't get out of the office much, but as far as I could tell, her presence had yet to tip the camera guys off to the fact that something out of the ordinary was underfoot. As far as I knew, they were still thoroughly unaware of our special guest, and I couldn't wait to see the looks on their faces when they found out.

Once everyone settled in and got some rest, we gathered for a meeting.

"So ... I have some news," Sandy said. "Tomorrow evening ... President Obama will be joining Tony for dinner on the show!"

After a minute or two of what looked like jet lag–related non-comprehension and a lot of blinking, Todd was the one to break the silence.

"Aww geez, a lame duck president?" he said.

THE FIRST DAY OF SHOOTS was always a bit bumpy, but this first day was going to be positively Himalayan. We hadn't taken any chances regarding the impending security cordon, so everyone and everything—including Tony—had made it through the restaurant's front door by noon for a 7:30 p.m. scene. But there was plenty of work to do, and I had a feeling time was going to move quickly. The first thing I noticed on arriving upstairs was the temperature.

"Please tell me the air conditioner is working," I said to nobody and everybody at the same time. "Perhaps it's just off at the moment to save energy?"

Somehow, attending to the air conditioner—the sole request from the White House—had slipped through the cracks.

"Oh no, oh no! We need to get a functioning AC unit *immediately*."

"You're not helping, go have a cigarette, I'll take care of this," Jared said.

While Ha and Phi attempted to figure out how to resolve the air-conditioning situation before the entire city around us shut down, Zach, Todd, and I set to work figuring out a seating plan. There were two upstairs dining rooms, each about thirty feet by fifteen feet. We chose the back room for filming, while the other would be used for staging gear and holding people.

Given that it was a pretty small space, there was no way to place light stands in the background without them being in the shot. So Zach decided the best option was to suspend the lights from a concrete support beam on the ceiling, right above the table.

"If the clamps come loose, the whole lighting rig would fall right on the president and Tony," I pointed out.

"It's strong, don't worry," Zach said.

"But what if the Secret Service doesn't agree?" I asked.

"Don't worry," Zach shot back.

"It's less about me personally worrying the lights will collapse and more that when a whole bunch of Secret Service agents rush here right before filming, one of them might have a concern about seven hundred pounds of sharp metal film equipment dangling above the president's head," I said.

I probably would have continued fretting about the death lights Zach was hanging, but I was distracted by two teenagers in flip-flops, carrying a massive box.

"The new air-conditioning unit has arrived," Jared said.

It wasn't the window type, but instead the kind that went on a wall with a big condenser outside. I remember thinking the install-ers looked like they couldn't be more than fifteen as I watched them climb out on the roof with a ladder, still wearing flip-flops. It had started raining, and one of them was clearly going to fall three floors to his death, which would probably mean the shoot with the presi-dent would be canceled. So we made the unpleasant decision to risk the heat and sent the air-conditioner boys home.

"What else could go wrong?" I said, instantly regretting having just jinxed myself. My mind involuntarily ran through a laundry list of worst-case scenarios. What if someone picks up a chopstick and stabs the president through the ear before the Secret Service could do anything? What if Tony only talks about Richard Nixon's obses-sion with cottage cheese? Are we going to get a scene out of this? And is that guy who carries the nuclear football going to be here?

I wasn't the only one stressing out. I noticed Tony was sitting by himself at a table in the corner looking withdrawn and nervous. He was never at his best around famous people, but his expression today was extremely unusual and unpleasant. I went and sat down across the table.

"Everything okay?" I asked.

Tony was deep in thought and barely acknowledged my pres-ence. As we waited in silence, I wondered what was going through his mind. Personally, I didn't feel worthy of the honor. I mean, we were getting paid to be in one of our favorite places on Earth and have dinner with a historic president. The bigness of the moment was frankly overwhelming and intensely humbling. I'd found what I was pretty sure were a couple of expired Valiums in a seldom used pocket of my suitcase, and I'd greedily swallowed them to help get me through the day. Given I wasn't wearing a straitjacket, it would be fair to say they were working.

"Ha, can you join Tony and me?" I asked, figuring a distraction might be helpful. Usually a local was across the table explaining the meal to Tony, but this time *he* was the "local." So to ensure Tony knew what he was talking about, we ordered a couple bowls and Ha explained the dish in detail.

"So you add the rice noodles and pork belly and meatballs to the soup," she said. "Then on top you put the fresh herbs. You can add fresh garlic, chilies, and vinegar as you like. . .Tony, may I ask you, why is this happening?"

"Fuck if I know," Tony said. "Obama only has six months left in office, he must be on his 'I don't give a fuck' tour."

Time, it seemed, was moving rapidly. Sandy made an announcement to the local crew that we were filming with President Obama, but like Ha, I was pretty sure they'd already connected the dots. The camera guys continued to work on the lighting setup while intimidating local security dressed in all black with big German shepherds came through the building sniffing everything. I joined Tony for a smoke on the small balcony and watched the gathering crowd on the street.

"I guess people in the city are starting to figure out the president might be visiting," I said.

"Could you have ever believed this was going to happen?" Tony said. "Not in a million fucking years . . . "

"It's pretty amazing, but I still can't figure it out either . . . " I said. "No offense, of course."

An hour before the president's arrival, the tension began to increase as people from the White House and the Secret Service started showing up. We all got checked with a metal detector wand several times. A very friendly man who seemed to be a dietary specialist checked out the kitchen. The meal was given a thumbs-up, but the president would be advised to stay away from the local greens.

Rachel and Nicole appeared thirty minutes before go time with a group of excited locals selected to fill out the dining room. Everyone was instructed to play it cool when we filmed and pretend they weren't in the same room with the president and a bunch of cameras. A man from the national archive showed up and explained they'd need an audio feed from our cameras for posterity. We ran multiple camera and audio tests, and I went over the plan with everyone several more times as the minutes whizzed by.

In the final sixty seconds before the presidential motorcade arrived, I could feel the energy in the restaurant intensify, almost like a charge of electricity in the air. This must be what a dog feels when it senses an earthquake before it happens, I thought.

"Make sure to get a good picture I can tweet," Tony called as Zach and I squeezed through the crowd of security personnel and bureaucrats on our way downstairs to film an entrance shot. We got into position just in time. Seeing President Obama walk through the restaurant's front door, everyone erupted into applause. He grinned ear to ear, waving back.

I can only describe what I felt as sort of a surreal, even out-of-body experience. It was almost like I wasn't actually there. Ironically, it felt more like I was watching the whole thing on TV.

I stood behind Zach as the president walked right past us with a big smile and a nod. Arrival shot in the can, Zach and I squeezed our way back up the staircase, which was now even more crowded with people. Zach got through first, then just as I reached the top of the stairs, the president moved through the narrow hallway landing from the holding room to the camera room. As I learned, when the president is on the move there's no time to say, "Please stand back." The Secret Service just pushes you out of the way. I started to fall backward down the stairs, but fortunately, in addition to pushers, they also have catchers.

I arrived in the dining room unharmed, and it was decided I would be the one to put the microphone on the president. He was relaxed, friendly, and kind enough to not mention anything about my trembling hands. In the dining room were fifteen local Vietnamese in the background filling the tables, Tony sitting with President Obama, the three cameras, and me, standing just next to the table. Jared was by the door next to the president's head Secret Service guy. The official White House photographer came in a few times to snap some pics. And that was it. The experience was unbelievably intimate.

The cameras were rolling; it was go time. I signaled to Jared who sent in the waitress. She placed white rice noodles, greens, fried pork rolls, two steaming bowls of broth, and two beers on the table.

"I feel a little awkward sitting in front of all this good food with you guys standing there working. Did you get something to eat?" President Obama asked before starting the scene. He was one of the few people in the thousands we'd filmed who inquired if the crew was hungry.

"Grab a spoon and chopsticks, hack off some noodles," Tony said, demonstrating. "Chilies to taste."

"That's good stuff," President Obama said, taking a bite of the bun cha.

Tony had done a good job of explaining the dish and how to eat it, though he was talking a little fast and laughing a bit too much anytime he thought a joke was being made—but I don't think that anyone other than Zach, Todd, and I knew him well enough to tell.

"Now if you were still running for office, enjoying this dish might be seen as a liability," Tony said with a chuckle. "I mean we live in a world where even enjoying arugula is apparently problematic. How did we reach this point in history? There's a fear, you can feel it, towards the other. Whoever they might be. How do we change that?"

"Well, first of all, I think it's important to recognize that America has always been of mixed minds about the outside world," President Obama said. "On one hand we're a nation of immigrants, and that's not going to change. That's one side of America. And another part of America is that we've been so big, we haven't always had to pay a lot of attention outside our borders. And so, we'll go through periods of time where anti-immigrant sentiment rears up or xenophobia. A lot of times it happens when people are feeling stressed. It is easy for people sometimes, for politicians at least, to use immigrants or foreigners as a scapegoat as opposed to talking about how we work through this together. Now, the good news is overall I think America is more tolerant, more mindful of the world than it's ever been, particularly the younger generation. So overall I tend to be optimistic . . . "

"I used to have a pretty dim view of humanity," Tony said. "But since I started traveling—particularly to places where I anticipated being treated badly—I am on balance pretty convinced that generally speaking the human race are doing the best they can to be as good as they can, under the circumstances, whatever they may be. I guess my hope is the more people see of the world, in person hopefully, or even on television, they see ordinary people doing ordinary things, so when news happens at least they have a better idea of who we're talking about. Put a face to some empathy, to some kinship, to some understanding. This surely is a good thing. I hope it's a useful thing."

"And this is why a show like yours is terrific," the president said. "Because it reminds people that actually there's a whole bunch of the world that on a daily basis is going about its business, eating at restaurants, taking their kids to school, trying to make ends meet, playing games. The same way we are back home."

I'd been worried Tony would choke and totally flub the interview, but it appeared Tony had, in fact, known what he was doing. It was actually so beautifully simple. Just two dads hanging out, having some noodles and a beer in Vietnam.

"As a father of a young girl, is it all gonna be okay? It's all gonna work out?" Tony asked. "My daughter will be able to come here. In five years, ten years, twenty years, she'll be able to have a bowl of bun cha and the world will be a better place?"

"I think progress is not a straight line. You know?" President Obama said. "There are gonna be moments at any given part of the world where things are terrible. Where tragedy and cruelty are happening. Where our darkest impulses pop up. I think there are going to be some big issues our children are going to have to address, because we didn't address them. But, having said all that, I think things are gonna work out. I think the world's a big place, and I believe that people are basically good. I think humanity is still in its awkward adolescent phase, but it's slowly maturing, and if we get a few big things right, I think we'll be all right."

Then all of a sudden it was over. We took a group photo, the president left, and his entourage began to disappear. The dietary specialist handed everyone a box of White House–branded M&Ms. Tony tweeted the picture I took, writing, "Total cost of bun cha dinner with the President: $6.00. I picked up the check. #Hanoi." I chuckled at that. Regardless of how you did the accounting, the meal had cost far more than six dollars. When you think about the production costs to cover crew, things like equipment, airfare, lodging, not to mention the fee for commandeering a restaurant. There was the money expended by the Vietnamese government in security personnel required to lock down a quadrant of Hanoi. Then of course there was the Secret Service and presidential entourage followed by the press pool of at least seventy, the jet fuel to move everyone and the motorcade, all the salaries plus the cost to rent the JW Marriott. I'm guessing the cost of that meal could easily have surpassed the annual GDP of a small nation, and now, having survived the experience, as far as I was concerned, it was worth every penny.

Chapter Fourteen

PLAYING WITH MY FOOD

IT'S BEEN SAID TONY USED FOOD AS A PASSPORT, AND WE DID. FOOD was a fantastic device, our way into a culture. Sharing a meal put people at ease, helped them forget the cameras were there, and inspired them to open up about their lives. Most importantly, food had become our cover, at least as far as I was concerned. In Iran and Laos, it was actually thought we were CIA like in the movie *Argo*. And in certain ways they were right. If it wasn't for the cover of a "food show," we never would have been able to get to the places we did. Season after season while planning the shoots, food had morphed from the show's *raison d'être* to almost an afterthought. By the end, it was a show about people far more than one about food.

"Did you eat the food? Was it good?" was something I'd been asked a lot. W. C. Fields famously said, "Never work with children or animals." He forgot to mention food. To be honest, I wasn't in it for the food. I always wanted everything to be perfect, and food was a difficult and highly perishable resource to work with. Despite constantly trying to keep all the plates spinning, over the years I experienced just about every possible food catastrophe imaginable.

Usually cramped, bustling, and extremely loud, restaurants were a difficult place to film. After promising we'd be "low impact" to business, the production would inevitably take over, much to the owner's horror. Whatever spot our DPs chose was sure to block the path from the kitchen or to the bathroom. Hitting a lunch or dinner rush so the establishment looked full was perpetually challenging. "Picture food" was either ready too soon or took forever, and Tony delivered all the good content over an empty table. Sometimes the sidekick was nervous and didn't eat at all, which looked awkward. Not to mention the sanitary standards I'd witnessed, which gave my already germaphobic imagination plenty to dwell on.

And it wasn't just the food on camera. All the food off camera was a disaster too. Feeding the crew was surprisingly hard. We often ate where we filmed the scene, but for a host of reasons that wasn't always possible. Probably because we ate at off-peak hours, the restaurant designated for crew meal would be overwhelmed by fifteen to twenty different orders, and the food would take two hours to arrive. The shooting schedule could barely even afford the one hour allotted for the break. The solution was to pre-order from a deli-type place, but, understandably, the crew didn't appreciate warm mayonnaise. Tony endlessly ridiculed the crew for eating "sawdust energy bars" and rancid sandwiches.

"I just don't understand cameramen. They load up at the hotel buffet, or I catch them eating those cardboard granola bars before coming to shoot an amazing meal like this. If they could just wait a little longer, then they'd enjoy one of the best meals of their lives," he'd say.

The reality was, by the time we were done filming the food, there often wouldn't be time to eat, or sometimes even any food left. The irony of going hungry on a food show was a recurring joke. I remember the crew eating van-temperature sandwiches out back by the dumpsters at several of the world's best restaurants.

I'm talking about the four-hour, twenty-five-course, several-thousand-dollar-plus per meal sort of places. Customers at these restaurants might wait months or even years to get a reservation. Others, possessing household names, dropped in by helicopter and snagged a table at the last minute. Well-heeled captains of industry, celebrities, hard-core epicureans, bucket listers . . . and me.

The kitchens in these restaurants were something to behold. Usually with an international collection of extremely talented and obsessively driven young chefs, there were often more people working in the kitchen than could be seated in the dining room. When you did the math, at restaurants like El Bulli or Noma, it wasn't too far-fetched to imagine your appetizer took a combined twenty man-hours to prepare.

As much as they did their best to remain "down to earth," there was an undeniable cult of personality surrounding whichever chef helmed one of these culinary cathedrals. Let's just say that calling the seven hours we would spend at a place like this a staggeringly extraordinary and intimidating experience would be a serious understatement. When we filmed at Noma in 2013, which had been awarded "World's Best Restaurant" three years in a row, chef René Redzepi created a customized menu just for Tony. Each ingredient was locally sourced or foraged and meticulously prepared.

BOURDAIN MENU

SNACKS:

- *Nordic coconut and flowers*
- *Blackcurrant berry with roses*
- *Reindeer moss and dried mushroom*
- *Edible branch with pine shoots*
- *Fresh peas and chamomile*
- *Cod liver and milk crisp*
- *Hay-smoked quail egg*
- *Aebleskiver*
- *Sorrel leaf*
- *Urchin toast and stock film*
- *Leek and cod roe*
- *Pike head and beach herbs*

MENU:

- ❧ *Shrimp, wild garlic, and rhubarb*
- ❧ *Onion and preserved pear*
- ❧ *Lobster tail, head sauce, and nasturtium leaves*
- ❧ *Lobster claw broth and nasturtium petals*
- ❧ *Asparagus and pine*
- ❧ *Potato and caviar*
- ❧ *Turbot and greens*
- ❧ *Pickles*
- ❧ *Blueberry and ants*
- ❧ *Bitters and woodsorrel*
- ❧ *Yeast and skyr*
- ❧ *Red seaweed danish*
- ❧ *Pork skin and dried berries*

While this is the sort of meal that people would—and have—gone to extraordinary lengths to partake in, I didn't mind not getting to try it. Somewhere along the line the food—regardless of what it was—had been too closely associated with the stress of the job, and usually, by the end of the shoot day, I'd lost my appetite.

Other members of the crew were not so afflicted. In fact, Josh was known to eat the things that even Tony refused to eat. That Tony was the guy who "ate all the weird stuff" was a misunderstanding that plagued him to the end. A good deal of this undeserved reputation can be traced back to a mistake he made on his first trip to Vietnam in 2000. Back then, before he'd got his sea legs, so to speak, he was much more suggestible, and was persuaded to eat the beating heart of a cobra on camera.

If Tony sniffed out that the producers were adding a scene or dish for the "shock value," he'd cancel it instantly. That said, Tony would eat nearly anything, but because he wanted to be a good guest. If the locals enjoyed it, he'd eat it—rotten fermenting shark meat, bull penis stew. If a diseased zoo animal, for example, was the local specialty offered to guests, it was an honor Tony couldn't refuse. He did always say he'd draw the line at eating dog. Fortunately, it never came up.

Tony never claimed to be an expert when it came to the food, despite his many years as a chef. There were a few particularly humorous examples of when he got it wrong. On *The Layover* Hong Kong episode, we stopped off for a last scene on the way to the airport. The restaurant supposedly served the best Peking duck in the city. It was a solo scene, and Tony raved on and on about how this was the best Peking duck he'd ever had. Just as we were about to finish, I got a tap on my shoulder.

"I've just been informed there was a mix-up in the kitchen," China Matt, our fixer, said, a distressed look on his face. "Tony's been eating suckling pig."

Thinking there might be some time to save the scene, I interrupted Tony, letting him know the Peking duck he'd been raving about wasn't actually Peking duck.

"Well . . . this is awkward," Tony said, putting down his chopsticks.

There was another time Tony kept raving about the pepper crab.

"Oh my god, this pepper crab is fantastic. The pepper sauce is so rich and nuanced, it's unbelievable," Tony said.

"Oh yeah! It is really good pepper crab," the sidekick said in agreement.

After Tony left and we went to the kitchen to film the food prep, the chef looked puzzled, explaining, "We don't have pepper crab. We don't have pepper anything."

Confused, I went to talk to the sidekick. As a local, he couldn't have also been mistaken about the pepper crab.

"Tony's the food expert," the sidekick said. "I thought I just couldn't taste the pepper."

BEING SICK WHILE TRAVELING IS never fun. But it's a lot worse when you're not able to sleep it off. We didn't do sick days and were always out in the loud, crazy, chaotic world and sweltering heat, constantly in the presence of food smells, kitchens, restaurants, and aromas.

After a scene in Haiti, everyone was eating, talking, and Tony was watching Todd. Halfway through the meal Tony said, "I guess you weren't paying attention during the scene *you* just filmed, Todd. Or you would have known a garden salad isn't the wisest dining choice in the middle of a *fucking cholera epidemic*."

Connecting the dots, though a little late, Todd rushed from the table to induce vomiting.

"It's okay, don't worry. I took three Cipros," Todd said when he returned to the table.

"I regret to inform you, Todd, that's not how it works," our medic said, shaking his head. "You may have just made yourself immune to Cipro."

We spent enough time out in the real world when the cameras were rolling, so when we shared a meal with Tony it was often at the hotel. He always enjoyed studying the crew's menu selections, then analyzing the choice. Spaghetti bolognese was the smart option. Hotel food was always more likely to get you than the local stuff. "Spag bowl," as Tony called it, was on every menu, hard to mess up regardless of location and unlikely to make you ill. Tony lived for the times the crew made amateur ordering mistakes. Offhand, here are a few of his favorites. There was a seafood medley in Iraq, a Caesar salad in Medellín, late-night gyros in Granada, gas station sandwiches in Ireland, Bob's Jungle Burger in the Amazon, and of course the time one of the producers ordered Louisiana-style jambalaya at the hotel in Namibia.

"Mark the time," Tony said, halfway through the meal. He went on to explain how in Namibia seafood jambalaya was an extremely poor menu choice, pointing out how far each of the ingredients had traveled to get to this landlocked central African country, and how long they'd likely been sitting in the back of the freezer, as jambalaya probably wasn't ordered often, and how it only took a single bad mussel or clam to shut you closed like a book. And then Tony would go on to remind you about the sanitary conditions of the kitchen, the statistical likelihood that at least one of the people who'd handled any single ingredient somewhere along the line hadn't bothered to wash their hands after coming back from taking a steaming dump. Then he'd explain in medical detail the types of bacteria and parasites likely to already be attacking you from the inside, and how—looking again at his watch—about three hours from now you were all but guaranteed to be shitting and vomiting at the same time.

Even if the food wasn't contaminated, Tony's monologue was enough to give almost anyone a bad case of psychosomatic food poisoning. Tony loved retelling these poor-food-choice stories time and time again during crew meals, and even during his speaking engagements in front of an audience.

But Tony wasn't immune to getting sick. The warthog anus in Namibia got him bad. Fortunately, his hotel had two bathrooms. As he explained it, he spent the whole night getting up every fifteen minutes to vomit furiously into one toilet then run across the room and shit in the other one. It was the only time I knew of when he'd actually been convinced to go see the doctor after returning to New York.

Tony got sick both times we went to Sri Lanka, and he came down with a particularly nasty stomach bug in Manila, likely from a fried tripe bar snack, and had to call out sick for a day.

"I was up most of the night experiencing chills and dementia, projectile vomiting bile and reptile parts, so we'll need to cancel the street food scene," he said.

I didn't get sick often, mostly thanks to my policy of not eating much. On the rare occasion it did happen, I did my best to keep it a secret—and usually succeeded—like in Toronto when I nearly blew the scene throwing up out back by the dumpster.

Tony only caught me sick one time. It was Sri Lanka, and I'd started feeling ill the day we took a train ride south down the coast. I repeatedly threw up in the train toilet, which was really just a hole in the floor. I continually ran back and forth between directing the scene and the toilet to barf. But I'd managed to keep it a secret from Tony.

By the end of the shoot, I was starving and feeling weak. When we finally made it to the airport lounge, I was about to collapse from low blood sugar. I saw some pizza underneath a warming light. Yes, I should've known better, it probably had been sitting there for a long time, and yes, it had some shriveled chicken looking thing on top. But my biggest mistake was allowing Tony to see me eat it. It didn't take long before I started to feel incredibly nauseated. Of course, not wanting Tony to see that I was ill, I calmly got up and headed toward the bathroom. As soon as I was out of sight, I started running down a maze-like series of hallways and made it just in time to projectile vomit into the toilet. Everything in my stomach forcibly ejected, I washed up and headed back to the group.

"Tom, feeling okay?" Tony asked, looking up from his iPad with a huge smile on his face.

"Fine, of course, why?" I said, reflexively wiping my mouth.

"Just checking," he replied.

Jared explained to me afterward that everyone could hear me vomiting, presumably through the ductwork. Tony brought up that cautionary tale for years to come. Despite all my hard work, I'd finally been added to his list of shame. Eventually I determined that not eating around Tony was the best solution.

Years ago I'd been scouting a high-end restaurant in Barcelona— the kind with obsessive waiter service where they were constantly at the table introducing and explaining each dish as it arrives. It can get distracting if you'd intended to have any conversation with your dining companion. To be fair, it was a molecular gastronomy–type tapas restaurant, so the food required a bit of an instruction manual. However, my opinion about the interruptions changed when Alejandro came to the table. He was extremely handsome and— unusual for me—we flirted a bit. He asked how I liked Barcelona, and I mentioned how much fun the nightlife was. Turned out Alejandro was of the same opinion and offered to show me a great spot, and we exchanged numbers. Score!

"Look, Tom, jamón de toro," said Lucy, our Spain fixer, pointing to the menu. "I bet you'll love it. What a perfect way to help you with your fish problem."

I didn't like peer pressure, especially when it came to fish, but maybe Lucy was right. She had been our fixer in Spain for years and was a food expert. The "jamón de toro" was actually tuna but supposedly tasted like ham. Tuna was the most vanilla of fishes, and I love ham, so I thought, why not? I'll give it a try! I'd gone out of my comfort zone and got a phone number as a result; I was on a winning streak. The more I thought about it, the more I decided Lucy *was* right, I'd been too much a prisoner of my phobias for far too long. Hey, who knew, I might end up liking it! Alejandro arrived and made a show of presenting the tapa.

"This is the jamón de toro," he said enthusiastically. "It is made of house-salted tuna belly painted with Iberian cured ham fat. *¡Que aproveche!*"

I waited for Alejandro to leave before trying the dish, just in case I didn't like it. It looked just like jamón. I hadn't eaten fish since 1984, but hey, this was going to be fine. I could do this. I took a deep breath. But after one bite I started heaving. It was a textural thing. I tried as hard as I could to stop the gag reflex, but I couldn't. I grabbed my napkin and threw up. Unfortunately, not only the jamón de toro came up, but everything else I'd eaten—just as Alejandro returned to the table with the next tapa. Alejandro and I never made it to that club.

WHENEVER POSSIBLE, WE'D FILM THE animal from alive to table, which usually meant me calling in a hit on a cute little fuzzy thing and then getting to meet it before the slaughter. In these admittedly uncomfortable situations, I tried to console myself with the knowledge that it's a part of life, and whatever animal we were offing was treated with infinitely more respect than factory-farmed livestock. I remember a darling fluffy little sheep tied to the bed of a pickup in Crete. She stood there meekly blinking at me. Despite sounding tough, Tony didn't like this part either. So of course, he came over, affectionately named her "Socks," and bleated, *"Why me-eeee, Tom?"* in mock sheep falsetto. I would hide behind the camera. Their death was for the camera's consumption, not mine. And if preparation took too long between slaughter and table, sometimes I'd have to order two.

There were also a few unfortunate instances where Tony's motto "Eat what the locals eat" resulted in us inadvertently consuming what turned out to be an endangered species.

"Well, Tom, in addition to the Romania scandal, now there's the 'mouse-deer incident,'" Tony said.

"Okay, well, I feel really bad about that," I said. "But who even knew the lesser Java mouse-deer was endangered?"

"Oh, let me think . . . Maybe the World Wildlife Fund, most responsible citizens, PETA, the Vietnamese government, the animal poachers who sold it to you, the sponsors pulling their ads, and the authors of that article accusing me of 'promoting the delicacy of endangered wildlife,'" Tony said. "Would you like me to go on?"

I'm not sure, but I think we might have been responsible for consuming the last giant Mekong catfish, and Tony didn't even like catfish. I'd once rescued a monitor lizard from a food market in Malaysia, intending to release it at the snake temple, where it would be safe. We all forgot, and it expired in the baking hot van. But I'm probably most haunted by my Portuguese rabbits Hip and Hop.

"I bought you a fish. His name is Pepe," Tony said, thrusting a lifeless sardine in my face.

"I don't want it," I said, recoiling.

"C'mon, you can adopt him and release him into the ocean. Or feed him to your bunnies?" Turning to the camera, Tony said, "Tom our producer bought six bunnies yesterday, to 'free them into the wild.'"

"Not funny," I said.

"*Lunch*," Tony fake-coughed.

First of all, it was two bunnies, not six. Second, I was the director, not the producer.

By the winter of 2017, having the best job in the world had left me resembling what can only be described as a complete and utter train wreck. My dating life was frequently on the rocks and my best friend, the black cat Frida—renamed "Mr. Whiskers" by Tony—was having kidney trouble and had been diagnosed with a heart condition. Lonely, nerves shot, and probably clinically depressed, I was so emotionally raw on the flight to Portugal that the part of the in-flight safety video with the child and oxygen mask caused me to sob uncontrollably, alarming nearby passengers. For way too long I had been eating, sleeping, breathing, and—increasingly over the years—drinking the job.

First day of filming we'd scheduled a typical pig feast scene, which of course meant we had to shoot the animal being killed, bled, scalded, scraped, skinned, eviscerated, butchered, cooked, and whatever else it was Todd filmed for a living. I looked into Piggy's eyes before the slaughter, knowing it wasn't too late. I could untie his rope and we could run off together. Knowing I had the power to grant him a stay of execution, and knowing that I wasn't going to do it—that Piggy, like so many innocents before him, was going to die because I had chosen it to be so—well, it was as difficult as it was irrational. I felt like I was teetering on the verge of a very public mental breakdown.

Adding to the malaise, rather than getting a production tan in our usual tropical February destination, I was shivering in northern Portugal. Seven cold, rainy days later I was barely hanging on by a damp, slippery thread. We were filming at Porto's historic Mercado do Bolhão, and I needed a break from the shouting and cameras and the butcher smells.

Wandering down a cobblestone alley near the back of the market, I came across a stall selling small livestock; it could have doubled as a pet store back in New York. Inside was a cage containing two of the most adorable little floppy-eared rabbits I'd ever seen! *Ever.* They were contentedly snuggled together like yin and yang. Possessing neither local currency nor fluency, I rushed back to our fixer Carla, and demanded she buy my rabbits immediately. Carla laughed, thinking it was a joke, and I burst into tears.

"You don't understand. If I can just save these two little rabbits, it might help make up for all my past sins! They can live on José's farm!" Carla wasn't laughing anymore, and I could tell by the look in her eyes she was worried I might climb one of the city's famous clock towers and start shooting. That afternoon we were headed to a beautiful farm in the Douro Valley; it was the perfect place for my rabbits to retire.

"My bunny hops over the ocean, my bunny hops over the sea . . . Bring back, bring back, oh bring back my bunny to me, to me," I sang while feeding them fresh lettuce and carrots.

"Jeez, Tom-o, are you cracking up?" Zach asked. I narrowed my eyes and glared at rabbit-hating Zach for a moment before deciding to pretend he didn't exist. I named the dark gray bunny Hip and the brown bunny Hop. I loved it when they wrinkled their noses. Arriving, we linked up with Todd, who was already at the farm, and I gave the cameras a list of things to film. Then I went back to the van and turned my attention to Hip and Hop. After an emotional goodbye, I reluctantly handed them over to a husband and wife who worked on the farm, along with strict instruction that, as a personal favor, my rabbits were to be well taken care of.

Feeling just better enough about the world to soldier on, I uncorked a wine bottle from one of the cases in the gear van and surveyed the dramatic sloping vineyard. It was a stunning view; Hip and Hop were going to be so happy at their new home. I actually felt a bit better about myself, the world, and the job. Later, with filming wrapped up, the cameramen returned for crew meal. I chose to remain outside, at peace in the quiet with my bottle.

When it was time to head back to Porto, I climbed in the van with Todd.

"Did you get good stuff today?" I asked.

"Yeah, but we missed you at lunch," Todd said.

"Oh? What did they make for you?" I asked, completely uninterested. "More tripe?"

"No," Todd said. "Rabbit stew."

IT WASN'T ALL BAD; SOME meals are just special—not necessarily because of what you're eating, but who you're eating with, and in what context. These sorts of meals don't come along that often, but when they do, you remember them for the rest of your life.

Our 2010 Naples shoot was a charmed trip, full of big char-acters, good times, great food, and beautiful scenery. It was also a family show. My dad, Zach's dad, and Tony's family came along for the trip, and Naples was turning out to be one of the most fun places I'd visited.

"You might experience Rome, but Naples experiences you," Tony said. "It's a city of people who drive against traffic, or *contro-senso*, which is a metaphor for how they live."

Narrow cobblestone streets were a free-for-all, crowded with shops, people, speeding scooters, and small cars fighting their way through. Drying laundry hung from every balcony, making Naples reminiscent of photographs from the early 1900s New York City Lower East Side. On many street corners, mountains of uncollected trash piled up, the result of a Mafia garbage strike. Catholic proces-sions weaved through the streets, barefoot performers clad in white playing music in the lead-up to Easter.

Any time we filmed in Italy, Tony insisted we include a nonna. We had one all lined up, but due to an illness in the family, our granny canceled, leaving sixteen hours to find a replacement. This sort of scene collapse had been typical of the shoot thus far. Naples was a tough location, but we all rolled with the punches. Every night around eleven p.m. the next day's scenes would somehow inevitably disintegrate. But in typical Neapolitan style, plan B magically ended up better than the original.

Josh and I were discussing the nonna cancelation issue with Emanuela and Lucio, our fixers, when Rosario, Tony's driver, overheard.

"I can solve your problem," he said excitedly. "My mother, she is the best cook in all of Napoli!"

Actually, if Rosario's mom was anything like her son, personality-wise at least, I could imagine she'd make for some interesting television. Rosario was forty-five, lived at home with his mother, worked the pedals of his BMW like Mario Andretti on the track, and could cut any travel time in half. He was short, bald, wore a leather jacket, and had all the southern Italian swagger you expect from a good Neapolitan mama's boy.

"Let's do it!" I said, since we didn't have alternative options anyway.

The next morning, we met the force of nature that was Rosario's mother. Nonna Giuseppina was a feisty eighty-year-old, chain-smoking grandmother with hair dyed jet black. Four and a half feet tall, incredibly animated, as well as opinionated, she possessed a powerful, high-pitched, gravelly voice.

"Perfect," I said. "Tony will love her."

Tony frequently said that his great sadness in life was that he wasn't born into a big Italian family. Maybe he recognized something fundamentally Italian in himself—using food as the ultimate expression of love, or as the ultimate weapon; anyone who has had the privilege of enduring a full family-style Italian meal knows that you are fed until the point of pain.

Rosario and Giuseppina lived in a fourth-floor walk-up in an apartment building in Centro Storico. Mother of seven, Giuseppina kissed her dead husband's picture each time she walked past. Giuseppina wore a blue patterned smock and smoked while cooking. She was making her famous Sunday ragout. She'd browned pork sausage, veal, pork ribs, and braciole, and had been stewing them for hours with tomato sauce. I watched in awe as Giuseppina somehow managed to be everywhere at once. She was tough, and even though she didn't speak a word of English, it didn't stop her from talking to us like we could understand. When Tony arrived, Giuseppina took the roses he brought, then put him straight to work.

"She is cooked for you, so you have to cook for her," Emanuela translated. The cameras had trouble keeping six-foot-four Tony and four-foot-six Giuseppina in the same shot. Tony loved that Giuseppina had the mouth of a sailor, and he didn't mind her occasional scolding of *"Nah, nah, nah, nah!"* when he'd done something wrong.

When the ragout was done, we filmed a wonderful and boisterous family meal.

"Your mother would be a TV star in America," Tony said to Rosario.

After we wrapped the cameras, the crew sat down around the dining room table to eat together. The ragout was fantastic, and the secondi tender after stewing for so long. Tony stayed the whole evening and even had a second helping. But it wasn't just the fantastic meal. In a way that I'm not sure ever happened before or since, I *really* felt like we were all one big extended family sharing this Sunday meal. The fixers, Josh, Mo, Zach and his dad, my dad, Tony, and of course our hosts. Nonna Giuseppina smoked, told dirty jokes, and kept the whole table doubled over laughing. Seeing how much my dad was enjoying himself, and how proud he was of me, brought tears to my eyes. At the end of the evening, Giuseppina came around and kissed everyone on the forehead as she poured us each a glass of amaro. It was an evening I won't soon forget.

A GLASS OF AMARO AT the end of a meal embodies the Italian point of view on life: You can't fully appreciate the sweet without a taste of the bitter. No meal is complete without it. The day after filming with Nonna Giuseppina, we went to Cetera, an old fishing village south of Naples. Leading down to the beach, narrow shops lined the street, where vendors were selling colorful fruits, vegetables, and meats—a picture-perfect Mediterranean postcard. Tony had been in good spirits all week, but today—in contrast to his gray sweater, black leather jacket, and black Persols—his mood was especially brilliant.

With a bottle of amaro, snifter glass, three cameras, and four producers in tow, Tony walked across the pebble beach and sat on the gunnel of a bright turquoise-and-red-striped fishing boat. It was one of those overcast days that did something strange to the light, amplifying rather than muting color. Clouds obscuring the sunset glowed an almost cotton candy pink and reflected off the shore.

"Into the sweet life where everything is beautiful and shiny and colorful and wonderful . . . a little something bitter," Tony said, taking a sip of his amaro while looking out over the teal blue Tyrrhenian. "Oh, that's good. This is ridiculously beautiful. Isn't it?"

Amaro is just as much a philosophy as it is a digestive, and we had a tradition of ending our Italy episodes with Tony enjoying a glass.

"Once again, life doesn't suck. If you really think about it, the fact that I'm here, and enjoying this, pretty much proves there is no God," Tony said. "Okay. I think we got some peppy commentary there. Cameras down, I'm done."

"But wait! Why *are* we here?" I said, tweaking because Tony was done filming when we'd only just started.

"That's like a season one *Cook's Tour* question," Tony said. "Why are we here on the Amalfi Coast? Why am I here in this idyllic town? In this most magnificent country in the world? Drinking amaro on the beach? Why the fuck wouldn't I? How could you ask me that?"

"That's answering with a negative," I said, blindly grasping at any way to draw out my filming minutes. "Could you try and answer with a positive?"

"So, Tom, step on in, let's get a podcast," Tony said, turning the tables around on me. "Let's face it, you are the gold standard of *No Reservations* producer-directors; what tips can you give to hopeful young film students who would like to be like you?"

The cameras pivoted and focused on me as I froze like a deer in the headlights. There were few things I disliked more than being on camera. The footage was thoroughly unusable for the episode, and I was only comfortable hidden behind the fourth wall.

"Can't we just talk about the beauty of the Amalfi Coast instead?" I asked, trying to back out of Tony's shot, but he caught me and wrapped his arm around my shoulder.

"What exactly were your hopes and dreams for this scene?" Tony asked.

"I thought, you know, we would set up why we came to Southern Italy," I said. "Cuz you have some pretty strong views on the subject."

"What kind of sick freak would not . . . I mean, look at this place . . . do you really have to ask . . . ? Do you think any viewers will wonder, 'Gee, why is Tony here in one of the most beautiful places on earth? Eating this amazing food?' Do you think this is something that people struggle with?"

"Well, I, umm," I stammered.

"What do you see in that lens, man? How could it all have become so twisted and distorted?" Tony asked. "Come on, Tom. Stop and smell the roses for once in your life! This is a good gig, right? This is what you need to understand, this is the secret in that tiny, tiny little ninth chamber . . . " Tony drew out the reveal for dramatic emphasis. "The secret is it's really not about the show. It's about having a *goooood* fucking time. So relax! Let's enjoy some downtime for a change. Your dad's here. Zach's dad is here. My family is here."

"You're absolutely right. It's a family show," I said. "It's a good time, thank you."

"Look, right over there, a nice bottle of amaro, we can drain that fucker, then let's go out for some gelato," Tony said.

"Oh, totally!" I said. "Can we film it?"

Chapter Fifteen

POLITE DINNER
CONVERSATION

IT HAD BEEN ALMOST YEAR SINCE TONY'S SUICIDE, AND AS MUCH AS I tried, no amount of blaming, alcohol, or running away could spare me from some difficult realizations. Everything I held true was starting to feel like it had been either a lie or a mistake. I'd considered Tony a role model pretty much my entire adult life. I'd thought he had it all figured out. Here was someone else with a similar appetite for trouble, a certain degree of social awkwardness, brave and smart enough to disregard all sensible advice and march to the beat of his own drum. I had looked at Tony, his triumphs, and my place in his band of misfits as proof I was on the right track. Knowing now where Tony's path had ultimately led, I was left to question the wisdom of my own choices.

Whether out of strength or resentment I don't know, but I resolved not to repeat Tony's mistakes. I owed it to myself to at least try and put the pieces of my life back together. Being at what was easily the lowest point of my life, I didn't really have anywhere to go but up. I'd been using alcohol to numb the pain, and for a while it worked. Until it didn't. So the choice to stop drinking cold turkey was an easy one. I started seeing a therapist. I liked her. As far as psychiatrists went, anyway. Most of the time I talked about Tony. I was still afraid if I talked about Tony too much, she would think I was crazy.

On the one-year anniversary of Tony's death, Todd hosted a small get-together at his house in Brooklyn. Josh, who'd moved to Los Angeles with his wife and two kids, flew in for the occasion. Everyone gathered around the piano, Josh at the keys, singing Bowie's "Oh You Pretty Things." I stood back watching, more comfortable at a slight remove. Todd picked up his guitar and took over the musical entertainment, which offered Josh and me the opportunity to catch up. The conversation, of course, gravitated toward Tony.

"You know, our jobs were to try to think like Tony," Josh said. "And he had great taste, so most of the shit he liked, I ended up liking. So much of who I am is wrapped up with Tony. Once I got to go with him to an Iggy Pop concert, and midway through the performance Iggy dove off the stage, right into my arms."

"Shut up!" I said.

"True story. I caught Iggy right in my arms like he was a little baby. And then carried him back up on stage. So the next night we were at dinner, and Tony introduced me to Iggy. He said, 'This is Josh, but you guys already know each other.' I'll be driving the kids to school, and my Spotify algorithm will play some Iggy and the Stooges. Takes me right back."

"I've been struggling with that. What's me? What's Tony? How much do I need to give up? How much can I keep?" I said.

"You know what I needed to do?" Josh said. "When I was in France on that last shoot, Haj was pregnant, and I went out shopping. I got little storks, some French baby books, knicknacks, shit like that. And when Tony killed himself, everything happened so fast, I just threw it all in my suitcase. Back at home my suitcase sat in my garage for a long fucking time. I didn't want to deal with it. Then one day, I just realized I needed to get that shit out of my house. So, yeah, in a way I'm still mad at him, but my suitcase and everything in it from France was what I needed to get rid of. Everything else belongs to me."

"That's smart," I said halfheartedly. Seeing I looked sad, Josh put his enormous hand on my shoulder and squeezed.

"You know, I did decide to keep *something* from France," he said.

"What?" I asked.

"Just before I left for the shoot, Haj and I found out that JJ was gonna be a big brother. I got to tell Tony that we were expecting a little girl. When I told him, Tony smiled, shook my hand, and said, 'Now you'll have your sun *and* your moon.' I really treasure that moment. It's sort of crazy too, Haj and I had already decided to name her Leila, which means 'night' in Farsi. So Tony called another one."

"I never thought it would end," I said. "It was one hell of a trip. Well . . . it was an honor to serve with you, Josh."

"That's right, brother! Storming the shores of Margaritaville! We won that day. Can you believe we used to do stupid shit like that all over the world? Like fuck. How lucky are we? It's important to acknowledge how lucky we are."

I smiled and nodded, but inside I didn't feel lucky. Acknowledging how lucky we were required admitting it was in the past. It also required admitting that, unlike other members of the crew, somewhere along the way I'd lost the ability to stop and smell the roses, too consumed with stress and worry to ever allow myself to enjoy the moment. Looking around the room, it seemed that, in spite of dealing with their own traumas related to Tony's death, everyone else had found a way to pick up the pieces. It was time to do something with my life, but going back to TV wasn't really an option.

I started writing about Tony and my travels because there was nothing else I could do. Searching for inspiration through old shoot notebooks, raw footage, and emails, I was startled how much Tony talked about death, on camera and off.

TONY'S SINGLE FAVORITE RECURRING MEALTIME icebreaker was "What would you choose for your last meal?" After hearing how his dining companion replied, Tony would often answer his own question, usually some blow-your-mind sushi type thing. "If I died with a mouthful of uni and some really good rice, particularly if it was made by Yasuda, I wouldn't complain, as I bled out on the hinoki wood bar." More useful advice, I once heard him say, "When facing death, it's a good idea to eat light."

Another of Tony's polite dinner conversation topics was describing the way he wanted to die, usually in vivid detail. The circumstances of his imaginary death mirrored whatever mood he was in at the time.

Terrified of a slow death in a hospital bed, Tony's original plan was that when the doctor found the inevitable lump, he'd disappear to an island somewhere in the South Pacific, spending the remainder of his days on the beach shooting up his dearly missed heroin.

After the birth of his daughter—a happy, optimistic period—Tony fantasized about being an old man in an Italian garden—like the scene in *The Godfather*—keeling over of a heart attack while chasing grandchildren, orange peel in his mouth.

When in a darker mood he might say, "I want to be run over by an ice-cream truck, get caught up in the wheel well, the oblivious driver dragging me down the street as happy ice-cream truck music plays, horrifying the children."

Another variant of this "death by amusement" rant centered around falling into a wood chipper and being sprayed into a crowd of unsuspecting department store shoppers. "People are trying on the free perfume and then suddenly, this giant blowhole starts shooting bone splinters and blood spray and bits of guts all over everybody."

Many years ago in Baja I'd asked Tony to make a comment to the camera about his first impressions.

"Jeez, you never give up, do you?!" he joked. "When I die, you'll be there at my funeral, poking me with a stick, asking, 'What are your first impressions of being dead?'"

Tony casually pulled off flamboyant and seemingly death-defying escapades on a regular basis. After watching him walk away from enough dangerously misguided stunts, skydiving mishaps, and spine-crushing ATV rollovers, I'd begun to think of him as invincible, if not immortal. He had nine lives, despite what seemed like a death wish.

I RUBBED FROST FROM THE window. Outside there was nothing but swirling snow and the bone-chilling howl of a late December squall blowing down from Siberia. Through the *thwop, thwop, thwop* of the windshield wipers, our headlights illuminated the occasional shadowy figure. Armed with a parka and broom, they were fighting a losing battle to sweep clear accumulating snow drifts on this unfrequented stretch of rural Manchurian highway.

"What do we have in the way of provisions?" Tony asked.

"There are some protein bars in here somewhere," I said.

"Now that would be a worst-case scenario if I have to eat one of those things," Tony said.

"I'm sure the storm will let up soon."

"Well, I hope you're right, because if we get stranded out here in the blizzard, we might be forced to make some tough decisions," Tony said. "Like which one of you we eat first . . . " The silence was eventually interrupted by a delayed reaction laugh from Todd. "With the threat of starvation, you'd be surprised how fast a situation can deteriorate," Tony continued. "It's important to think these things through while we're all still of sound mind."

"Easy, we draw straws," Todd said.

"Amateur move," Tony said. "There are just too many important variables at play to leave it to chance . . . For instance: useful skills that might possibly aid in our survival, ease of dispatch, and perhaps most important, who's likely to make for a crap meal."

I watched the driver concentrating on the highway amid the relentless lashing of the storm. It had ended up being worse than predicted and didn't give the impression of letting up anytime soon. Tony looked around the dimly lit van, studying his prey, weighing pros and cons while mentally running through a list of recipes. I found the hunger in his determined gaze . . . unnerving.

"What about the driver?" I said.

"Well, that would just be cruel. Besides, if we ate him, then who's gonna drive us out of here when the weather finally clears?" Tony said, shaking his head condescendingly. "Let's see . . . in the increasingly probable event we're forced to resort to intra-crew cannibalism . . . ability to operate a camera is of little use to the greater good." Slowly looking Todd up and down, Tony's eyes came to rest on his legs. "Those meaty calves would be fantastic slow-roasted with rosemary. But I don't think Todd would go gentle into that good night . . . "

"Plus, I don't know where we'd get rosemary around here this time of year," Todd said.

"Zach might scratch, but he would definitely be less of a challenge to take down," Tony said. He reached over and palpated Zach's arm, causing him to squirm. "There's not much meat on those bones, and what there is feels stringy. After a good deal of tenderizing he'd probably have to be stewed in a ragout for an extraordinarily long time. It's a lot of work for minimal yield, and Zach *does* have first aid skills."

"I mean, if we really end up going full-on Donner Party, somebody probably *should* film it," I said. Then I instantly realized the error of speaking up. "Umm, also, I absolutely, definitely wouldn't go down without a fight either." I wanted to make sure that was on the record. Just in case.

"*Ppphf.* Yeah, right," Tony said, rolling his eyes before studying me for a moment. "Tom would probably need to be barbequed with a *lot* of spice," Tony said. "Kansas dry rub perhaps. Livestock raised under extreme stress tend to have a bitter taste. They're called dark cutters."

"I guess that leaves me," Jared said.

"Too valuable to the operation," Tony said. "You have the money and cigarettes. And I'll need a witness whose testimony would hold up in court."

"What if we all vote to eat Tony?" Zach asked.

"This is not a democracy," Tony said. "Besides, if we've learned anything from making this show, it's that, left to your own devices, within ten minutes you'd all be running around bashing open each other's skulls, indiscriminately sucking out brains."

Blessed with a gift for elevating the mundane to the absurd, Tony's imagination was so powerful he could literally make his own reality come alive. I loved the way he reinterpreted the gray everyday, making it more colorful. It might not have always been easy living in Tony's world, but it was never boring.

Tony had inherited his wicked sense of humor from his father. Pierre Bourdain worked for Columbia Records and instilled in Tony a love of music and cinema, showing him films like *Doctor Strangelove* from an extremely young age. Pierre died unexpectedly at fifty-seven, and Tony never really got over his passing.

"You know my father used to scrapbook bus plunge newspaper clippings," Tony said, watching a heavily laden bus with worn brake pads careening toward us at full speed while rounding a blind curve. I made the mistake of looking out the window, and down at the narrow winding dirt road. The wheels of our Land Cruiser were mere inches from a 1,000-foot drop off the cliffside into a remote Himalayan chasm.

"Bus plunge?" I asked, an octave or two higher than usual.

"Yeah, editors used them when they had to fill empty space in the paper. They always seemed to be stories about buses plunging off a bridge or cliff into a remote gorge or canyon in some faraway place like . . . well . . . the Himalayas. The more gruesome the wreck, the more interesting. Extra points if there was a noteworthy group of people aboard, like a funeral party or scientist's picnic."

Though his reckless behavior suggested he had a death wish, Tony was uncomfortable with the concept of dying. Like other things that upset him, he used gallows humor as a defense. Tony would say, "Painful is funny, one of the essential rules of comedy. The shit that really hurts, your greatest humiliations, they're funny, you know?"

Tony always said, "Butchers have the best sense of humor. Hacking up body parts all day gives you a hilariously twisted perspective." Tony could put any butcher to shame. His talents were never more apparent than when we found ourselves in an uncomfortable situation.

In addition to his macabre sense of humor, Tony constantly and flippantly mentioned suicide, and I just as casually included his references in the shows because they were, well, entertaining. The way Tony openly spoke about fears, weaknesses, angst, and death prevented even those close to him from seeing how deep, dark, and destructive these feelings really were. After Tony died, one of the first things people asked was if he left a note. I was horrified when I realized I'd been unwittingly helping him make one for sixteen years.

Chapter Sixteen

KARMA

"WHERE ARE YOU HEADED?" MY NEIGHBOR ANDREA ASKED.

"Java and Bali," I said, hoisting my suitcase into the car. "That is if I make the flight." I was late, as usual, having waited until the last minute to pack, again.

"Are you going to film a funeral?" she asked. "I was invited to join one when I was in Indonesia; it was the highlight of the trip."

My ears perked up. Over the years we'd filmed nearly every manner of festival and celebration imaginable, but *never* a funeral. Apparently in Bali a funeral was quite a raucous party. After arriving in-country, I brought up the idea at our first production meeting.

"Funerals in Bali are like nothing else," Desak, one of our local fixers, said. "Cremations are a big party!"

I was intrigued. There were, however, some daunting logistics to consider. How would we fit the funeral for someone who wasn't dead yet into a rigid production schedule? Would the family of the deceased want us there? Would Tony even agree to the scene? Was pursuing such a long-shot a valuable use of limited resources? But a funeral that was also a party fit in perfectly with the episode's theme of duality in Balinese culture. In stark contrast to the more rigid

Western way of thinking, on the island of Bali, seemingly contrasting opposites—light and dark, the seen and unseen, life and death—are interdependent and coexist peacefully. It was a concept perfectly epitomized by the belief that a person's death was something to be celebrated. So despite the risks, I decided to roll the dice.

"I will pray somebody dies, so we can get our funeral." Desak smiled.

"Thank you," I said, feeling a little uncomfortable at having once again found myself in the awkward position of courting misfortune to benefit the show.

But with each passing day came a statistical decrease in the likelihood we'd be able to include a funeral. In the week and a half since I'd arrived in Indonesia, just about everything that possibly could had gone wrong. Emblematic of the comedy of errors befalling our tropical misadventure thus far, the only time we *weren't* stuck in traffic was the one time we'd scheduled to film traffic jams. During a scene in Jakarta a cat gave birth to a single dead kitten, which seemed like it might be a bad omen. Threatening to erupt, Bali's volcano started smoking for the first time in fifteen years, and we missed the shot. It felt like anything that involved leaving the hotel was causing the production to collapse under its own weight.

So I shouldn't have been surprised on discovering that the catamaran we'd chartered for the day's sailing beat didn't have working sails. Nonetheless, I was doing my best to keep a positive attitude and ignore the sputtering, loud twin outboard motors messing up the audio. The cameramen struggled to keep both a steady shot and their footing as the bow lifted skyward before settling back again, rolling over ten-foot swells.

"I grew up reading books about pirates. Conrad and *Lord Jim* very much resonated with me," Tony said. "I guess it goes a long way to explain why I'm doing what I'm doing."

"This is one of the three most piratical places on the planet," Lawrence said, adjusting his eye patch. A British expat with a PhD in psycho-anthropology, Lawrence had spent the better part of the 1970s sailing across the Indonesian archipelago with his brother and a sixteen-millimeter camera. "I lived for six months with the Boogies," he continued. "They're a wild, seafaring lot believed to have given the word 'boogie' or 'bogeyman' to the English language. I also filmed with the cannibal tribe who ate Michael Rockefeller."

Lawrence and his brother produced a documentary series about their adventure, after which they'd decided to stay. Out of Indonesia's 17,000 islands, they'd chosen Bali to call home.

"When we arrived, there were only a handful of foreigners who lived here," Lawrence said. "No electricity, only one telephone at the airport."

"I was in Bali eleven years ago," Tony said. "And so much has changed."

On that first trip for *No Reservations,* Tony had been enchanted by the island's lush green rice paddies, ancient temples, religious ceremonies, trance-inducing gamelan music, and warm welcome from the local population. Returning for this shoot in spring 2018, Tony was chagrined to find the once bucolic island paradise had been transformed into a maze of gridlock traffic. Retail shops, hostels, bars, yoga studios, and restaurants had replaced what had once been rice paddies. Tourists and luxury hotels crowded formerly unspoiled beaches. Plastic garbage was everywhere, blowing like urban tumbleweeds across what Tony called a post–*Eat Pray Love* apocalypse. So a trip across the Lombok Straits to a comparatively undeveloped island seemed like a good idea.

"I think we'll be arriving soon," I said. "This might be a good time to talk about where we're headed."

"Well, Nusa Penida was once a penal colony for Bali," Lawrence said. "And they also believe that it is the home of the Leyaks, the witches, the black magicians."

"This island has not been invaded by tourists like Bali?" Tony asked.

"No," Lawrence said. "Somehow it hasn't."

Drawing closer to Nusa Penida's rugged coastline, I could make out odd-shaped rock formations protruding from dense jungle canopy. The island appeared timeless, unmarred by the scourge of tourism. Rounding a jagged escarpment, we entered a protected cove and dropped anchor. Our destination—a stunning white sand beach surrounded by bright turquoise water—couldn't have been more beautiful. There was a feeling of having stumbled upon a hidden treasure, as if the island's cliffs and dense vegetation colluded to keep this place their jealously guarded secret.

"Well, we certainly have it all to ourselves," Lawrence said.

Surveying the landscape, it was hard to believe we were only twenty kilometers from Bali's discos, hotels, yoga studios, and exhaust fumes. Landing on shore, however, an unpleasant surprise awaited.

"That's the trouble, even the wildest and most remote beaches still have garbage washing up on them," Lawrence said.

In addition to the usual styrofoam, shredded fishing nets, and plastic bottles, we collected five hypodermic syringes. With the beach restored to its natural state, it was time to set up. Everything needed for the scene—tables, chairs, umbrellas, a barbeque, giant spiny lobsters, as well as a local chef—had come with us by boat. Keeping one eye on the cameras filming b-roll and food prep and the other on Tony, who'd gone for a swim, I took a moment to sit down in the sand and breathe in the fresh sea air. It was a perfect day, late afternoon sun glinting off the lagoon, the only sound crashing waves. I took a couple hits from the bottle of duty-free Johnnie Walker stashed in my backpack. After the cheek-by-jowl chaos of Bali, something felt almost eerie about the emptiness.

"All right, everyone, let's reconfigure to the table," I called over the walkie. I didn't consider myself superstitious, but I'd heard nothing but creepy stories about "Black Magic Island," as it was known locally, and missing the tide would mean being marooned here overnight.

"These are the biggest local lobsters I've ever seen," Lawrence said as the massive crustaceans hit the table with a thud. "Actually, those are really crayfish, aren't they?"

"If that's a crayfish, I don't want to meet the lobster," Tony said, digging in.

While cameras rolled, the conversation meandered between topics such as psycho-anthropology, reincarnation, and Balinese religion.

"We call Bali the Island of the Gods. That's the slogan for the tourism industry, but it's equally an island of the demons," Lawrence said. "The Balinese believe the universe is a balance of light and darkness, good and evil. One cannot exist without the other."

"We've been talking about this throughout the show," Tony said. "In the West we tend to think of things in a binary way. There's good and evil, capitalist and communist, life and death. But in this part of the world those notions of light and dark, good and evil, are not absolute ones?"

"Not at all," Lawrence said. "It's particularly the case in Bali with the Hindu Buddhist. They see it in terms of balance."

"So they know things we don't?" Tony asked.

"Absolutely," Lawrence said.

Spirituality and magic were so interwoven into the fabric of everyday life that Bali had more temples than houses. In contrast to the rest of Indonesia—the most populous Muslim nation on Earth—Balinese practiced a unique form of Hinduism that blended elements of Buddhism with ancient beliefs of ancestor worship and animism.

"No matter where I am, there's always a little voice outside of me second-guessing the experience," Tony said. "There's always an *I would like to be here now.*' But very rarely have I been able to feel so . . . unless aided by some psychoactive drug. I wish I could free myself of the analytical part of my mind."

Over the last couple years, I'd seen Tony exhibit a genuine motivation toward personal philosophical growth. Perhaps it was because he was getting older, or more mature. Whatever the reason, his attitude in regard to religion had evolved from a generally snarky distain to a sort of intellectual curiosity, for certain elements of Buddhism in particular. A couple months before Indonesia, while in Bhutan, I'd been surprised by his considerable knowledge of Buddhist teachings. He'd been impressed at how the Bhutanese considered it therapeutic to spend time every day reflecting on death.

"Maybe Lawrence can tell us about funerals?" I asked.

"Yeah, tell me about the funerals," Tony said. "Hopefully we're attending one."

"You are?" Lawrence asked. "Well, a Balinese funeral is a very sobering phenomenon, especially for us Westerners who distance ourselves from death. It's quite an extraordinary thing, that you actually light the match that consumes your loved one."

"Yeah, I wonder . . . I've thought about, as one does, how I want to go," Tony said.

"You want them all to cry, don't you?" Lawrence asked with a chuckle.

"No, leave me in the jungle," Tony said. "I don't want anybody seeing my body. I don't want a party."

"Okay," Lawrence said, unsure of where Tony was taking the conversation.

"What actually happens to my physical remains is of zero interest to me, unless it could provide entertainment value . . . I mean in a perverse or subversive way. If you could throw me into a wood chipper and spray me into Harrods, you know, at the middle of the rush hour. That would be pretty epic. I wouldn't mind being remembered in that way . . . " Tony thought for a moment, looking out at the ocean. "But other than that, yeah, I wouldn't want my loved ones to be inconvenienced or burdened with the responsibility of having to emulate some concern, affection, or sense of loss when really, they're just thinking about . . . you know, 'It's two for one chicken wings at Applebee's.'"

LATER THAT EVENING I SAT reclined on an oversize purple banquette watching well-heeled vacationers sip designer cocktails. The DJ played techno dance music beneath a polychrome of lights pulsing aqua, violet, and magenta. The ambiance was more beachside nightclub than hotel bar, but everything about the W Bali was over the top.

"It's like a whole room," Tony said. "With a rain shower. Then next is a garden with an open roof and a giant marble bowl that's a bathtub. That's another room."

"You have a bathtub room?" I asked.

"I have a bathtub room," Tony said. "And a private lap pool. Why don't you move into my place, man? Seriously."

"Well, I don't want to bother you," I said, not knowing quite what to make of the invitation.

"There's a guest wing that's like a whole other apartment complex," Tony said. "In between there's a communal living area. So move your shit over, man. Leave your oppressive lodgings. Seriously."

Being invited to move into Tony's hotel suite—or villa complex, in this case—wasn't an everyday occurrence. In the last year or so Tony had become more volatile, but also generally nicer to me than he'd been in the past—which, ironically, had only made me more nervous. The truth was Tony scared me. Was I going to say something stupid and embarrass myself? Was he going to do something mean? Was this a gesture of kindness, or just another impulsive mood swing that could reverse itself at any second? I didn't trust my own judgment when it came to Tony. I worried if I let down my guard, it was going to be all the more painful when he inevitably pulled out the rug. Somewhere along the line, I'd learned it was safer to keep a distance.

"Crazy what Lawrence said about the hotels, huh?" I said, eager to change the subject.

"Yeah," Tony said. "We're sitting on a mountain of skulls."

Another of the episode's intended through-lines was the still-unfolding aftermath of anti-communist massacres in 1965 known as "the year of living dangerously." Three million Indonesians had been killed, by some accounts. It was a poorly kept secret that the luxury hotels lining the beach had been constructed on top of unmarked mass graves. I had an image of corpses emerging from beneath the swimming pool to seek revenge on oblivious hotel guests, like in *Poltergeist*.

"One order chicken wings, two orders french fries, two orders margarita pizza, two orders burgers, and four double Johnnie Walker Black and a Coca-Cola," the waiter said, delivering our standard international off-camera dinner.

"You haven't said anything about the picture," I said once we were alone. I'd been carrying around a framed photo of my cat Frida—the one Tony had renamed Mr. Whiskers—waiting for him to notice. But after four days and a few drinks, I was getting impatient.

"Mr. Whiskers died the day before I left for Indonesia," I said, my voice cracking a little. "She knew I was leaving. I buried her in the backyard under our favorite rose bush."

"Aww, I'm sorry, Tom," Tony said, sympathetically looking up from his iPad. After a long pause, he said, "Asia's been offered a role as judge on that Italian TV show *The X Factor*. I think it's a really bad idea. It's a tough schedule and going to take up a huge amount of her time."

Tony was fully aware how close I was to that cat, and I felt hurt by his seeming lack of interest in my life, even though I knew it wasn't really the case. Not unlike me, one of Tony's strategies for dealing with uncomfortable situations was to change the subject.

For years, I'd had to pretend to care about whatever Tony's current obsession was—Brazilian jiu jitsu or the Marvel versus DC Universe, and for the last eighteen months all he'd wanted to talk about was Asia Argento. I knew he wanted me to ask what *The X Factor* was, but I just didn't have the energy to humor him tonight. Instead I let silence fill the empty space between us.

Tony stared at orange paper lanterns strung between the palm trees swaying in the ocean breeze before he got up, saying, "All right, I'm heading out. Let me know if you want to move in tomorrow, man. I'm telling you there's a whole fucking extra building. You get your own pool."

"WE'RE ROLLING," I SAID.

"So this, too, is Bali, I guess. Or it is now. Thank you, Jimmy Buffett, for taking a big dump on the world," Tony said to the camera.

He sat in a poolside lounge chair wearing a black shirt, jeans, and jet-black Persols and couldn't have contrasted more with his surroundings. All around us there was laughter, splashing, and leisure. We were filming a solo scene at the hotel's impressive five-level lagoon-shaped interconnecting swimming pools, which cascaded down from the mezzanine to the beach. Couples in bright pastel bikinis and Speedos suntanned on lounge chairs while other guests frolicked on oversize rainbow-colored unicorn pool floats. Australian bros chugged beer while high-fiving each other. Everyone was enjoying themselves, except for Tony, who was looking hilariously miserable.

"I have to say, this is not the Bali I remember. It's different . . . It's, like, crowded," Tony said. "Why can't I be happy? I do not smell the spices of the East. I no longer hear the gamelan, *bing-bong-boong*, like I first did when I came here." Tony sipped his W Bali signature mango margarita.

"Anyway, guys, we're having a few buckets of chicken later at my place. It's a pool party, nothing high-profile," Tony said by way of an invitation to the crew. In the last year or so, Tony had displayed more interest in wanting to hang out, regularly inquiring when we'd be getting back to the hotel. Usually it was too late for the camera team, which meant it was just me meeting him at the bar. But we were finishing early tonight, already at the hotel, and Tony had discovered there was a KFC nearby, so it was going to be a party.

"Don't forget to order mac and cheese and biscuits," Tony said after the scene. "I'm hungry as fuck."

"NOT JUST ONE, BUT THREE people from my village have died," Desak said. "And one of them is even a high priest."

"You're kidding? That's fantastic!" I said before catching myself, toning down the excitement. "I mean, my condolences to the family."

I couldn't believe Desak had pulled it off. Despite all odds, I had got my funeral after all. The next morning, and last day of the shoot, we prepared for Tony to share a simple breakfast of rice, sambal, and chicken steamed in banana leaf with a local man named Kadek. He wore a traditional sarong with batik headscarf, T-shirt, and a gentle smile on his face.

When Tony arrived, he sat down cross-legged at the table and saw I'd placed the small picture of Mr. Whiskers next to an offering in the background of the scene. He glanced quickly at me with an expression I couldn't exactly decipher, but said nothing.

"It's a joyous occasion, especially the cremation. It's a big party to send the spirit to the afterlife," Kadek said.

"Because people firmly believe that we are not talking about the end, so this is something to be happy about?" Tony asked.

"Life is cyclical," Kadek said, nodding in agreement. "The state of mind at the time of death is very important for your next journey . . . Cremation frees the soul, purifying it by fire. This allows the dead to rejoin the cycle of reincarnation."

After we filmed breakfast, the crew reconfigured for the cremation parade and celebration. Cameras rolled as the body of the high priest was washed and wrapped in white cloth before being placed inside an elaborate multi-tiered pagoda shaped like a bull. Made of bamboo and paper and the height of a two-story house, the bull was white with gold horns and draped in gold jewelry, scarves, and headdress. Intended to carry the deceased to the next life, it was an unbelievably beautiful piece of sculpture designed to last for only twenty-four hours before being burned.

The funeral procession began with the banging of drums, chanting, and ringing of bells. Several hundred members of the village were there, laughing and yelling, some taking pictures or filming with their phones, others carrying offerings of food or flowers. Everyone gathered around the bull, which was lifted onto the shoulders of about twenty young men. The music kicked up a notch, and the cavalcade got underway. As promised, a party-like atmosphere prevailed. Everywhere there were huge smiles; the feeling was more victory parade than funeral, at least compared to what I'd experienced before. There was no denying the event was an impressive spectacle to behold.

"The priest is throwing out rice along with money to confuse and misdirect the spirits that might try to follow the procession," Kadek explained.

Dressed from head to toe in white, the band beat drums, cymbals, chimes, gongs, and gamelans, some small, others massive, over four feet in diameter, keeping time to an increasingly frantic tempo.

"I love the sound, it's beautiful," Tony said.

"It's slightly off tune always, so they create that big noise that reverberates throughout your body," Kadek said above the din. "The idea is that it shatters the illusion between the seen and the unseen worlds."

Chanting and cheers swirled together, with the cacophony increasing in intensity and building toward a crescendo. Men carrying the bull began yelling and shouting, spinning the deceased in circles and shaking him up and down.

"Who's that?" Tony asked, pointing to someone who'd appeared on the bull, riding it like a rodeo cowboy while holding on for dear life.

"The son of the deceased," Kadek said. "It's a big honor to be on the float."

We were swept along in the ever more raucous festivities until the procession arrived at an open field. The pagoda was set down, offerings placed around its base.

"Shit, it's hot in the sun," Tony said, out of breath. "We got anything to drink?"

We had a little bit of time before the cremation began, so I brought Tony to the courtyard of a nearby house arranged as a rest area and a place to stash our gear.

"I've started seeing a therapist," Tony said out of nowhere.

I was a bit surprised; he'd always stalwartly refused the notion of therapy. Tony was someone I had always looked to for answers, that millions of fans had looked to for answers. To hear him voluntarily admit that he didn't have all the answers and was seeking guidance was uncharacteristically vulnerable.

"How's it going?" I asked.

"Good, she makes me feel better about myself," Tony said. "You know, sort of that I'm not such a bad person after all."

I studied him for a moment. It was hard to know what he was grappling with behind his sunglasses. Was he regretting his personal and professional choices? Did he feel a need to make amends with the people he cared about?

One thing was clear, Tony was thoroughly exhausted and could use a vacation. Tony had an addictive personality and was without doubt a workaholic, choosing to travel over 250 days a year for as long as I'd known him. Whenever I used to suggest he take some time off, Tony would say, "Television is a cruel mistress. She does not let you cheat on her, even for a while." I'd learned that the truth was he couldn't rest. Tony always needed a distraction, a project, a problem to solve. And, for better or worse, the show provided that in spades.

"When was the last time you had some real downtime?" I asked.

"Last summer in Italy with Asia. Five or six days on a boat; it was glorious," Tony said, lighting up with excitement. "I did all the cooking. I had the boat stocked with fresh truffles, foie gras, caviar, a couple cases of really good wine. I even brought my own omelette pan. Occasionally we'd go ashore in disguise wearing hats and sunglasses, and line up with all the housewives to get fish from the market. It was fucking great."

"Are you doing it again this year?" I asked.

"We were hoping to, but if Asia gets the job on *X Factor* it's going to be difficult," Tony said, deflating somewhat. "She's going to move to New York in the fall; I'm really looking forward to having her there."

"I know what you mean," I said. "I've been feeling pretty lonely too."

"Get rid of that fucking house," Tony said. "You could move into my building."

"Yeah," I said with a smile. No matter how much I tried to keep up a wall, it wasn't successful, because Tony was at the absolute center of my personal and professional life. It was equally hard for me to consider the possibility that I was only of use to him as a director, as it was that he could have really cared for me and loved me. Times like these made it hard for me to keep my distance, as I could feel his genuine affection coming through his kind, although completely unrealistic, comment. Even though there was no way I could afford $16,000 per month for an apartment in Tony's building, I sincerely appreciated that he'd made the suggestion.

"We're going to Seattle this summer for the speaking tour," Tony said. "Is Jennifer O'Degan still there?"

Tony's question caught me completely off guard. It had been seven years since I told him about my elementary school nemesis, who had punched me in front of the whole class to the cheers of all the kids watching. I couldn't believe Tony had been listening, let alone retained details.

"You remember her?" I said, as a wave of emotion swept over me.

"Of course I do," Tony said. "There's a bucket of pig's blood with her name on it."

This blew my mind. Even though it was a small gesture, it erased years of bad feelings. My tenuous state of mind over the past few years had led to some tension between me and the New York office, but we'd patched things up a bit lately, and I was working on getting my personal life at home more under control. I'd been making some adjustments in the name of mental health, figuring out how to stay sane for the long haul and survive on the show.

"Come over now!" the walkie screeched. "They're lighting it up!"

Tony and I hurried back across the street, and he got into position next to Kadek. Family members placed lighted incense and matches at the base of the bull, igniting the funeral pyre. Once it was fully engulfed, a man with a massive flamethrower sprayed the body with a jet of fire while another jabbed around with a poker, ensuring it was fully burned. A column of smoke reached into the sky, buoyed by the sound of gongs, drums, and joyful chanting while relatives and loved ones watched.

I stood away from the crowd and lit a cigarette. I couldn't know it at the time, but after all those miles, a lifetime of gonzo adventures, I'd just finished the last scene I would ever film with Tony. Fitting, then, somehow, that it was a funeral. Not in a million years would I have believed within the month Tony would disappear into flames.

Looking back, I didn't see the warning signs, although there were some. It was less about his musings on death, karma, and spirituality, and more so his attempts to show me that he cared. Repeated requests to hang out are what stand out most. Tony's ability to hide his fears behind his dark humor, combined with his near unflappable façade of strength and impenetrability, prevented me from seeing these requests for what—in hindsight—I realized they were: the actions of someone lonely and depressed, trying his best to come to terms with himself.

Later, I would think about something Tony said at the end of the shoot. At the time I hadn't paid much attention. Of course, in retrospect, what Tony said takes on new meaning.

"I would like to be thought of as a good guy. I mean, I don't want people walking over my grave—if there is even a grave—or see a picture of me—in the unlikely event anyone bothers to look—and for them to say, 'Oh, that son of a bitch. I'm glad he's dead.' I'd prefer not . . . I don't know that I'm trying to accrue good karma specifically, but I'm definitely trying to avoid bad karma these days. I am thinking about how I'm going out and on what terms . . . "

Shortly before Tony's departure for France and his death, he asked me to have dinner with him. We'd just returned from Indonesia, and I was busy preparing our India trip, so I declined the offer, figuring soon enough I'd be seeing Tony every day whether I wanted to or not. I'll probably never stop asking myself if I could have changed things had I accepted the invitation. I'll also probably never forgive myself. But what I can see now, that I didn't back then, is that ultimately Tony was a man who was trying his best—to free himself of his analytical mind, to find a belief system that was more forgiving of his spiritual ambivalence, to express his love to the people he cared about, to reconcile the contradictions that embodied his internal and external life and ultimately defined his persona. His best was enough for millions of fans, but it wasn't enough for him. Throughout the years, both before and after his death, I've struggled with persistent questions of whether he actually cared enough about me to give me his best. But ultimately it doesn't matter: I'm just grateful for the time I had with him.

EPILOGUE

HOW DO YOU END A STORY LIKE THIS? THE TRUTH IS I DON'T FEEL DONE or remotely satisfied with what I've written. All along I'd been clinging to the naïve hope that, given enough time, I'd be able to find the missing pieces of the puzzle.

When I came across a long-lost USB memory stick buried in the back of my desk, I thought maybe I'd found what I'd been looking for. A year before Tony's death he'd put it in my hand, looked me in the eye, and deliberately said, *"Whatever you do, don't look at this."* What had he meant? Actually don't look at it? Or don't look at it, wink, wink, as in, do look at it? Was it a prank or a test? Ultimately I'd decided to play it safe, and I put the drive away. With the craziness of life and work, I'd forgotten it even existed.

I held my breath as I inserted the drive and double-clicked it open to find a document named "Hungry Ghost." My eyes raced back and forth across the pages of what appeared to be an unfinished manuscript Tony had been working on before his death. It was the story of his travels—our travels—to many of the same places I'd chosen to include in my own book. His writing was lyrical, almost stream of consciousness, riddled with errors and omissions, but exquisite nonetheless. I found it humbling how, even in an early draft, Tony succeeded at effortlessly capturing the dislocation of moving through space, the blur of a life spent in motion.

It took a moment for me to realize how different it was than Tony's other work. Instead of the curiosity and humor that usually characterized his writing, Tony described himself as wandering from place to place, haunted by crushing loneliness. A lost soul trapped in a perpetual state of dissatisfaction, always longing for more, he was the very embodiment of a hungry ghost.

Over the next eighty pages Tony wrestled with some of the questions that had been eating away at me for years. Writing about Libya, he examined why we'd gone to such dangerous places and whether it was worth the risk. Every time I'd asked Tony those questions, he'd given me some unsatisfying non-answer. Until now.

> I looked around the room at my closest colleagues and friends. People I'd spent the greater part of my waking hours with for YEARS. More than my wife or my child or anybody I called a friend. What was MY responsibility to them? Tom, my producer, who'd been with me in one capacity or another for nearly 100 shows. I knew he'd walk straight into a fusillade to get a good shot. But that was Tom. What about Todd, who'd been with me from nearly the very beginning—nearly 15 years of putting up with my shit, my moods, my personal ups and downs, while walking backwards holding cameras in Borneo, in Liberia, Mexico, and Beirut? I knew his wife, his kids. Zach had been with me for some years too. Josh was new. He surely hadn't signed up for THIS shit.

Tony went on to recount how during our Hazardous Environment Training the crew was advised to continue performing CPR long after someone had died. When Tony asked the point of expending the energy, the answer was so that you would be able to truthfully say you'd done all you could. "I did NOT want to go back to any of these people's wives or girlfriends or children and have to have that conversation," Tony wrote.

I was overcome by the uncanny realization that in a very literal way Tony's voice was speaking to me from beyond the grave. But it was what was written on the last page that hit me the hardest. "I DO want to tell you the story of Tom's birthday in Iran," Tony wrote. ". . . It was an extraordinary moment." He stopped shortly afterward, the setup to something never finished.

It was a powerful metaphor for Tony's life—incomplete and interrupted. Even more powerful, the writing expressed the feelings Tony had struggled to communicate while he was alive, the same feelings I'd had such difficulty accepting when I'd heard them. Here was my longed-for missing clue, and yet, finding it, I only felt a deepening emptiness and regret. Faced with tangible evidence that Tony had cared, would I finally have to admit that I'd convinced myself he hated me so I wouldn't have to accept the magnitude of the loss?

Maybe the real question was, how do you end a story that you don't want to be over? I'd assumed writing this book was an attempt to process the last two decades of my life. Was it possible instead I'd figured out a way of keeping Tony alive? The more I mulled it over, the more the realization sunk in that I'd been living in a delusion, surrounding myself with artifacts from a world that no longer existed. There are consequences to living in the past, however. The boundaries between my life and work were less defined now than they'd ever been. That's the danger of a ghost: it follows you wherever you go. Trapped, simultaneously overwhelmed and left longing, it turned out I was the hungry ghost.

My good friend Alicia, who'd regularly offered her perspective on my writing, had to continually remind me to include myself in my own memoir. Convinced I'd just poured my heart out on the page, Alicia would say to me, "Okay, so that was Tony's experience. What was it like for you?" I usually didn't know how to answer that question. I didn't even realize most of the time unless it was pointed out that Tony's experience wasn't the same as my own.

Alicia was right. Ultimately this is my story; it begins and *ends* with me.

So what did I learn from my time traveling around the world? What meaning have I found in writing this book? I've learned that it's time to put away my pictures, souvenirs, and shiny objects and figure out who the fuck I am. But I've come to the realization that moving on doesn't mean giving up all my extraordinary experiences. They were mine all along, even if it didn't always feel like it at the time. Clearly I still have a lot to unpack.

ACKNOWLEDGMENTS

I'M FILLED WITH GRATITUDE FOR THE PRIVILEGE OF KNOWING SO MANY wonderful people who have shown me kindness and guidance throughout my life. There's no way to include everyone, but in the brief space I have I'd like to thank a few particularly instrumental people.

Thank you Catherine for the inspiration, encouragement, and counsel!

I genuinely appreciate the support from my agents Steve and Jamie as well as my editor Lauren. I never would have made it without my dear friend Alicia who worked with me tirelessly up to the bitter end.

All my love to my mother Ann, father Frank, sister Katie, brother Ed, uncle Michael, aunts Jean, Betty, Cindy, Sheryl, and cousins Mathew, Andrew, Anna, Tessa, and Wendy. Same goes for David, Samantha, Tom, Priscilla, Kristina, Pat, Barbra, and my muse Andrea.

Out of the multitude of influential educators who played an outsized role in making me who I am, I would like to express my appreciation to Mr. Hearn, Mrs. Ivayni, Mrs. Circosta, Miss Hayes, Mr. Ryder, Mrs. Ovino, and Professor Cohen.

Thank you to Michael, Rob, Nigel, Paul, Sandy, Chris, and Lydia for encouraging my career and giving me a shot.

Cheers to my collaborators and friends at Zero Point Zero including Nicola, Anna, Joe, Nick, Meghan, Adam, Sally, Alex, Tracey, Diane, Rennik, and Mike.

Stunning cinematography was one of the defining features of our work. Zach, Todd, Alan, Alex, Fred, Jeremy, Josh, Jerry, and Mo, you guys are the best in the business. The shows were truly made in post.

I will be forever indebted to the hard work and brilliance of Hunter, Jesse, Mustafa, Chris, Yeong-A, Angie, Tim, Hannah, Shawn, Parker, Julia, Benny, Brian, Pat, Andrey, Lou, Steve, Manny, and our composer Mike who provided the soundtrack to my life.

There wouldn't have been anything to shoot, edit, or score without the input, expertise, grit, and talent of our local producers and fixers. Sara, Yin, Raja, Natalia, Lucy, Ishan, Ivan, Inky, Girlie, Bindu, Ayman, Camelia, Carleene, Lisa, Laura, Hary, Nok, Esra, Joe, Shinji, Carola, Gus, Susana, Ha, Phi, Matt, Emong, James, Carla, Mariana, Oliva, Shoba, Paddy, Hulya, Annika, Razan, Marcello, Annalisa, Emanuela, Patrick, Dan, Jigme, Jason, Yeganeh, Joe, and Desak you will always be in my heart!

Last (but certainly not least!) I would like to send an *extra* special thanks to Jeff, Josh, Jared, Helen, Jon, Ottavia, Chris, Laurie, Philippe, Fuen, Nari, our faithful travel agent Lorraine, and of course Tony.